# SENTENCING IN THE AGE OF INFORMATION:

## FROM FAUST TO MACINTOSH



glasshouse press
London • Sydney • Portland, Oregon

# SENTENCING IN THE AGE OF INFORMATION: FROM FAUST TO MACINTOSH

Katja Franko Aas

glasshouse press

London • Sydney • Portland, Oregon

First published in Great Britain 2005 by
The GlassHouse Press, The Glass House,
Wharton Street, London WC1X 9PX, United Kingdom
Telephone: + 44 (0)20 7278 8000 Facsimile: + 44 (0)20 7278 8080
Email: info@cavendishpublishing.com
Website: www.cavendishpublishing.com

Published in the United States by Cavendish Publishing
c/o International Specialized Book Services,
5824 NE Hassalo Street, Portland,
Oregon 97213-3644, USA

Published in Australia by The GlassHouse Press,
45 Beach Street, Coogee, NSW 2034, Australia
Telephone: + 61 (2)9664 0909 Facsimile: +61 (2)9664 5420
Email: info@cavendishpublishing.com.au
Website: www.cavendishpublishing.com.au



British Library Cataloguing in Publication Data
Aas, Katja Franko
Sentencing in the age of information: from Faust to Macintosh
1 Sentences (Criminal procedure)
I Title
345'.0772

Library of Congress Cataloguing in Publication Data
Data available

Paperback ISBN 1-904385-38-9
Paperback ISBN 978-1-904-38538-7
Hardback ISBN 1-904385-39-7
Hardback ISBN 978-1-904-38539-4

1 3 5 7 9 10 8 6 4 2

Printed and bound in Great Britain

*For Eva and Maria*

# Preface

This is a deep book on how we are prevented from going deep.

The book presents a picture of modern judges in modern courtrooms equipped with computers, electronic information systems, and with sentencing tables that prescribe the 'right' punishment – it simplifies decision-making. Right decisions, or wrong decisions? Right, if the predetermined procedure is followed correctly; wrong if the procedure is not followed correctly.

But the deep problems, those Faust wanted to penetrate, those he deposited his soul to understand, become redundant in this new setting. What is it all for? What sorts of problems are there to make decisions on? Most importantly: are the decisions not only technically right, but also morally right? Are they kind? Are they decent – or wise? These large questions are forced into the background by a situation now defined in terms of strict rules on how to decide on the base of an assembly of pre-determined elements.

Maybe the judge has more wisdom than she or he can be programmed for? Maybe we all have?

The old-fashioned judge in a penal case attempts to understand what sort of person she or he is facing. Slowly, the judge builds a story of what has happened. To the judge, and hopefully also to others, this is a comprehensible story; in the best case, a creation of a piece of art. Through that story, the judge intuitively comes to a conclusion – the final sentence.

But this is a complicated process – one with many variables at play. It is a process often based on most of a life on the bench and on experience and intuition. It is also a story where the outcome, the final sentence, is difficult for politicians and their managers to control.

Today it appears that all these problems are to be solved through the modern trend of using sentencing tables or statistical information on the standard sentence. These pre-determined forms will capture the judge and eliminate discretion, while the accused will be converted from a whole person in a whole story to a carrier of a risk configuration according to a grid of pre-determined factors.

But then come the costs: the original meaning of individual was 'indivisible' – that is, something that cannot be divided. Now, it seems, the individual can be divided into a set of factors. But, thinking of Faust, maybe this is when the devil comes back; when we are not individuals any more, but only divided parts without souls – parts that can be handled like parts.

That is what this important book is about.

*Nils Christie*

*Oslo, January 2005*

# Acknowledgments

I am grateful to a number of people who have contributed in various ways to this book. In particular, Nils Christie, who provided guidance and inspiration. Grateful acknowledgments also to the former and present colleagues and students at the Institute of Criminology and Sociology of Law in Oslo, including Hedda Giertsen, Ragnhild Hennum, Nicolay Johansen, Heidi Mork Lomell and Lill Scherdin. Helene Oppen Gundhus has been all one could hope for in a colleague and a friend. I am also grateful to Craig Calhoun, Thomas Hylland Eriksen and Clifford Shearing for their inspiring courses, as well as to other participants for the discussions. Further thanks to Richard Jones, Thomas Mathiesen, Iver B Neuman, Annick Prieur and Jonathan Simon for their constructive criticism. Different versions of some of the material also appeared in *Punishment & Society, Journal of Scandinavian Studies in Crime Prevention* and *The New Punitiveness* (edited by John Pratt, David Brown, Simon Hallsworth, Mark Brown and Wayne Morrison). I am grateful to the editors and the reviewers for their comments. Norwegian Research Council generously provided the financial support for the project. Finally, thanks to Beverley Brown and Sanjeevi Perera from GlassHouse Press for making the book possible.

The mistakes, of course, are mine alone.

Special thanks to my families, Slovenian and Norwegian. First, as always, to Per Christian, Eva and Maria, and to Iztok and Tanja for their frequent visits and the joy they brought with them. To my mother and to my grandparents for making me feel I still had a home with them. And finally, to my father.

*Katja Franko Aas*
*Oslo, January 2005*

# Contents

# Introduction

[T]he essence of technology is nothing technological. (Heidegger 1977: 35)

This is a book about sentencing. This is also a book about computers. It is a book about the relationship between people and computers, and how out of this relationship new stories about crime and offenders and new images of justice are being born. Furthermore, this is a book about the changing nature of our thinking and our sociality, about how our perceptions of the appropriate ways of reasoning and governing social institutions are being transformed in the technologically-mediated social world. Our notions of our own and others' identities are mediated by a growing number of technologies and governmental strategies – also, or even more so, when it comes to the administration of justice. Today, we are required to adopt technology-friendly identity and language when communicating with a bank, when we want to order a plane ticket or enrol at a university, just as criminal justice officials are required to fill out an increasing number of forms when evaluating their clients and reporting about their own work. In almost every aspect of our daily lives and work we are encountering new communicational situations, new modes of expression, thinking and identification. This book is an attempt to gain insight into and to grasp some of the effects of the new technologies of justice and the emerging images of identity.

A while ago, I tried to find out how many PIN (ie, personal identification numbers) codes and passwords I actually use in my daily life. I gave up after reaching 24, fully aware that this was by no means a complete list. The password to my computer, my library code, bank code, online bank code, medical code, online garden shop code, online children's bookstore, code to enter the university building, mobile phone code … I could go on. What are all these strange numbers and letters? Kqty7!U – this is me. This is my identity, as confirmed to a bookstore, and I have at least 23 other such identities that I have to present to various institutions in order to function normally. Presenting my name, my signature, my picture or myself in person would have been both unnecessary and, even more importantly, *insufficient* for a database to recognise me. I have to know the magical letters and numbers. What a change from the time when one had to stand in line and sign numerous documents in banks, various government offices and libraries in person!

However, it may be useful to remember that, historically, pen and paper signatures, just as PIN codes, became accepted as a guarantee of legitimate identity due to modernisation and the fact that people and organisations became more mobile (Lyon 2001). PIN codes and passwords are therefore merely a continuation of this trend towards abstract relationships in modernity and late modernity. Living in an increasingly global world means doing things and identifying oneself at a distance. We make sense of the world through technological systems and, often, cannot imagine facing our surroundings without a mobile phone or a computer. We operate as 'man-machine-interfaces' (Lash 2002: 15). These technological forms of life make it possible to experience life and culture at a much greater distance than ever before. For someone living in Oslo, it might feel as if London or Copenhagen is much closer and more familiar than a neighbouring town 30 kilometres away. This is 'culture-at-a-distance' – disembedded and 'lifted out' – whose context is, as Lash argues, 'no context at all' (2002: 21). It is most obviously represented in generic spaces such as airports, McDonald's restaurants and department stores. 'As lifted out, they take on increasingly less and less the characteristic of any particular place, and can be any place or indeed no place' (Lash 2002: 21). These are places that are interchangeable. One McDonald's restaurant is like another. Their identity is predictable. Using information and communication technologies facilitates and accentuates the trend.

So far, the story probably sounds familiar. However, it may be interesting to ask whether the fact that our identities become abstract and generic when doing things at a distance also changes the ways we identify ourselves and others when we are (or should be) proximate. A librarian who cannot lend me a book, because I have forgotten my card with a code, does not do so because she does not 'recognise' me, but simply because that type of recognition is not accepted by the library system. Moving to penal systems, a question can be posed regarding what kind of identification patterns they have, when technology increasingly seems to be the magical solution to so many problems. Electronic bracelets and video surveillance cameras are obvious examples. Nevertheless, I will suggest that changes in identification may be less obvious and, at the same time, more pervasive than that. The world of technology may provide us not only with more efficient ways to trace people or with more information and better ways to handle the information, but also with new images of people and new narratives regarding crime and punishment. If the technological systems enable a bank or an online bookstore to identify me through a PIN code, what forms of identification and what presuppositions about human identity do they bring to a penal system? This book suggests that cultural shifts in perception of identity are not only limited simply to the 'obviously technological' areas such as electronic bracelets and surveillance cameras, but may also affect the images of offenders in other areas of punishment such as, for example, sentencing.

My discussion draws primarily on the analysis of certain sentencing developments – sentencing guidelines and sentencing information systems – and tries to pin down the changing images of justice, knowledge and offenders that these developments embody. If we were to imagine a picture of justice, the Roman goddess Justitia would probably come to mind. The image of Justitia, holding scales of justice in one hand and a sword in the other, adorns numerous courthouses, city halls and other civic buildings throughout the Western world. Justitia wears a blindfold, indicating that the scales and the sword are to be used regardless of skin colour, social status and other more or less sympathetic qualities in those who appear before the courts of law. However, if we are to look at the various real-life statues of Justitia that have been made throughout history, we may notice that the blindfold is quite often absent. The different images are not simply a historic peculiarity, but indicate a more profound duality in the nature of Western penal law. On one hand, there is the demand, envisaged by Beccaria and his contemporaries, that punishment should be equal for all and that justice should be blind. On the other hand, one of the most influential penological ideas since the 19th century has been that one should know the ones who are being punished. As Foucault memorably put it: 'During the 150 or 200 years that Europe has been setting up its new penal systems, the judges have gradually [...] taken to judging something other than crimes, namely, the "soul" of the criminal' (1977: 19).

However, in the past 30 years Western penal systems have increasingly been put under pressure to adopt the image of justice with a blindfold (Christie 1993) – one that sees and understands less (and maybe therefore also punishes more), one that puts priority on uniform rather than individualised treatment of offenders. In Chapter 1 I examine the developments which led to the shift from individualised to more standardised or 'tariff' sentencing, and the solutions that have been adopted. The book suggests that the move towards 'tariff' penalties is not simply a form of renewed emphasis on 'blindness', but also a question of creating new fields of visibility. Parallel with the demands to make offenders' individual differences less relevant, there has also been a trend to make judicial decisions and decisions of other penal professionals more transparent. They should be visible to the outside world and to the system managers. The purpose of the book is partly to explore these new fields of visibility: how are they being created? What are the rationalities behind them? How does the fact that our knowledge today is to such a large extent created and communicated with the help of information technologies influence how penal professionals see and communicate about their work?

In Chapter 2 I turn to information technology and media studies to gain some insight into the emerging new fields of transparency and visibility. Contemporary societies tend to be described as 'knowledge societies', 'information societies' or 'technological societies', yet it is less frequently discussed how these terms relate to governance of contemporary penal institutions and the nature of penal knowledge. Are we still to hold on to the concept of power and knowledge coined by Foucault (1977, 1980) over 20 years ago, without taking into account the new technological developments? Can we discuss knowledge and power/knowledge today, without addressing the issues of information technology? Here, David Lyon poses a vital question:

> But what if the computer is more than a modern machine? What if the computer is implicated in the social and cultural transformations of modernity itself? And what if it thus requires novel modes of analysis appropriate to this putative transformation? ... Does this mean that older models, such as the panopticon, require revising or rejecting? (Lyon 2001: 108)

Information and communication technologies have become vital tools of contemporary social governance. However, criminologists often seem to have somewhat ambiguous feelings about technology. While we acknowledge the powers of technical devices, for example, to intensify surveillance, we seldom seem to acknowledge that we, in turn, are also being formed and transformed by these devices. This book argues that computers cannot be simply described as tools or technical devices. They are, to borrow Andrew Barry's (2001) term, 'political machines'. Living in a technological society means that technologies in many ways 'dominate our sense of the kinds of problems that government and politics must address, and the solutions we must adopt' (Barry 2001: 2).

The book does not argue for a simple cause and effect relationship between technology and penal change. Rather, it tries to situate penal developments in the context of late modern and information societies. This contextualisation touches upon a number of social and cultural features. Therefore, it is important to note that technological change should by no means be seen as apolitical or not involving social actors, but rather as essentially social and cultural – having as much to do with social actors and meanings as with the technical devices and their uses. New technologies are 'being looked for and developed with certain purposes and practices already in mind', is how Raymond Williams memorably expresses the thought (1974: 7). Mark Poster points out that when analysing modern bureaucracies, computers should certainly be seen as an essential element in their increased capacity for systematic surveillance (1990: 38). A computer is, however, not enough. What is needed is the encoding of language – creation of language without ambiguity that suits the medium of a database. Consequently, not only a technological change is needed, but also a cultural and linguistic change.

This duality of cultural and technological change has been precisely my point of interest when it comes to punishment. What is at issue here is not technological change *per se*, but rather the conceptual shifts that accompany it. As Ericson and Haggerty argue:

> The material technology of computers, cellular telephones, video, radio, and telecommunications infrastructures determines nothing. It does provide new technical means for sensing and representing the environment ... However, it is only its particular uses within culturally specific interpretative frameworks and visions of social organization that result in cultural and social effects. (1997: 411)

Such intricate connections between the technological and the cultural would, therefore, render it futile to try to predict social change on the basis of technological developments. This is perhaps especially the case with penal policies. As Michael Tonry (2001) points out, while new technologies, such as electronic monitoring and prison security equipment, can be transferred between countries in a matter of months, penal policies are slower to follow.

However, the intriguing issue for penal analysts today may be precisely the blurring lines between the spheres of technology and penal policy. The new information and communication technologies are transforming the nature of penal knowledge itself, and thereby also the discursive parameters within which penal policies are discussed and implemented. The distinction between the political, technological and cultural is becoming increasingly difficult. Lash makes a vital argument when he suggests that technological change should be primarily seen as a change in the nature of our sociality. The information society, he argues, is an order 'in which the principle of "society" becomes displaced by the principle of 'information". An order in which sociality becomes displaced by a certain "informationality". Sociality is long-lasting and proximal. Informationality is of short duration and at a distance' (Lash 2002: 75). Chapter 2, therefore, examines the nature of information in the information order, particularly its increasing disembodiment and ability to travel at a distance. A critical examination of the information order does not need to imply technological pessimism and a wish to return to the past. It does require, however, a challenge to its seeming objectivity.

Chapter 3 applies the analysis developed in Chapter 2 to the field of penal practice. It suggests that contemporary sentencing may be adjusting to the new information order, in the same way as it once adjusted to the disciplinary culture

(Foucault 1977). In many ways, it may appear as if penal power today is no longer ashamed to punish (Foucault 1977), and that it freely professes to understanding less and punishing more. However, the book suggests that 'understanding less' is also a way of understanding. It is a paradigm that has its resonance in the contemporary cultural climate and its striving for standardisation and uniform means of communication. The book explores how punishment is becoming part of the so called 'information society'. It touches upon the issue of computers, databases and information itself. However, first and foremost, it is an inquiry into the societal aspect of the information society and the social aspect of punishment. As we shall see, it may not primarily be about computers and information, but about distance – punishment-at-a-distance.

The book is, therefore, essentially an inquiry into the nature of penal knowledge. In talking about knowledge, a question always arises about the subject and object of penal knowledge. Who are we, when we think about crime and punishment? What is a judge's, a parole officer's or a researcher's position? I wish to point out, however, that the focus of the book is not principally on the contents of knowledge (sentencing theory, ethical justifications of punishment, objectives of punishment, etc), but rather on the form of knowledge. Forms of knowledge and discourse (databases, narratives, numerical guideline forms, risk assessment forms, etc) will be studied not only as neutral transmitters of content, but rather as active participants in its creation. In addition, while the content of penal knowledge usually tends to be in focus (incapacitation theories, just deserts, risk thinking, etc), the form is relatively rarely taken into consideration. However, decision-making forms are the vital aspects of modern governance (Ericson and Haggerty 1997). They are the instruments that ensure that scientific discourse is transmitted throughout governmental institutions in required ways. I will suggest that decision-making forms encourage penal practitioners to construct offenders' identities in certain ways rather than in others. Forms are, to a large extent, technologically transmitted and they direct human communication, thus influencing the perceptions of ourselves and others. Chapters 4 and 5 therefore address the possible implications of formatted communication for our conceptions of offenders' identities, thus introducing a term 'categorical identity', and comparing it with Foucault's (1977) model of a 'delinquent'. The book concludes that the new forms of decision-making introduce and privilege a certain mode of thinking which is based on working on the surface, rather than on in-depth understanding. Symbolised by the Macintosh computer with its easy-to-interpret icons, this new mode of thought represents a culture where work becomes 'transparent' and one can get things done without needing to understand them.

The book is written in the hope of being able to write about technology and culture without sounding deterministic, although I am fully aware that the attempt has not always been successful. Throughout the writing process, I was continuously reminded of the essential difficulty of talking about the 'social impact of technology' without promoting the belief that the social and technological aspects were two independent spheres. Hutchby (2001) argues that one of the difficulties with embracing a social constructivist view of technology is that it casts into doubt the validity of asking questions about the nature of technology and social interaction as such. This is certainly a dilemma that I was presented with throughout the book.

Can we ever ask questions such as 'Are penal decisions influenced by the technological framework through which they are executed?' without sounding simplistic and deterministic? Or should the technological always be seen as essentially social? My answer to the first question is a reluctant yes. However, to be more accurate, what is at issue here is not simply the computer and information technologies as such, but rather the relationships between people and various technologies. These relationships are always determined not only by the technical properties of computers, but also by the choices and objectives of the people using them. This is a complex process that cannot be studied independently of organisational and ideological change within contemporary penal systems. So, while studying the role of information technologies in sentencing reforms, my objective has been to place these reforms within the broader context of organisational and paradigm shifts. Sentencing reforms and the striving for greater uniformity in decisions are a result of a combination of political, organisational and technological developments. It will be suggested that the rise of the demands for so called 'transparency' is an important aspect of these developments. The pressure to change an unstructured and 'non-transparent' sentencing process may come from sentencing being a 'cultural anomaly' in a system that so highly values transparency, rather than from the existence of the technical means to do it. Lyon tries to clarify the complex relationship between technological change and social change (in this case, social disembodiment):

> [N]either do I want to imply that communication and information technologies are the cause of social disembodiment. They are indeed its primary means, but how this occurs is a complex matter of socio-technological relationships. New technologies are the products of particular social patterns and purposes that in turn affect those patterns and purposes. A subtle process of co-construction takes place. (2001: 17)

***

Writing these lines, I feel a certain discomfort. On closer inspection, I realise that there may be several reasons for this. First of all, writing about one's own approach is, in many ways, an exercise in labelling – something which most criminologists tend to be quite knowledgeable about. However, in this case, one is labelling oneself, which makes it significantly more difficult and uncomfortable. Another reason for my discomfort may be the realisation that throughout the book I am moving in territories that I cannot quite call 'my own'. Throughout the book, I travel between several disciplines – criminology, criminal law, sociology, media and technology studies – without being able to cover any one of them exhaustively. I do not regard myself as an expert in any of these domains and have, therefore, to live with the constant awareness of 'black holes' in my knowledge in each one of them.

Furthermore, when crossing the borders between several disciplines, one becomes aware of the disciplinary nature of the word 'discipline'. As Ingunn Moser (2001) points out, academic disciplines are based on a maze of power relations that define their objects of research, their borders, the definition of methods and what the legitimate problems are, as well as what should be left outside. The function of academic disciplines is often to mark intellectual turfs and to ensure that outsiders do not come in, and if they do come in, they should 'use the same vocabulary as we do, or leave' (Moser 2001: 59, my translation). Thus, disciplines have borders that, in many ways, resemble states. As a cross-disciplinary scholar I found myself in the same position as a foreigner who does not really fit in a new country, but who, after many years abroad, also feels distant from his or her native land. One can thus become unsure of which culture one really belongs to. The only way out of this dilemma, of course, is to accept that one is a mixture, that one is both, and yet none of the options in their pure form. So much for the drawbacks. Doing cross-disciplinary research also in many ways resembles living in a multicultural society and that, for me, has a number of advantages which undoubtedly outweigh the drawbacks. Throughout the research process, I have had to enter new areas, such as the works of Marshall McLuhan, David J Bolter, Lev Manovich, David Lyon and Mark Poster. These areas have, precisely because of their novelty, brought new light and excitement, new perspectives and ideas to my existing knowledge and understanding. I cannot claim to have understood them correctly (if there is such a thing). However, they have been a tremendous source of inspiration.

Last, but not least, I wish to admit to one of the offences that academics often regard as one of the most serious but nonetheless seem to commit with a certain regularity – that of simplification. Penal practice is and has always been a complex mix of various ideologies, models and theories – co-existing with each other, although often conflicting in their intentions. In many places, the old rehabilitative apparatus still persists alongside new discourses such as just deserts and risk thinking. The discursive relations may have been changed, but there are few clear lines between the 'before and after'. In trying to shed some light on penal developments, I found it necessary to simplify in order to facilitate understanding. The differences between different models may be somewhat exaggerated and clearer than what could be evident from a closer look. Therefore, despite the use of words such as 'change' and 'shift', I choose not to view the new cultural conditions as a radical break with the past. The language of change is sometimes employed for pedagogical reasons, rather than with the aim of describing a totally new reality. As Manovich points out:

> New media does not radically break with the past; rather, it distributes weight differently between the categories which hold culture together, foregrounding what was in the background, and vice versa. As Frederick Jameson writes in his analysis of another shift, in this case from modernism to post-modernism: 'Radical breaks between periods do not generally involve complete changes but rather the restructuration of a certain number of elements already given …' (Manovich 2001a: 229–30)

When terms such as 'information society' are used, this is only a typified model whose difference from its predecessors is somewhat exaggerated. While some authors explicitly acknowledge and argue for the novelty of the so called information age, information order (Lash 2002) and technological society (Barry 2001), others, on the other hand, point to the fact that there are strong lines of continuity with the past (Giddens 1985, Mathiesen 1999, Winston 1998). As Giddens argues:

> modern societies have been … 'information societies' since their inception. There is a fundamental sense … in which all states have been 'information societies', since the generation of state power presumes the reflexively gathering, storage, and control of information, applied to administrative ends. (1985: 178)

Similarly, Mathiesen (1999) suggests that the use of information technologies does not necessarily imply the end of industrial society. On the contrary, certain uses of technology further reinforce and strengthen the social structures of industrialism, particularly the class divisions. Some even argue that all societies could, in a way, be described as information societies because knowledge and organised exchange of information are necessary conditions for any society (Finnemann 1999b: 362). Such continuity with the past should not, however, be a reason for avoiding the term information society or trying to coin a new one. In the same way as industry had been present in societies that were not termed industrial, so too does information take a special place in social organisation today. Thus, information and its specific qualities can and should be distinguished from 'other, earlier socio-cultural categories' (Lash 2002: 2). This book is written with the intention of directing focus on the nature of information and information gathering that are vital elements of contemporary governance, including governance of penal systems.

However, my purpose is neither to join the 'prophets' of the digital age – either prophets of its overly pessimistic or optimistic nature. I agree with Lyon (1995), however, that information society should be granted the status of 'problematic', that one needs to be aware of its ideological and uncritically optimistic connotations. History is far from being a constant process of progression and improvement, and we are far from achieving a world free of industrial production, pollution and physical work. The problematic status is therefore intended to question the uncritical celebration of technology, the visions of a radically new era, or 'silicon idolatry' as some have called it, without overlooking its significance for social change. This book is written in the hope of contributing to the debate in a way that, as Katherine Hayles puts it:

> embraces the possibilities of information technologies without being seduced by fantasies of unlimited power and disembodied immortality, that recognizes and celebrates finitude as a condition of human being, and that understands that human life is embedded in a material world of great complexity, one on which we depend for our continued survival. (Hayles 1999: 5)

# Chapter 1
# 'Sentencing-at-a-Distance'

## Making sentencing transparent

In most Western societies judges are considered to be in a position of considerable power and social status and held in high public esteem. Although this may be slowly changing, judges still tend to be predominantly upper and upper-middle class white males (Mathiesen 2001, Forer 1994, *The Independent* 2002). The financial rewards of a judicial office may sometimes be lower than those offered in the private sector, but the rewards are still high in terms of professional respect and social status. However, this tradition of judicial power and respect is not something that can be taken for granted. A number of socialist regimes succeeded to a considerable extent in curtailing both the power and the public status of the judiciary. In a number of contemporary Western penal systems as well, the traditionally strong status of the judicial profession may not be as stable as before. Not only are judicial decisions subject to increasing media focus and public criticism, the judiciary is also under increasing scrutiny and its power subjected to a growing number of restrictions from within the penal system. This eagerness to reform has probably come furthest in the US.

Naturally, such changes have not been unproblematic and, as changes usually are, have not been implemented without protests. The protests have, in some cases, been so strong that they cannot simply be explained as the usual reluctance to change. Some judges for the first time found themselves in conflict with the legal system whose laws and values they were supposed to implement and protect. Particularly in the US, resignations in protest are not uncommon. Some observers have even used terms such as 'judicial guerrilla warfare' (Tonry 1992). The question is: how can such a seemingly powerful profession, one of the cornerstones of state power, suddenly be in conflict with the established system of government? How can a profession, traditionally endowed with an aura of respect and even wisdom, suddenly be subjected to massive distrust and governmental scrutiny?

In this chapter, I look at how the change took place in the case of judicial decisions about sentencing. There are few spheres of penal policy that have received more attention and caused more heated debate in the past 30 years than sentencing. A great number of reforms have been introduced even more have been suggested: mandatory sentences, 'three strikes and you're out' laws, sentencing guidelines, 'truth in sentencing' reforms, increasing penalties for certain types of crimes, decriminalisation of others, introduction of new types of sentences, etc. To describe all these phenomena would be beyond the scope of this book, particularly as they often have so little in common, except for their reforming fervour. What follows is a selective story of sentencing reforms: a story about numerical sentencing guidelines and sentencing information systems (SISs).

The US experience with the so called *numerical sentencing guidelines* will serve as the initial example. However, as we shall see, although extreme in its extent, the curtailing of judicial sentencing power in the US is by no means unique. Other jurisdictions such as Australia, Scotland, England and Wales and the Netherlands exhibit some similar trends. A common trait of these reforms is that they try to limit the discretionary powers of the judiciary and make sentencing a more transparent, predictable, standardised and less discriminating process. The methods they use to achieve the goal are different, yet there are clear points of continuity. Therefore, this book intends primarily to examine numerical sentencing guidelines not as a US-specific sentencing technique, although in practice guidelines inevitably remain just that. Rather, it will be argued that guidelines can be seen as an embodiment, albeit extreme, of a more general trait within Western penal systems towards regulating the minutiae of penal decision-making and exercise of discretion. Numerical sentencing guidelines are characteristic of a specific style of governance which puts a premium on transparency and standardisation of penal decisions.

Furthermore, it will be suggested that numerical sentencing guidelines, similarly to SIS and risk assessment forms, are instruments of justice with so called *Macintosh traits*, offering pre-programmed, on-the-surface answers and solutions. Through their emphasis on standardisation and programmability, guidelines share an intrinsic structural likeness not only with other formalised decision-making tools, but also with other, technologically-mediated, systems of contemporary knowledge production. In their striving for structural beauty, explicitness of knowledge and focus on information gathering and analysis, guidelines are, I will argue, 'a child of the information age'. They are essentially 'computer-friendly' decision-making tools.

However, the history of sentencing guidelines cannot be told in clear and simple terms. These are complex phenomena and have many aspects and 'stories' which need to be told: first, the story of chronological events (when and how the reforms started, who the proponents were, and when and how they were implemented); secondly, the story of the political constellations and objectives behind the reforms (what did the various actors wish to achieve?). There is also the story of the practical implementation (which objectives were achieved and how the reforms were implemented 'on the ground'). Needless to say, populist pressures have always been particularly prevalent in sentencing. Finally, there are the broader shifts in penal culture and constellations of penal power that need to be taken into consideration (Garland 2001). Most of these developments have been well documented, and attempting to repeat their project would probably be unproductive (see, for example, Tonry 1992, Tonry 1996, Clarkson and Morgan 1995, Rex and Tonry 2002, Tata and Hutton 2002).

This book therefore offers a selective history of sentencing reform. I say selective, because none of the types of stories mentioned above are the main focus of the book, although they are all mentioned in part. Rather, the main focus is directed towards the various techniques, rationales and *forms of knowledge* represented in the chosen sentencing reforms. Two main questions are asked: what has been the rationale behind the reforms and growing distrust of the judiciary's sentencing power, and what have been the objectives of the new solutions adopted by the reforms? The second, and crucial, question is how has the nature of judicial sentencing knowledge changed through the process? The starting point will be an assumption that, since law is essentially a knowledge profession, the power shifts within judicial practice are necessarily reflected in, and fought through, the shifting perceptions of what is the accepted and legitimate knowledge base for legal decisions.

## Sentencing guidelines

The origins of sentencing guidelines lie in attempts by liberal reformers and human rights activists in the 1970s to design a more just and equitable penal system. Prior to that, sentencers had wide and, in some jurisdictions, virtually uncontrolled discretion. In the US, the majority of states had no appeal against sentence. Defendants had a right to appeal only if the sentence was illegal, ie, it exceeded the statutory maximum. In many states, sentences for serious offences were indeterminate or partially indeterminate, their duration being determined by parole authorities exercising almost unlimited discretion (Clarkson and Morgan 1995). In the 1970s, many reports and studies strongly criticised indeterminate sentencing practices and pointed to the abuse of power to which they were open. The dominant view was that indeterminate sentences, tailored to the personal characteristics of the offender – education, job, marital status – gave judges and parole boards the discretion to penalise black and lower-class offenders (Rothman 1994).[1]

The idea of proportionate punishments and sentencing grids gained momentum with the 1972 publication of Judge Marvin Frankel's book *Criminal Sentences: Law Without Order*, Norval Morris's *The Future of Imprisonment* in 1974, and the 1976 publication of *Doing Justice – The Report of the Committee for the Study of Incarceration*. Andrew von Hirsch became perhaps one of the most influential proponents of the so called just deserts movement that stressed the importance of offence-focused rather than individual-focused sentencing policy. He argued that 'desert' should have the central role in deciding criminal sanctions,[2] and that punishments should be *proportionate* to the seriousness of criminal conduct. At the same time, rehabilitation programmes were regarded as a sham – giving the illusion that prisoners were locked up for their own good, and thus making imprisonment seem legitimate and desirable. Reformers proposed to reduce substantially discretionary powers of judges and parole boards. Sentencing practice should be determined only by crime and criminal record, regardless of offenders' personal and social characteristics, such as race, gender, occupation, employment record, etc.

In this effort to limit judicial discretion, left-wing liberals came later to be supported by conservative thinkers who believed that indeterminate sentences were too lenient, that they released prisoners too early, and thereby jeopardised public safety. The right-wing critics opposed the release of prisoners after a third or a half of their sentences had been served, and demanded 'truth in sentencing' – that offenders should serve out their time. The rise in reported crime was blamed on soft

1 Wolfgang and Riedel's (1973) study, for example, showed that black offenders were more often sentenced to death, and for lesser offences, than white offenders. Furthermore, actual executions were also carried out discriminatorily.

2 However, von Hirsch does allow other objectives, such as crime control, to be taken into consideration. Later, we will see that most of the reforms that used the desert principles as their basis also took other objectives such as incapacitation and general prevention into account.

liberal judges, who imposed sentences which were much shorter than offenders deserved and which failed to prevent crime. Forer (1994) argues that since US federal judges serve for life and most state judges for long terms, the removal of unco-operative judges would not have been easy. The solution was to deprive them of their discretion in sentencing. The interesting point here is, as Rothman (1994) suggests, that the oddness of the alliance with conservatives at first did not seem to weaken liberals' enthusiasm. They believed that sentencing reforms would in fact lead to a less punitive penal policy. Unfortunately, their beliefs have proven to be unfounded.

Sentencing guidelines, created by sentencing commissions, became widely accepted in the US penal system. It needs to be pointed out, however, that the majority of US states still have a system of indeterminate sentencing. Reitz thus rightly asserts that in spite of the considerable reforming fervour, 'the traditional indeterminate structure remains the single most prevalent model of US sentencing practice' (2001: 231). The federal system and roughly one-half of the states now use some sort of guideline systems or are considering their use. Some states adopted advisory or voluntary guidelines, while 10 states and the federal system opted for the presumptive guidelines (Spohn 2002: 72). Unlike voluntary guidelines, the presumptive guidelines require judges to follow them in each individual case, or otherwise provide reasons for departure. Some guideline systems also specify reasons which cannot be grounds for departure from the rules and, as we shall see later, the grounds for departure can be in some cases quite limited.

However, in spite of the initial hopes that the creation of sentencing commissions and sentencing guidelines would be able somehow to 'insulate' sentencing policy from the popular punitiveness and political pressures, the effects were quite the opposite of what their liberal proponents originally wanted. With the exception of a few jurisdictions, prison populations have increased and the effect of the guidelines on disparity in sentencing has been disputed. Minnesota, for example, was one of the first jurisdictions to have developed guidelines, in 1980. The guidelines were carefully crafted to adjust imprisonment levels to the already existing correctional resources. A so called 'prison population impact model' was used to ensure that the overall prison population level would remain stable. Similarly, in Oregon, the primary objective behind the guidelines was to link sentencing policy to available prison resources (Tonry 1996). However, as the guideline model spread to other US states and the federal system, such considerations were mostly abandoned. Also in Minnesota, originally committed to the objective of keeping the prison population growth under control, the 1989 Crime Bill fundamentally changed the commission's originally stated purpose of punishment and made public safety and higher penalties for violent crimes the priority of sentencing. Spohn (2002) reports that severity of sentences increased in most guidelines jurisdictions, as well as the percentage of offenders who are sentenced to prison.

Sentencing guidelines, therefore, were not only unable to curtail popular punitiveness, but they may have created a system that is even more vulnerable to being hijacked by politicians. The US Federal Sentencing Guidelines are especially severe and have greatly increased the levels of imprisonment, particularly during the 1980s war on drugs. The average time served in prison has increased from 24 months in July 1984 to 46 in June 1990 (Rothman 1994). In addition, in a number of states, sentencing commissions had to give in to political pressure to increase sentences for certain categories of crimes. This has been the case in Minnesota, where the penalty levels were increased twice. In 1989, for example, following the public and political pressure, the penalty for aggravated robbery was increased from 24 to 48 months, thus doubling the sentence with a single decision (Clarkson and Morgan 1995). Therefore, not surprisingly, the guidelines have been subjected to considerable debate. The US Federal Sentencing Guidelines, enacted in 1987, have received the most fervent criticism, both from judges and academics. They have been termed 'the most disliked sentencing reform initiative in the US in this [ie, 20th] century' (Tonry 1996: 25). By 1989, over 200 judges had either written judgments or concurred in finding the US Federal Sentencing Guidelines unconstitutional – although the Supreme Court disagreed with this view and ruled in 1989 that the guidelines were constitutional. Judges have complained about the loss of discretion that results in unjust sentences.

Another question is, of course, whether the sentencing levels would have been raised anyway due to the wave of increasing punitiveness that marked the US penal landscape. Reitz (2001: 231), for example, points out that one should not assume an existence of an automatic correlation between sentencing guidelines or indeterminate sentencing and more severe or less severe sentencing practices. He points out that the state with the highest per capita incarceration rate, Texas, built its prison population with an indeterminate sentencing model. So did the state with the lowest incarceration rate, North Dakota. Reitz (2001: 231) makes an important point that what seems to distinguish the guideline from the non-guideline states is not their lesser or greater punitiveness or lesser or specific sentencing patterns, but rather that the guideline states are marked by '*uniformity* in sentences imposed, *planning*, *predictability*, and *systematic* oversight' (2001: 231, emphasis added). These are, among other, also the issues that will be the focus of this book. My purpose here is not primarily to write yet another critical account of the guidelines with regard to their punitiveness. An abundance of literature already exists on the subject, particularly on the subject of the US Federal Sentencing Guidelines. The objective will be, therefore, to situate the guidelines in a broader cultural and political context of contemporary information societies, where the guidelines can assume a broader significance and transcend their specifically American character.

The question is, naturally, whether the guidelines have any relevance in a European and wider international context. We may choose to dismiss them as an exclusively US phenomenon; in a way, they have been just that. No other country has followed the US example and imposed detailed numerical sentencing guidelines, although there has been a certain amount of interest. For example, the British Government has recently published a White Paper proposing the introduction of some form of guidelines (Home Office 2001). Consequently, a Sentencing Guidelines Council was established and held its first meeting in March 2004. In addition, the Parliament of Western Australia has recently adopted a bill proposing a sentencing matrix (Morgan 2002).[3] However, I would like to suggest

3 Morgan (2002) reports that the Australian proposal was directly inspired by the US sentencing grids, although the scope of Australian judicial discretion differs strongly from that of the US. Australia already has an established tradition of appellate review, and desert principles have been strongly represented. Morgan therefore suggests that the guideline model has been driven by the right-wing law and order politics.

that there are salient reasons for further examining the sentencing guidelines phenomenon.[4] The structure and the rationale behind the guidelines are consistent with a general trend in contemporary penal culture: the implementation of transparent and, as we shall see later, 'computer-friendly' auditing tools. My purpose is, therefore, to examine the guidelines as a specific *technology of governance*[5] of penal decision-makers. Guidelines share a certain structural likeness with a number of other methods that are used in contemporary penal systems to achieve accountability of penal practitioners. Furthermore, it will be suggested that these methods or technologies for achieving accountability and transparency of decisions are marked by specific ways of ordering decision-making processes, and conceptualising what it means to think and act, and what it means to be a decision-maker and an offender. Therefore, it is interesting to look at the guideline design *itself* and explore why it became as widely accepted as a new architecture of penal power in the US.

## The matrix design

The guideline method, as a form of decision-making, has not been reserved to sentencing only. In fact, the guidelines matrix has become so widespread that it has been described as 'the new design of penal power in the USA' (Simon 1993; see also Walker 1993). The guidelines approach has been developed first for structuring parole decisions, and subsequently for bail and pre-trial release and for classification in jails and prisons in the USA (Gottfredson and Tonry 1987, Blumstein *et al* 1986). In these classification systems, the focus has been on dealing with offenders according to their risk rather than the seriousness of offences. The guidelines are formal prediction-oriented rules, based on statistical calculations of risk.[6] They are a result of collaboration between social scientists and decision-makers to improve the efficiency and effectiveness of criminal justice decisions. In addition, as Gottfredson and Tonry (1987) point out, the biggest reform in the US in the last 20 years has been precisely the widespread incorporation of research-based risk assessment methods into decision-making:

> Just a decade and a half ago, most decisions concerning defendant and offenders were ad hoc and intuitive ... Today nearly every state has attempted to incorporate scientific knowledge about predictions – of future crimes, of violence, of suicide proneness, of victimization vulnerability, of amenability to treatment – into explicit decision standards. (Gottfredson and Tonry 1987: vii)

---

4 The guidelines have also placed a certain pressure on the judiciaries in other countries to [illegible] preventing the implementation of the (often disliked) guidelines system. The guidelines have been viewed by the judiciary as a possible penalty if it does not voluntarily accept some other form of curtailing of their discretion.

5 For a further discussion of the term 'technology' see Chapter 2, below. 'Technology' is not meant to describe technical qualities of certain objects, but rather refers to a number of rationalities, objectives, artefacts, etc for structuring social action.

6 As the Panel on Research on Criminal Careers describes the guidelines: 'Such empirically based rules require development of scales that relate prediction variables to estimates of future offending and transform every offender's scale score into a risk classification level, such as high risk or low risk. The risk classification of each offender is then considered as one factor in making individual decisions' (Blumstein *et al* 1986: 164).

However, it might be interesting to note that the use of guidelines as a form of decision-making is nothing new in penal history. Statistical prediction tables were already in use in the 1930s to determine release dates for prisoners in the US. Nevertheless, prior to the 1970s, 'forms played a widespread but minor role as one part in a large dossier of information available to the decision-maker' (Simon 1995: 5). When it came to the courts, guidelines were 'quite removed from the judicial role which remained the symbolic if not operational center of sentencing' (Simon 1995: 5). That, however, was fundamentally changed during the reforming fervour of the 1980s.

One of the primary objectives of sentencing guidelines has been to reduce judicial discretion and make decision-making more transparent and predictable. Their proponents argued that sentencing decisions lacked a coherent structure, that they were a 'law without order' (Frankel 1972). To achieve a just and democratic sentencing process, judicial discretion[7] should be limited, or at least regulated. The whole process should be made more predictable and accountable. Proportionality, consistency/uniformity and rationality/transparency are thus the core principles behind the numerical guidelines:

- Proportionality means that punishment should be in proportion to the seriousness of the offence.
- Consistency and uniformity prescribe that offenders convicted of similar crimes and with similar criminal records should receive similar sanction.
- Rationality and transparency mean that the reasoning behind a sentence should be clearly articulated, open and observable (Lubitz and Ross 2001).

The main imperative of sentencing reforms has been that decision-making should be more *explicit*, that the rationality and information behind judges' decisions should be specifiable and traceable. Judges should explicitly state the reasoning behind their decisions. Decisions should consistently follow certain rational goals, and the information used to achieve the goals should be visible. It was argued that, in the past, judges' sentencing decisions were not subjected to rules, and that the lack of rules could result in unfair and unequal treatment of offenders. Therefore, the goal was to make sentencing as objective as possible: to minimise the dependence of the rationality of the process on individual judges' personalities and create maximum equality for offenders. A natural continuation of the reforms was, therefore, to design *objective* formal structures for decision-making that would translate sentencing rationalities into exact decisions. Sentencing guidelines were the result. On the one hand, guidelines satisfied the requirements for greater transparency and rationality of penal decisions. On the other hand, they addressed the demands for equal treatment of offenders. Guidelines promised to achieve objectivity with regard to decision-makers as well as offenders. Perhaps we could give another name to the phenomenon – programmability? *Programmability* means that people or machines respond with unvarying precision, and that their actions

7 Judicial discretion is the power of the court to do as it sees fit (for example, grant a remedy, evaluate evidence, etc). Discretion is usually regarded as the opposite of rules and laws. It denotes a situation where, instead of deciding a question by recourse to a fixed rule, the court is able to decide between alternative courses of action. This means that the existence of discretion presupposes an element of choice, and that there is no prescribed correct answer to a given problem (Pattenden 1990).

are uniform, because the instructions that guide them have been standardised. In order to translate human agency into a programme, certain conditions have to be met: the process needs to be rationalised and events in the process standardised. Rationalisation and standardisation were also central elements of the guidelines' design.

Most guidelines are designed in the same way, in the shape of two-dimensional grids. Decisions are scaled according to crime and criminal record. Guideline grids vary in detail. Most divide crimes into 10 or 12 categories, some more. The Minnesota guideline grid, presented in Table 1 in the Appendix, has 11 vertical grids. In the extreme, the US Federal Sentencing Guidelines, presented in Table 2 in the Appendix, take the form of a grid with 43 offence levels on the vertical axis and six criminal history levels on the horizontal axis. The task of the judge is to look up the point on a grid where the offence level intersects the criminal history. He or she then passes a sentence according to the grid, unless there is an explicitly defined reason to depart from it. In principle, the process is similar to calculating income tax – the process is complex and intricate, but, in theory, leads everybody to the same conclusion (Simon 1995).

The strong emphasis on criminal acts is partly a result of the just deserts rationale, but also partly a result of the view that crimes can be scaled and calculated according to seriousness. Thus, even when guidelines are not explicitly based on just deserts, due to their design, crime and criminal record are still in focus. The US Federal Sentencing Guidelines, for example, which are not explicitly based on just deserts or any other explicit rationale, in practice still resemble a deserts system (Tonry 1996). As Tonry (1996) writes, a grid axis cannot handle factors that are not linear. However, he points out that many ethically important considerations are not linear. They vary from case to case and may be mitigating in some and aggravating in others.

## Formalisation as the new ideology

Critics have often pointed out the incompatibility between just deserts, deterrence and incapacitation theory, and that some guideline systems, by accepting all, lack a coherent ideology. Just deserts ideology is often presented as the opposite of the utilitarian reasoning embodied in deterrence and incapacitation theories. However, I would like to explore some coincidences between these policies. Could it be that, while the utilitarian and desert theories may be contradictory at the level of philosophical principles, they are not so when it comes to their application in practice? Minnesota Sentencing Guidelines are one obvious example. As mentioned earlier, Minnesota was at the forefront of the proportionality and just deserts movement, and the first state to implement presumptive numerical guidelines in 1980. However, due to the change of political climate, the Minnesota Sentencing Commission had to change the goals of the guidelines and put priority on the utilitarian considerations of public safety. Today, the Commission specifies the goals of the guidelines as follows:[8]

8 Source: from the Minnesota Sentencing Guidelines Commission website: www.msgc.state.mn.us.

1 *To Assure Public Safety*: The violent offenders who pose a danger to the community are likely to be incarcerated and for longer periods of time;

2 *To Promote Uniformity in Sentencing*: Offenders who are convicted of similar crimes and who have similar criminal records are to be similarly sentenced;

3 *To Promote Proportionality in Sentencing*: The guidelines support a 'just deserts' philosophy by recommending to the sentencing judge a proportionally more severe sentence based first, on the severity of the conviction offense and second, on the offender's criminal history;

4 *To Provide Truth and Certainty in Sentencing*: The period of time to be served in prison is pronounced by the judge at sentencing and that time is fixed. Those sentenced to prison will serve at least two-thirds of their executed sentence in prison;

5 *To Co-ordinate Sentencing Practices with Correctional Resources*: To assure available resources, the guidelines recommend who should be imprisoned and for how long. The need for prison resources is therefore more predictable and the Legislature can fund accordingly.

This varied mix of goals is by no means specific to Minnesota, but can, with modification, be applied to most guideline systems. The guidelines may, therefore, be marked not so much by their ideological connotations, since they can be used for just deserts as well as utilitarian purposes, but rather by their *formalisation*. Perhaps formalisation, as a phenomenon, describes sentencing guidelines across jurisdictions more accurately than their ideological orientations. Better still, perhaps we should consider formalisation as the new 'ideology' of criminal justice. Thus, it becomes easier to grasp why managerialist thinking can coexist and thrive within the new penal paradigms, although it had problems with rehabilitation. While deserts theory conflicts with managerialism and incapacitation on a deontological level (Bottoms 1995), it still is amenable to, and in fact demands, the rationalisation and predictability that is at the heart of the managerialist project. As the Panel on Research on Criminal Careers has said: '[F]our general concepts are of central importance in the implementation and evaluation of decision-making guidelines: visibility, rationality, equity, and effectiveness.' Further on, it states:

> The concept of rationality suggests that guidelines should assist in relating decisions made to the goals specified. These may be predictive in nature (eg, associated with desired offender outcomes), but they may be of another nature (eg, of ensuring just deserts or of increasing equity). (Blumstein *et al* 1986: 252)

The belief that decision-making can and should be predictable is the basic principle of the just deserts theory. However, as Nils Christie (1980) has pointed out, here lies also its 'hidden message': 'The world is simple. Sins can be clearly classified in advance.'[9] Implicit in the just deserts theory is that criminal acts can be reduced to their 'essences', and that it is possible to find *quantitative* equivalents of pain that would correspond to every act within a certain category processed through the system. Throughout the 1980s, the just deserts movement popularised the principle of *equality* as one of the most important goals of criminal justice, and made disparity into a number one 'enemy'. However, Tonry makes an important point that the overemphasis on the equality principle cannot be simply blamed on just deserts

9 My translation.

theories. The overemphasis on equality is a 'by-product' of the sentencing format – the two-dimensional axis grid which inevitably puts emphasis on crimes and criminal record, while obscuring other factors (Tonry 1996: 14).

It has been argued that the preoccupation with formal equality has in fact been a great source of *inequity* in contemporary penal systems (Tata 2002).[10] The system of formal equality, which stresses the sameness of individuals before the law, is based on an assumption of overlooking social differences. The fact that a prison sentence may have a particularly grave impact on a sensitive gay man, or on a family with strained economic resources, is overlooked in order to preserve the illusion of sameness. At the same time, the focus on equal treatment does not really guarantee that the law itself is unbiased. The racial bias of the US drug laws is one such blatant example.[11]

Therefore, a question that could be raised at this point is: why has equality become such a highly prioritised value in modern justice? Until 30 years ago, the need for treatment and individualisation of sentences was clearly one of the leading and undisputed paradigms of penal discourse and the welfare state. In a number of countries this is still the case. One could, of course, argue that the principle of equality, promoted by the guidelines proponents, has a long tradition in Western legal systems, formulated clearly in Cesare Beccaria's *On Crimes and Punishments* ([1764] 1986). Beccaria's argument that the punishment of a nobleman should not differ from that of the lowest member of society ([1764] 1986: 39) formed one of the bases of a number of 19th century penal codes. However, as Garland points out, the welfarist fervour for treatment and expert evaluation undermined the legalistic discourse of formal equality:

> Where once the leading principle had been *nullem poena sine crimen* ('no punishment without a crime'), in the world of penal-welfarism it came instead to be *no treatment without diagnosis,* and *no penal sanction without expert advice.* (Garland 2001: 37, original emphasis)

The contemporary just deserts arguments clearly take up Beccaria's claim that punishments are to be estimated, 'not by the sensibility of the criminal, but by the harm done to society' (Beccaria [1764] 1986: 39). Interestingly, however, Beccaria also argues that the injury to society 'is augmented by the high rank of the offender' ([1764] 1986: 39), thus modifying his seemingly objective position. Like the guidelines' creators, Beccaria, too, entertained a vision of mathematical accuracy and geometric precision in punishment:

> If geometry were adaptable to the infinite and obscure arrangements of human activity, there ought to be a corresponding scale of punishments, descending from the most rigorous to the slightest. The wise lawmaker, however, will rest content with noting the chief points and respecting their order … (Beccaria [1764] 1986: 15)

---

10 Tata describes *equity* as having the meaning of substantive justice and fairness, as opposed to the narrower formal meaning ascribed to *equality*.

11 The US federal legislation designed to reduce disparity in sentencing also institutionalised penalties for 'crack' cocaine (stereotypically used by poor blacks) which are far more severe than those for any other type of drugs. The sale of one gram of crack is punished as harshly as the sale of 100 grams of powder cocaine (stereotypically usually used by more affluent groups).

Beccaria's vision had a number of followers in the Enlightenment and post-Enlightenment period. Stith and Cabranes (1998) point out, with some irony, that Enrico Ferri's 1919 Italian Penal Code Commission proposed similar solutions to the ones adopted by the guideline commissions almost a century later. Ferri proposed:

> 'a new and autonomous systematization of legislative norms in accord with the advance of scientific doctrines'. The Ferri system insisted on a comprehensive specification of factors relevant to a sentence, along with instructions on penal arithmetic for adding these factors together ... It is worth noting that Italy never sought to implement Professor Ferri's elaborate system. (Stith and Cabranes 1998: 13–14)

However, the revived focus on equality and better uniformity in some recent sentencing reforms is not merely a continuation of this age-long tradition. On the following pages, I will suggest that the contemporary insistence on equality is situated in and is supported by distinctly late modern cultural and technological environments. While relying on the Beccarian philosophical frame and striving for formal rationality, the new sentencing trends are marked by their distinctly late modern context, which is the context of information societies.

## Judicial thinking under attack

One could say that guidelines have programmed decision-making to achieve a higher degree of predictability and system rationality.[12] However, this approach not only proposed to limit disparity and arbitrariness of judicial decisions, but also introduced a break with the existing models of judicial thinking and knowledge. As a consequence of the guidelines, both decision-makers' and offenders' experience of punishment have been fundamentally changed. Explicit rules have been introduced regarding how judges should think and express themselves about sentencing. Many judges have experienced guidelines, especially US Federal Sentencing Guidelines, as mechanical, arbitrary and impersonal. The US Federal Sentencing Guidelines are marked not only by extreme complexity – the manual has more than 900 pages and weighs close to five pounds; in comparison, the US Internal Revenue Code weighs under four pounds (Stith and Cabranes 1998: 3) – but also by their severity. They have therefore been subjected to considerably more criticism than the state guidelines. Human factors, it is argued, have to a large extent disappeared from the sentencing process. To use one judge's words about the US Federal Sentencing Guidelines:

> They have established a system of wholly mechanical sentence computation which desensitizes those associated with it, and converts a sentencing proceeding, which might otherwise have some salutary effect on the offender, to a mathematical and logistical exercise ... (Lasker 1997)

---

12 Another question is whether the reforms have succeeded in limiting discretion. Some research indicates that discretion has simply been transferred from judges to prosecutors, and that while judges' decisions have become more predictable, the system as a whole has not (Freed 1992). The inflexibility of numerical guidelines makes the pre-trial decisions, where the charges are negotiated, more significant. The system may have become more predictable when it comes to the outcome of judicial decisions, but not with regard to the system as a whole. It may be that the outcomes now depend even less on the nature of the offence and more on offenders' negotiating skills (Morgan 2002).

Judge Lawrence Irving resigned in 1990, describing the process as having become 'a numbers game … It's a game I just can't continue to play … You are a robot now on the bench' (Simon 1995: 6).[13]

The case of Rosa M, described by a former judge, Lois G Forer, illustrates the inflexibility of the guideline system, in this case, guidelines for bail:

> Rosa was pushed into my courtroom in a rickety wheelchair. She had only one leg. She was on trial on charges of arson, risking a catastrophe, recklessly endangering others, and several other crimes. As the case unfolded it became clear that Rosa was not a dangerous felon but a very sick, 64-year-old widow. She was living in a slum at the time of the alleged crime. Her key had broken off in the lock on the inside of her apartment and she became trapped there. Rosa had no phone so she opened the window and screamed for help. But with the noise of TVs, boom boxes, crying babies, and fighting adults, no one heard. In desperation she placed a wastebasket on her windowsill, put a piece of newspaper in it and lit a fire. As she expected, a neighbour saw the flames and called the fire department. Firefighters broke down the door and rescued her. The police also came and arrested Rosa … At the police station Rosa was interviewed by a young lawyer employed by the bail project. He went through his guidelines: Rosa was not employed; she had lived in that slum only a few weeks; she had no family; she had no credit cards. He recommended that bail be denied. Rosa M was in jail almost six months before I saw her in court … The purpose of bail is to assure that an arrestee will come to court when his or her case is called for trial. But where was an indigent old woman with only one leg going to go? … I asked the lawyer why he didn't recommend that Rosa be released without bail. 'She didn't meet the guidelines,' he responded. (1994: 57)

Rosa's case is not an isolated example. Guidelines are a system based on the *nomenclature* of crimes rather than on seriousness of individual acts. The system often has difficulty in accounting for the fact that offences with the same name may be very different with regard to their moral seriousness. A charge of theft, murder or arson (described above) may be used for a variety of different circumstances. Another often cited example is the case of Dane Yirkowsky:

> ... a man serving 15 years in prison for possession of a single 22-calliber round of ammunition that was discovered by police during a search of his residence. Although he had no weapon and no history of using one in a crime, prosecutors in the US Attorney's Office in Cedar Rapids, Iowa, filed charges of felony possession of ammunition against Yirkowsky, an ex-convict. The tactic was an attempt to pressure him to yield information about other crimes in which they believed he had been involved. Yirkowsky, who had previously served time for burglary, claimed that he found the bullet under a carpet in his home. However, he pleaded guilty to the charges. Given his record, and the restrictions on the possession of ammunition for convicted criminals, Yirkowsky's mandatory sentence was based upon his categorization as an 'armed career criminal' under federal sentencing guidelines. This was done although he had never been convicted of committing a crime with the use of a weapon. (*The Washington Times* 2002)

---

13 Another issue that has been addressed recently is whether some judges have given up exercising the discretion still left to them under the guideline system. It has been argued (Tata 2000, Provine 1998) that some judges appear to have convinced themselves that their 'hands are tied' and decline to use their discretion when this is still possible. Provine (1998) points out that the situation is similar to that under the Fugitive Slave Act 1850. At that time, judges were also appalled by the harshness of the law, yet nonetheless declined to use their discretion to ameliorate its worst effects.

The just deserts framework has thus resulted in equal punishment for crimes with the same name, but it has not necessarily achieved fair punishment for people according to their 'deserts'. It has resulted in the problem of 'just deserts in an unjust society'.

## Just deserts in an unjust society

The guidelines have fundamentally changed the reasoning process behind sentencing. How is the quality of justice changed when a judge can no longer 'look a defendant straight in the eye', but has instead to use the lenses of two-dimensional guideline grids? Formalisation in sentencing has been achieved at the expense of richness of language and narratives and – as we have seen from the cases mentioned above – human dimensions as well. Inherent in the guideline approach is a large degree of impersonality. The only information permitted for consideration is standards prescribed beforehand. Information not contained in words cannot, therefore, be interpreted. This approach has difficulty in reflecting offenders' private thoughts and subjectivity. The factors that are taken into consideration are objective factors that do not require an understanding of complex subjective rationalities. A two-dimensional grid focuses judges' attention to the elements of the grids and away from other considerations.

In the old system, justness in sentencing was (at least in principle)[14] explicitly determined by examination of a wide variety of factors. Judges looked at education, employment, family life, mental health, character and a variety of other 'human considerations'. In the guideline system, on the other hand, this entire dimension has been removed from analysis and even, as in the case of US Federal Sentencing Guidelines, determined as 'not ordinarily relevant'. The US Sentencing Commission concludes in its Guidelines Manual that age, education and vocational skills, mental and emotional conditions, physical condition (including drug or alcohol dependence, abuse or gambling addiction), employment record and family ties and responsibilities are '*not* ordinarily relevant in determining whether a sentence should be outside the applicable guideline range' (November 2003: §5H1.1–5H1.6, emphasis added). The factors a federal judge may use to reduce a guideline sentence are the offender's 'acceptance of responsibility' (a guilty plea), which can result in a minor reduction, and his willingness to provide 'substantial assistance' to the government (turning state's evidence and implicating others) which can lead to a major reduction (Rothman 1994).[15]

In addition, the Minnesota Sentencing Guidelines, although far less harsh and more flexible than the US Federal Sentencing Guidelines, explicitly state among the factors that should *not* be used as reasons for departure:

---

14 It must be pointed out, of course, that the extent to which these considerations were in fact taken into account in practice varied considerably. However, in principle at least, a sentence was meant to reflect a wide variety of considerations.

15 The US Federal Sentencing Guidelines also introduce so called 'real offence' sentencing, requiring judges to take into account not only the specific offence but also other offences which an offender had committed (including the ones he had not been charged for or even had been acquitted of).

c Employment factors, including:

(1) occupation or impact of sentence on profession or occupation;

(2) employment history;

(3) employment at time of offense;

(4) employment at time of sentencing.

d Social factors, including:

(1) educational attainment;

(2) living arrangements at time of offense and sentencing;

(3) length of residence;

(4) marital status. (Minnesota Sentencing Commission 2003: 24)

On the other hand, in Pennsylvania, where judges are allowed to depart from the guidelines if they provide their reasons, Kramer and Ulmer (1996) report that the most usual reasons for departure are precisely the above stated factors: 'defendant is remorseful/good candidate for rehabilitation, guilty plea/plea bargain, defendant is caring for dependants, court is unwilling to disrupt family ties, defendant is employed, court is unwilling to disrupt job ties, offense prior record is qualitatively less serious than the guideline score indicates' (Spohn 2002: 230). Kramer and Ulmer's study thus shows that the old tradition of individualised sentencing is still quite strongly present in judicial reasoning.

The rationale behind the provisions prohibiting consideration of offenders' personal circumstances has been that if judges were allowed to take personal and social circumstances into account, this could lead to biased decisions favouring middle-class offenders, who are more likely to have a job and stable family life. Tonry argues that this rationale is empirically misconceived and even perverse. Only a small proportion of offenders sentenced by courts today come from middle- and upper-class backgrounds:

> The normal range of socio-economic backgrounds of common law offenders range from deeply disadvantaged to the merely deprived. The chimerical middle-class offender is conspicuous by his absence ... Thus, policies designed to prevent unfair treatment of disadvantaged offenders as a class have the likely effect of unfair treatment of disadvantaged offenders as individuals. (Tonry 1994: 76–77)

The preservation of formal equality, therefore, prevents judges from focusing on the minimisation of suffering and parsimony (Tonry 1994). In order to maintain the notion of formal equality, a disadvantaged offender is assumed to be the same as the abstract (homogenous) subject of law.

These provisions have in practice led to results that conflict with many trial judges' perception of what is fair and just. The case of Frederick Eiselt, charged with possession of a firearm, is one example:

> Eiselt had held the same job for seven years. He earned $11 an hour and health benefits for his entire family; he had a baby boy and his wife was pregnant. Eiselt's criminal history consisted of several old misdemeanour convictions, none of which resulted in a prison sentence. The sentencing Guidelines committed Eiselt to 10 to 16 months in prison. But in light of Eiselt's family responsibility and modest criminal history, the

> judge considered that sentence too severe. He concluded that Eiselt was 'not a model citizen' but that Guidelines calculation over-represented his actual dangerousness. 'If we put him in jail, he will lose his job; and his wife and baby will be on welfare. I don't know that's going to do anybody any good,' the judge declared. He sentenced Eiselt to three years' probation with six months of community confinement. The Court of Appeals reversed. (Coalition For Federal Sentencing Reform 1997)

As one judge's report shows, Eiselt's case is not isolated:

> I also had a lady before me who was a courier. The guidelines called for a year prison sentence. She was the mother of three children, one of which, the youngest, was being breastfed at the time of the sentence. When I departed downward in order to allow her to be with her child for the first two years of her life, I was reversed by the Court of Appeals which said I had not sustained a case for departure. (Sporkin 1997)

Forer (1994) reports that before the reforms it was unusual to impose prison sentences on pregnant women and mothers of young children for property and drug offences. Now, judges are forced to do so by law. As a result of these gender-neutral sentencing laws, the female prison population in the US has increased substantially.

In addition to illustrating how sentencing guidelines take away the power to listen from the courts, these examples also show the harshness of US mandatory sentencing laws on drugs (a subject that goes beyond the scope of the present study), and the rigidity with which appellate courts enforce the guideline legislation.[16] Trial judges and lawyers, who are closely involved in sentencing, to a greater or lesser extent resist the two-dimensional view of individuals imposed by the guidelines. Appellate courts, on the other hand, are further removed and, seeing only lawyers and papers, seem to be more comfortable than trial judges in treating people as stereotypes rather than as individuals (Tonry 1996). As Freed (1992: 1681) writes, appellate judges no longer have to look defendants in the eye. They no longer see large numbers of worried faces in front of them. Thereby, they can treat the guidelines as if they were 'written in stone' and reverse a significant percentage of departures. This is especially true when departure is based on offender characteristics. Sporkin (1997) argues that the development allows an individual, in effect, to be *sentenced* in *absentia*. What is seen by a judge is only the offence which has been committed: the purest form of just deserts – of justice with a blindfold. Christie suggests that the image of justice as blindfolded would be, in the case of the US Federal Sentencing Guidelines, in fact misleading:

> In this situation, Lady Justice does not need to be blindfolded. She has nothing to look at, except a Table. Central authorities in the form of a Sentencing Commission have decided. And there is no need for scales. The weighing too, is done in the Table. The task has been simplified. No wonder things are speeding up, an advance for modernity. But her sword is easier to use than ever. A sword directed by a table. (1993: 145)

The guideline grids make crimes and criminal records distinct and the human characteristics of offenders invisible. To use one judge's words: 'Whereas sentencing once called for hours spent reflecting on the offence and the person, we judges are

---

16 It needs to be pointed out, however, that there is considerable variation with regard to departures from the guidelines. While the US Federal Sentencing Guidelines have become almost mandatory, in Minnesota, there is a departure rate of almost 30% (Clarkson and Morgan 1995).

becoming rubber-stamp bureaucrats' (Federal Judge Weinstein in Rothman 1994: 37). Guidelines are based on a belief that one's responsibility should be determined only by a particular criminal act and not by wider social circumstances. However, critics point out that this solution would be only just in an ideal world. In reality, there are no identical criminal acts that can be punished in a standard way. Offenders differ according to their personal and social circumstances, and that necessarily affects their responsibility. A long abused wife who attacks her abusive husband or a child who attacks her father calls for a different judgment of moral culpability from when the same act is committed by the husband.

Tonry (1994) suggests that because of its reliance on objective legal measures of deserts, the theory of proportionality is unable to take into account the subjective degree of moral culpability of the offender under particular circumstances and conditions. Barbara Hudson also argues that culpability (as a personal characteristic of the offender) has been under-emphasised in the just deserts perspective.[17] She further suggests that blameworthiness should take into account wider social and personal circumstances of the offender, thus considering the problem of just deserts in an unjust society. Offenders who 'through poverty, mental disorder, racism or other obstacles have been denied chances of achieving through lawful means the goods to which we all aspire' may be less blameworthy than those who have not lived under such constraints (Hudson 1995: 65). At the same time, punishment does not only affect individual offenders, but also their families. The prison sentence for the mother of three mentioned above will necessarily cause more suffering to the innocent than the same sentence given to a single woman. As there are no standard offenders, punishments are not standard either. A prison sentence will necessarily have different effects and consequences on different individuals. Today, just deserts exist in an unjust society – and ironically, as can be seen, often make society even more unjust.

## Sentencing: art or science?

Guidelines attempt to make punishment a rational and transparent process. Their aim has been to *explicate* the information contained in judges' decisions and translate it into a formal procedure, thus making sentencing less dependent on individual offenders' and judges' personalities. Sentencing is lifted to a higher level of abstraction. However, a question can be asked as to the implications of making sentencing knowledge explicit. An argument of many judges has been that a sentencing decision is an *intuitive* synthesis and that factors, or a combination of factors, relevant in a decision can never be fully prescribed in advance. Each case is unique with its special circumstances and should be treated as a 'whole'. When describing their work, judges stress the importance of personal experience, feelings and intuition (Tata, Wilson and Hutton 1996). This view is, for example, clearly expressed in *R v Williscroft* [1975] VR 292, a judgment where the Full Court of the Supreme Court of Victoria declared that:

17 Simon points out that the 'requirement of providing a culpable mental state has long been recognized as a critical component of the common law's respect for individuality' (1999: 1,010). Strict liability, on the other hand, represents a move away from individualism and shows that lawmakers are primarily concerned with a risk *group* rather than the individual. Feeley and Simon (1992) have described this move from individuals to groups as the 'new penology' and actuarial justice.

> Ultimately every sentence imposed represents the sentencing judge's *instinctive synthesis* of all the various aspects involved in the punitive process. Moreover, in our view, it is profitless … to attempt to allot to the various considerations their proper part in the assessment of the particular punishments presently under consideration.[18]

This is only one among a number of judgments that express the judicial view that a sentence is essentially a subjective judgment based on intuition as much as on rational principles. Judges therefore tend to see their work more as an art or a craft, rather than a precise science. As an art, it is argued, the sentencing process cannot be reduced to a mechanical application of a few rigid formulae. A work of art requires experience, time, diligence and personal skill (The Canadian Sentencing Commission 1987). As one Pennsylvania judge argued regarding sentencing commissions and the data they collect:

> Sentencing commissions, in general, and the release of sentencing data, in specific, attempt to quantify something which is not able to be quantified because they fail to recognize that sentencing is an art, not a science. Thus, the numbers, charts, and graphs which are released to the media and the public do little to illustrate what a judge must consider when a human being, as opposed to a newspaper headline, is standing before a judge for sentencing. (Cardwell Hughes 1999: 20)

On the other hand, the proponents of guidelines insist on the understanding of sentencing cases as similar and comparable. They stress the importance of formal rationality, rules and consistency in decision-making. In fact, one of the striking aspects of von Hirsch's desert theory and his concept of proportionality is its continual allusion to mathematical terminology (Davis 2002). Von Hirsch uses terms such as 'establishing a metric', 'formulae', establishing an 'explicit harm-scale' and 'penalty scale', which can then be 'deflated or inflated', 'net harmfulness grades', 'converting values', etc.[19] Julia Davis argues that since mathematics is the most precise of all human languages:

> by shifting from the traditional image to this mathematical imagery, von Hirsch has given his model some of the cachet and precision that we associate with measurement, and the authority, rigour and objectivity that we associate with science. (Davis 2002: 333)

Davis points out that this allusion to science masks a vital difference between law and science. She suggests that, while science is an activity that aims to discover regularities in the world, law *creates* them.[20] 'The numbers imposed by the law are imposed as an act of will … It is order that is chosen, not discovered, and it is enforced by acts of power, not by the force of nature' (2002: 334). Therefore, when guideline creators and deserts theorists refer to proportionality between punishment and the seriousness of an offence, they do not talk about phenomena that can be objectively measured, such as temperature, for example. Seriousness of an offence, Davis argues, is like the 'deliciousness' of an ice cream or the

18 Information from the High Court of Australia at www.highcourt.gov.au (emphasis added).

19 Von Hirsch himself (2002), however, opposes the view that he is looking for exact mathematical notions of desert or proportionality, despite the use of the above-mentioned vocabulary.

20 An argument can be made, of course, that not even science is a simple process of discovery of knowledge, but that scientists, too, have a creative role in the definition of ontological phenomena.

'friendliness' of an act – a *subjective* quality. Its evaluation might perhaps tell us more about ourselves than about the nature of the phenomenon itself.

The argument about whether sentencing is an art or science is not simply an abstract academic discussion, but rather marks an important transformation in the nature of professional knowledge. As we shall see later, the discussion has taken place in a number of other professions which have gone through the transition from traditional craft knowledge to objective, often computerised, expert systems (Zuboff 1988, Lyotard 1999). What we see here is a dichotomy between two different ways of thinking and decision-making, and between two different visions of justice: one concrete, case-oriented and *subjective*, the other abstract, system-oriented and *objective*. The two approaches contain important implications for the nature of knowledge and skills, as well as power, in criminal justice systems. The suggestion that knowledge of a certain profession is objective and can be explicated carries with it an implication that individual professionals can easily be replaced and, therefore, reduces their professional status. Furthermore, the subjective and objective visions of justice also embody two fundamentally different conceptions of human identity. Guidelines are based on what is commonly described as a 'mechanistic world view' (see, for example, Dahlbom and Mathiassen 1993). Mechanistic thinking relies on rules and logic in order to create exact and explicit knowledge. It is a way of thinking that seeks to strip ideas of subjective material such as colour, taste and smell, in order to map the world in a clear and exact way. The objective is to *formalise* not only ideas and symbols, but the thinking process itself, in order to make it more exact and to avoid misunderstandings (Dahlbom and Mathiassen 1993). This is also, as we will see later, the world-view that is embodied in computer programming.

## Punishment-at-a-distance[21]

By turning sentencing from an 'art' into an activity that can be programmed, the guidelines have created new possibilities for the control of the judiciary and exercise of power. As Dahlbom and Mathiassen point out: 'To follow the rules in our thinking is to control our thinking ... A society governed by rules can be controlled by those formulating the rules' (1993: 14). Now, those formulating the rules and programmes for sentencing are people sitting in sentencing commissions and legislative bodies. In fact, the US Supreme Court Justice Antonin Scalia has described the Federal Sentencing Commission as 'a sort of junior-varsity Congress' and as a 'new branch' of government (Luna 2002), appropriating tasks that have been by constitution vested in the legislature. It has been argued that the Commission lacks a clear line of accountability and that its work is quite invisible to the general public (Luna 2002: 6). For example, Luna (2002: 8) points out that the above-mentioned prohibition on considering a defendant's age, employment, family situation and substance abuse was in fact not ordered, nor even 'implicitly suggested' (*sic*!) by the legislature. 'Instead, the commission made those and other decisions of its own accord and without a clear legislative mandate' (2002: 8).

21 The terms 'action-at-a-distance' and 'government-at-a-distance' originate in Rose and Miller's development of Bruno Latour's work (see Rose and Miller 1992, Rose 1999: 49; see also Chapter 5, below).

Originally, sentencing reformers hoped that this kind of transfer of power from judges to sentencing commissions would make sentencing less political and, thereby, also less punitive. However, the American experience has shown that, all too often, this has not been the case. Stith and Cabranes (1998) report that the appointment of the members of the Federal Sentencing Commission in the mid-1980s was a highly politicised activity, which offered President Reagan another weapon in his war on crime. Although a number of state commissions saw as one of their objectives to control the rise in prison populations, they have generally not managed to insulate sentencing policy from penal populism.[22] Sentencing has become more of a political issue than before – with the result that now when commissions decide to increase penalties, they increase penalties for entire categories of crimes, not just individual cases as judges used to do previously (Rothman 1994).

Therefore, despite the fact that the control of correctional resources can be and has been incorporated in some guidelines systems, the ability instantly to raise punishment levels, and to monitor the implementation in detail, makes guidelines a potentially dangerous political instrument. As Garland writes:

> These methods of fixing sentences well in advance of the instant case extend the distance between the effective sentencer (in reality, the legislature, or the sentencing commission) and the person upon whom the sentence is imposed. The individualization of sentencing gives way to a kind of 'punishment-at-a-distance' where penalty levels are set, often irreversibly, by political actors operating in political contexts far removed from the circumstances of the case. The greater this distance, the less likely it is that the peculiar facts of the case and the individual characteristics of the offender will shape the outcome. (2001: 179)

With the introduction of sentencing guidelines, control over offenders' destinies in concrete cases has been lifted to a yet higher level of abstraction. This has recently been expressed in *AB v The Queen*, a 1999 judgment by the High Court of Australia, where the court argues that:

> If the judge first formulates an objectively determined sentence, he or she has only relied on part of the relevant circumstances and has effectively allowed that part of the circumstances to determine the sentencing process. Worse still, there is a danger that the objectively determined sentence will be formulated by reference to abstractions derived from the circumstances, rather than by reference to the concrete facts of the case. ... Abstraction replaces the convicted person's circumstances in determining the appropriate sentence.[23]

With numerical sentencing guidelines, power has, to a large extent, been transferred to people who we may describe, to use Robert Reich's (1991) term, as '*symbolic analysts*'. They are the people whose work is based on the manipulation of abstract symbols. They seldom come in direct contact with the totality of concrete reality; their job is to simplify real-life situations into abstract symbols. For example, Tonry

22 As mentioned above, the goals of guidelines have varied greatly from state to state. While some states stated the increase of punishments for certain categories of crimes as their goal, others have seen the guidelines as a tool which would promote the use of non-prison sanctions, and thus reduce prison overcrowding (Lubitz and Ross 2001).

23 Source: information from the High Court of Australia at www.austlii.edu.au/au/cases/cth/high_ct.

(1992) reports that members of the Federal Sentencing Commission were all people with limited day-to-day knowledge of criminal courts. Even though three members of the Commission were judges, they were all appellate judges with very limited trial experience. The other members consisted of three academics and one correctional administrator. American judges have, therefore, to some extent played a minor role in reforming sentencing. This is particularly the case with the Federal Sentencing Guidelines, while in some states, individual judges did have some influence on sentencing reforms.

Furthermore, the objectives of consistency and proportionality that have guided most sentencing reforms aspire to be based on detailed scientific knowledge of the *system as a whole*, of past decisions, and even possible future consequences. A judge who is traditionally educated to resolve *concrete* conflicts lacks competence and information about the large-scale processes. At the same time, judges often believe it to be inappropriate to take an active part in policy-making and debates, which makes judges poorly organised and politically weak (Tonry 1992). The crucial question here is, therefore: on whose terms is the sentencing process being conducted? Who, in fact, is the *creator* of the new sentencing models? Due to the nature of their work, which is to solve concrete cases, judges are not, to use Stein Bråten's concept of *model power*, actors who are strong in terms of having models and concepts. On the contrary, today, the predominant concepts and models of the sentencing process have largely been created and articulated by academics and various government agencies. According to Bråten (1983), the fact that someone is a user rather than a creator of a certain concept or a model has significant consequences for the nature of their power relations. Bråten describes the concept of model power in the following way:

> 1 For an actor A to control x, a model of x is presupposed, developed on A's terms (that is, as seen from A's standpoint).
>
> 2 For two actors, A and B, to enter into dialogue, it is presupposed that they have access to models of the issues to which they are referring, and of each other. It follows from the latter point that, for an interaction situation between A, who is strong in models, and B who is weak in models:
>
> 3 The B who is weak in models will try to acquire the models of the A who is strong in models. From 1 and 2 it follows that:
>
> 4 The more B succeeds in acquiring A's models, which are developed on A's terms, *the more B comes under A's control*. (Bråten 1983: 25, translated from Norwegian by Mathiesen 1987)

While traditional models of judicial control, such as sentencing precedents and guidance are coming from the appellate courts and are created by the judiciary itself, numerical sentencing guidelines and SISs, which will be discussed later in this chapter, are largely designed by experts who are not themselves judges, although individual judges sometimes do participate in the process. Even more importantly, sentencing guidelines and SISs are based on a model of justice that is 'foreign' to the way judges think and work (Tata 2000).

## Judicial guerrilla warfare

American judges have strongly resisted sentencing reforms, particularly the US Federal Sentencing Guidelines, from the beginning, although some state guidelines have received a more generous reception. Feelings of exclusion from policy-making, diminished judicial authority and quality of justice are the main reasons. Within the first two years of their taking effect, more than 200 district judges rejected the guidelines and all or part of the Sentencing Reform Act on constitutional grounds (Tonry 1992). The US Supreme Court, in *Mistretta v US*, upheld the guidelines' constitutionality. However, judicial dislike of the guidelines continues and is quite extraordinary. Simon (1995) reports that, while public dissent by federal judges is otherwise rare, particularly regarding procedural issues, two federal judges, both with lifetime tenures, resigned on the express grounds that applying the guidelines repelled them. More than 50 federal judges have declined to hear drug cases because of their reluctance to impose the sentences required by the guidelines (Forer 1994). Forer (1994: 5) reports of a judge, Harold H Greene of the US District Court in Washington DC, who refused to impose a guideline sentence of 17.5 to 21.5 years' imprisonment for selling one tablet of Dilaudet, arguing that such a sentence would violate the Eighth Amendment, prohibiting cruel and unusual punishment.

Spohn (2002: 239) reports that in most states that have imposed sentencing guidelines, most judges comply with the guidelines and that departure rates are relatively low, depending also on the type of offence. It must too be pointed out, however, that the US Federal Sentencing Guidelines are considerably less flexible than state guidelines. Judges are allowed to depart from the US Federal Sentencing Guidelines only when circumstances exist which have not been 'adequately taken into consideration by the Sentencing Commission' (18 USC 3553(b)). This leaves relatively little ground for departure, especially since factors such as employment, stable home life and effects of the sentence on dependants are expressly *forbidden*. Factors such as age, education, vocational skills, mental and emotional conditions, drug dependence and alcohol problems are factors considered to be 'not ordinarily relevant' for departure from the guidelines. A recent act of Congress, the so called PROTECT Act 2003, requires of the Sentencing Commission further to limit departures from the guidelines as well as to release data files containing individual judges' sentencing records to the Attorney General. The Act also reduces the number of judges who may be members of the Sentencing Commission.[24]

In 1990, the Federal Courts Study Committee questioned 270 people: judges, prosecutors, probation officers, defence lawyers, etc, and only four (*sic*!) of those questioned (three Commission members and the US Attorney General) favoured the guidelines in their current form (Tonry 1992). The rest of those questioned supported a proposal to make the guidelines less rigid, to increase the authority of trial judges to select a sentence outside the guideline range and to take into account defendants' personal characteristics and history. In the 1996 Federal Judicial Center Survey the strong judicial opposition to the guidelines was confirmed: 61.5% of

24 The act was strongly criticised by the Chief Justice William Rehnquist, who declared that it would 'seriously impair the ability of courts to impose just and responsible sentences' (Bazelon 2003), while the chief judge of the US District Court for Massachusetts asked: 'Why does Congress hold the courts in such a low regard that they were uninterested in obtaining the views of those whose duty is to fashion fair and just sentences in every case?'

federal judges expressed their strong opposition to the current mandatory sentencing guidelines, while only 16% expressed their support for the system. Tonry even describes the remarkable judicial resistance, especially against the US Federal Sentencing Guidelines, as 'judicial guerrilla warfare':[25]

> Five years after the implementation of the US Sentencing Commission's Guidelines, something like judicial guerrilla warfare continues. Even in law-abiding Minnesota where judicial acceptance of sentencing guidelines was common, though not universal, as Richard Frase has shown, judges have created doctrines to justify departures from guidelines on rehabilitative grounds that the commission expressly rejected. (1992: 163)

At the same time, the diminishing of judicial discretion has also added greatly to the powers of prosecutors.[26] Since the base sentences are largely decided by the charges brought by the prosecution, and the judge must sentence according to the prescriptions for a specific offence category, the balance of power has shifted in favour of the prosecution. Some commentators have pointed out that the use of the term 'guidelines' is in fact somewhat misleading in the federal system, since the guidelines do not offer guidance but are rather binding for the judges (Stith and Cabranes 1998). Daniel J Freed (1992) describes a judge in the guideline system as a 'handcuffed decision-maker' rather than the 'black box' decision-maker of the past. 'Guidelines are administrative handcuffs that are applied to judges and no one else' (1992: 1,697). A judge's sentencing range is now chained to the prosecutor's choice of charges and facts. Defendants and their lawyers understand that judges no longer control sentencing, and thus opt for bargaining with prosecutors.[27] For a guilty plea, for example, a prosecutor might charge a defendant for a category that carries a lesser penalty.

Thus, disparity and discretion do not disappear from the penal process; rather, they are transferred within the system, and perhaps made less visible on paper. Tonry (1995) reports that in the federal system, judges have devised a number of ways to circumvent guidelines they view to be unjust. They may, for example, refuse to find facts (such as a large quantity of drugs or a firearm) which, if found, would require a much harsher sentence. Alternatively, they may order probation officers to omit key facts from their pre-sentence reports. Sometimes they simply ignore the guidelines, and, unless one of the parties appeals, this is the end of the matter (1995: 272).

Luna (2002) argues that the prosecutors, according to their priorities, rather than the judges, now decide who is eligible for leniency. He describes a case of a small drug ring in northern Virginia where:

---

25 Sentencing has often been the subject of a battle of wills between judiciary, the legislature and executive. The resistance to the US Sentencing Commission is not unique. Leith (1998), for example, reports on the resistance in the UK to using judicial case management as an attempt to improve court productivity.

26 Caplow and Simon (1999: 101) point out that a number of recent administrative reforms in the US penal system have shifted discretion towards those agents who are most sensitive to populist pressures to punish more, especially prosecutors and legislators. The cost of a more formal and 'due process' oriented penal system may be, therefore, more incarceration.

27 Tonry (1992) reports that prosecutors often manipulate the guidelines to avoid unduly severe sentences (hidden plea bargaining). This is even the case in the states that consider their guidelines to be a success – such as Minnesota, Oregon and Washington.

> Federal law enforcement personnel documented sales totalling more than 50 grams of crack cocaine, the minimum amount needed to trigger a mandatory 10-year sentence for every individual associated with the drug ring. More than a dozen suspects were arrested, most of whom were in their early 20s ... The punishment each defendant received, however, was not a function of whether he was a major participant in the ring or just a bit player. Instead, those who co-operated with federal prosecutors by turning in their friends secured lower sentences through 'substantial assistance' departures. The drug ring's lieutenant and two major dealers admitted their active involvement in distributing crack cocaine, sold out their colleagues, and in turn received sentences of five years or less. In contrast, three minor dealers (two of whom were teenagers at the time) refused to co-operate with prosecutors and were sentenced to 12 years in federal prison. (Luna 2002: 9)

The fact that federal prosecutors in the period between 1991 and 2002 appealed in less than 0.1% of cases (Bazelon 2003) also indicates that the balance of power has tipped in prosecutors' favour. The largest part of departures from sentencing guidelines come from prosecutors' plea bargaining; however, prosecutorial discretion, and the inconsistency and disparity that result from it, is seldom addressed as a problem that needs to be subjected to strict rules.

Freed (1992) goes so far as to describe the judicial branch of power as 'a victim of a hostile takeover'. There have been discussions regarding whether controlling sentencers' discretion (legally) breaks with the principle of the independence of the judiciary (Ashworth 1997, Tonry 2002). However, regardless of legal definitions of judicial independence, one can see that guidelines are instruments aiming to control human thought and expression. They are forms which, in common with forms in general, are created to achieve government control over public knowledge and the 'uniform identity of human creatures' (Fussel 1975: 185). They are connected to bureaucratic control of knowledge and communication. However, the degree of control that is involved, especially in the US Federal Sentencing Guidelines, has made judges describe their work as a 'numbers game', a 'cold calculation of numbers' and, even more interestingly: 'nothing more than *computers wearing robes*' (Simon 1995: 6, emphasis added). In fact, the connection between guidelines and computers goes beyond the mere feelings of individual judges, and as I shall proceed to argue, can be found on several levels.

## Sentencing information systems

Even though no other country has adopted the US style *numerical* guidelines as described above, a number of countries have opted for some form of judicial guidance. Reduction in sentencing disparity, the main goal of the guidelines, has been accepted by a number of other jurisdictions. Canada, Australia, Sweden and Ireland have set up sentencing commissions to provide reports on sentencing. This has often resulted in the acceptance of so called narrative guidelines in legislation. Such guidelines are now in operation in Sweden, in Victoria, Australia, and have, to some extent, been developed in England.[28]

---

28 Extensive overviews of the various styles of guidance are provided in Ashworth (1992), Clarkson and Morgan (1995), Tata and Hutton (2002), Rex and Tonry (2002).

Another way of curtailing sentencing disparity has been the use of computerised SISs. Often, the motivation behind employing computerised information systems has been precisely to prevent implementation of US-like sentencing guidelines. In a number of countries, judges themselves have realised that sentencing discretion is a politically contested issue that needs to be reformed. They have therefore supported the implementation of information systems that would make judicial decisions more uniform. The purpose of SISs has therefore been not only to reduce unwarranted disparity in sentencing, but also to retain judicial 'ownership' of the sentencing process. They have become a 'weapon with which to beat off political interference' (Tata 1998: 155).

Thus, even though sentencing guidelines and SISs share the same goal of achieving consistency in sentencing, their values appear to be different. Guidelines are based on a rational model of sentencing which involves a precise notion of what decision-making should be like. The answers are constructed from abstract principles decided by 'outsiders'.[29] This is why judges have tended to resist them, while they have shown greater acceptance for sentencing information systems. SISs are often considered to be neutral because they do not provide judges with solutions, but simply with information relating to previous judicial decisions, leaving them with the choice of finding the right solutions in individual cases.

SISs provide judges and other users with information concerning the range of penalties which have been passed for a particular type of case in the past. An SIS usually consists of databases which provide sentencing statistics about predominant sentencing patterns, as well as databases containing full text or abbreviated judgments and commentary on sentencing principles. The system provides no guidance about what the appropriate sentence should be. The sentencing decision is open and left to the judge to decide. However, the statistical information provided shows the highest and lowest sentences previously passed, and the availability of this information is, in itself, thought to promote higher consistency of decisions. Even though a judge is under no obligation to accept a particular sentence, the hope is that his wish to pursue consistency would lead him to choose a sentence within the statistical average. While promoting the image of judicial independence, SISs strive for consistency. Therefore, the distinction between an SIS and sentencing guidelines may have more to do with the authority attached to the system than with its technical properties (Hutton 1995: 550). In short, SISs may have the same normative effects as the sentencing guidelines.

Today, SISs are operating in a number of jurisdictions. One of the earliest systems was produced in the 1980s by Doab and Park in Canada. The system operated for six years in four provinces (British Columbia, Manitoba, Saskatchew and Newfoundland). However, it is no longer operative, probably due to lack of use by judges (Tata, Wilson and Hutton 1996).

29 Tonry (2002) argues that guidelines have a greater chance of success if the judiciary does not feel excluded from the process.

## New South Wales

The best documented and longest operating SIS system is in use in New South Wales, Australia. It is administered by the Judicial Commission of New South Wales, established in 1986. The system provides judges with legal, factual and statistical data concerning sentencing practices. The system provides judges with instant access to relevant information, without placing any limits on their discretion. The SIS has several components:[30]

- full text judgments from the Court of Criminal Appeal as well as criminal cases decided by the High Court of Australia. Cases can be retrieved by case name or word search;
- summaries of the Court of Criminal Appeal judgments (when there is an important sentencing principle stated in a judgment, a hypertext link is provided to the sentencing principles database);
- a sentencing principles database (containing commentary on sentencing principles as well as key passages from judgments expressing the principle in question);
- The Sentencing Statistics Component, which is the earliest and most used component of the system. It provides statistical data for local courts (about 170,000 cases over the past two years) and the District and Supreme Courts (20,000 cases over the last six years). The information appears in the form of graphs showing the range and frequency of penalties imposed for particular types of offences. A judge may also supplement the search with specific details regarding the offence and the offender (age, prior convictions, etc);
- a component about legislation, containing electronic versions of all New South Wales and Commonwealth Acts;
- a sentencing facilities component about various facilities for drug and alcohol counselling, community service and periodic detention, cross-referenced by geographic location and type;
- a 'Sentencing Date Calculator', used to calculate the exact dates for the beginning and ending of a sentence;
- a publications component.

According to Schmatt (2001), the system is used extensively, having approximately 700 users every month and has been mentioned by the Court of Criminal Appeal in over 200 judgments.

## Scotland

Scotland has also developed an SIS for its High Court of Judiciary. Interestingly, the initiative for this came from the judiciary, and judges were closely involved in the design of the system. As in New South Wales, its aim is to pursue consistency simply by providing information concerning previous sentencing patterns, without binding judicial decisions. The Scottish system contains mainly numerical

30 Sources: Tata (2000), Schmatt (2001) and information from the New South Wales Sentencing Commission on the internet.

information, with over 6,000 first instance cases from the past six years, and all decisions of the Appeal Court concerning sentences. Unlike the New South Wales system, the Scottish SIS has no official 'institutional home'. It is an unofficial collaboration between the senior judiciary and academics. While this allows for more creative solutions than simply relying on official recording practices, Tata (2000) reports that this also renders the project more vulnerable to resource pressures and changes in judicial leadership.

### *The Netherlands and Israel*

Experimental systems are now in operation in the Netherlands and Israel.[31] A system called NOSTRA has been developed in northern regions of the Netherlands. NOSTRA was inspired by the Scottish system. It is limited to around 600 cases of relatively uncomplicated offence categories with regard to sentencing. NOSTRA is only one of the attempts by the Dutch system to combat sentencing disparity. The Netherlands recently also adopted numerical guidelines for prosecutors (Tak 2001) and a complementary information support system. The system provides advice to the prosecutors as to which sentence should be demanded, based on certain circumstances (for example, the amount of money stolen, use of weapons, etc).[32]

Obviously, information systems are used in more countries than are mentioned here. Judicial decisions and sentences are increasingly available to judges, defence lawyers, prosecutors and the general public, on the internet (eg, the Norwegian information system Lovdata). Even though these do not necessarily contain sentencing statistics, they generally contribute to greater visibility and scrutiny of judicial decisions. The information that previously required hours of searching to retrieve is now immediately available to the public.[33]

## Why judicial ambivalence?

Despite the judicial preference for SISs over sentencing guidelines, and despite considerable academic and initial judicial interest, SISs have not been an unconditional success. Tata (2000) reports that the judiciary in general still seems to be reluctant to institutionalise them. He suggests that such judicial reluctance cannot be explained exclusively as judicial conservatism, unco-operativeness and reluctance to change, or as a protection of the 'ownership of their decisions', although these all may play a part. Another part of the answer may be that judges have problems with the concept of 'sentencing incoherence' and the vision of justice employed by computerised sentencing information systems and sentencing guidelines.

Tata (2000) suggests that judicial reluctance to use SISs may stem from the fact that the judiciary has a different vision of justice from its critics. It does not see its

31 For more information about the various systems, see Tata (1998) and Hutton (1995).

32 Source: http://pubs.cli.vu/pub161.php.

33 This shows how the fact that the same (content of) information is available in a new *form* may have profound practical consequences. I explore this contention further in Chapters 2 and 3. We may perhaps compare this to what happened when Norwegian citizens' income and property taxes became available on the internet instead of in print. Visibility became greater (for some too great), simply because the information became available via a new medium.

job as simply that of applying formal rules, but rather as a balance between two competing visions of justice: '"formal-rational law" (in sentencing with its concern for rational calculation, formal rules, openness and predictability) and "substantive-irrational" law with its concern for individual cases and apparent uniqueness' (Tata 2000: 311). Judges see their job as combining these two visions of justice: as creating a balance between the *formal* and *substantive* vision of justice – between the 'tariff' and the individual case. Their discretion is an essential precondition for that. In this context, law is not exclusively a formal discourse, but also a social practice and performance that is woven into a constantly changing social fabric (Tata 2000).

The dichotomy between the formal and the social, the abstract and the concrete, has been a source of constant tension in modern law. In fact, it has often been described as one of modern law's defining traits. For example, in his history of supreme court judges, Edward G White (1976) describes as one of the most important shifts in the American judicial tradition the abandoning of so called *'oracular judging'* for a liberal vision of justice. The oracular tradition, predominant in the 19th century, viewed the law as a body of timeless principles and universal truths that had to be discovered. A judge's role was simply to find those principles and profess them without adding his own views. His role was that of a passive law-finder, rather than a law-maker. He was an 'oracle' for the law. The *liberal* view, on the other hand, did not see the law as a static phenomenon that could be uncovered. On the contrary, the content of legal norms changes with changing social conditions and values. The judicial role is therefore to give space to the competing notions of justice and give new contents to legal norms, rather than simply profess an eternal, pre-existing entity. A judge's role was seen as active, rather than passive. The liberal vision was aided by the fact that, in the 1920s and 30s, it became increasingly obvious that the oracular tradition was by no means objective and value-neutral. In fact, judges who supported the unchangeable vision of the law, especially relating to property rights, were the cornerstone of the conservative attacks on Roosevelt's New Deal and the workers' movement. The formalistic vision of justice was revealed to be politically biased and embedded in the historically distinct economic and social order of 19th century capitalism.[34] The opposition to innovative judging revealed itself to be a preference for one set of economic and social views over another.[35]

Taking a cue from this short leap back in history, we may take a closer look at the social and cultural conditions behind the present formalistic visions of justice and the fight against sentencing discretion. White's story shows that the oracular tradition was eventually discarded when it became obvious that it was incompatible with the new economic and social order of the welfare state. A question thus arises about which social conditions again favour the passive role of

34 White (1976) points out that the absolutistic protection of individual property rights and freedom of contract was essential to the economic expansion of 19th century capitalism. However, by the 1930s, the economic depression made obvious the need for stronger state involvement in the economy and a need to regulate business activities and property rights. The judicial belief in the unchanging nature of law and constitution was clearly hostile to the New Deal welfare legislation and governmental attempts to regulate business.

35 White's argument does not touch upon a number of intricate legal philosophical debates with regard to legal realism and formalism. However, entering the discussion would be beyond the scope of the present study. I propose to use White's argument as a starting point for a debate, rather than a sufficient explanatory analysis in itself.

the judiciary, trying to make them again into law-finders rather than law-makers. How can we explain the sudden belief, now gaining predominance in sentencing, that judicial decisions should be extracted from universal principles? In what follows, I suggest that the present formalistic visions of justice, although having a long history, are nevertheless based on a particular conception of knowledge that is characteristic of contemporary information societies. I argue that concepts such as disparity, sentencing incoherence, proportionality, judicial accountability, etc are concepts that have gained special prominence as well as specific meaning in contemporary penal culture, which is focused on information processing, system management, accountability and transparency.

By no means do I wish to question the salience and importance of striving for greater equality and justness in judicial decisions. However, I would like to examine the language that has been used to promote the critique of judicial decisions, as well as the solutions that have been adopted. These are culturally embedded phenomena, and my purpose in the following chapters is to explore the nature of this embeddedness, as well as, in Chapter 4, their consequences for our understanding of offenders' identities.

# Chapter 2
# How Information Lost its Body

New technologies alter the structure of our interests: the things we think *about*. They alter the character of our symbols: the things we think *with*. And they alter the nature of community: the arena in which thoughts develop. (Postman 1993: 20)

## Technologies and cultural change

There is by now a well-established link between cultural change and penal developments. Changing cultural patterns and mentalities leave their mark upon patterns of punishment. As Garland suggests: '[T]he frameworks of meaning through which we generally lead our lives are likely to guide the ways in which we design our penal institutions' (1990: 200). Penal practices derive 'their sense and credibility from their ability to resonate with established ways of thinking and understanding' (1990: 210). Changes in cultural patterns thus have a resonance in the ways in which penal systems think about offenders' identities: what it means to be a delinquent, a man, a woman, a juvenile offender, etc. Cultural perceptions of offenders have changed from the time when they were, according to theology, viewed as sinners, to the view of offenders as rational, calculating individuals and, further, to views of offenders as abnormal human beings shaped by genetic, psychological and social factors (Garland 1990: 207, 208). Since the 1970s, with the fall of rehabilitation and the rise of competing paradigms, new images of offenders have been created in contemporary penal systems.

Undoubtedly, the recent technological changes, particularly the rise of information and communication technologies, have had a significant impact on the ways we lead our lives, design our institutions and produce our knowledge. We are witnessing a rapid growth of these technologies in virtually all areas of our daily lives. They are increasingly ingrained in such mundane tasks as communicating with our spouses and children, paying bills, gaining access to places of work and leisure or booking hotel rooms and cinema tickets. Academic work, although largely remaining print and speech based, is also incorporating new innovations such as e-mail, presentation of courses, persons and books on the internet, electronic publishing, distance learning and, of course, there are few academic texts today which are written without the help of computers.

Not surprisingly, a number of authors have pointed out the cultural significance information technologies have had in our society. However, criminologists have not been overly eager to join the discussion. Lyon (1988) was perhaps among the first, writing that computers today provide 'metaphors for thinking about people and social organization'. He wonders if the computer today is 'performing a role which in some significant respects is analogous to the clock, culturally *and* socially?' (1988: 133). Since the 17th century, the clock has served as a prototype for the mechanisation of a variety of tasks and as a model of a precise and ordered world, accessible to human reason. Similarly Jay D Bolter (1984) and Neil Postman (1993) have argued that, just as the clock defines humanity in terms of a clockwork image, the computer alters this so that people view themselves as 'information processors' and view nature itself as information to be processed. The argument can be, justifiably, criticised for its apparent technological determinism. The idea that computers or any other technology *itself* could be an autonomous agent of social change has been repudiated. By contrast, cultural analysts have asserted that technological change and development has to be understood within the larger framework of social change. This increasingly influential group of researchers points out that technology operates in a social context, that it can have unforeseen and unintended consequences, and that it can have different meaning to people in different social and organisational positions.

The role of technology as an agent of social and cultural change is obviously at the crux of a wide-ranging and ongoing debate within the field of media studies. It is not difficult to agree with Rasmussen (2000), however, that the increasing embeddedness of information and communication technologies in forms of everyday life makes it even more difficult to see these technologies as isolated in their social effects. 'No longer do they belong to the "sub-stratum" which merely *effect* cultural processes. As with television, they are *themselves* cultural products' (2000: 5, original emphasis). On the other hand, one should be wary of seeing technologies merely as social constructs, as projections of social relations into material and immaterial objects. Andrew Barry (2001) tries to bridge the gap between the social and the technical by suggesting that we should focus instead on concrete arrangements of people and technical products in various forms and circumstances:

> [I]nstead of drawing a line between the social and the technical, one might instead analyse *arrangements*: of artefacts, practices and techniques, instruments, language and bodies. These arrangements make up what we tend to think of as persons and institutions: states, markets, families and so on. They are collectivities which include technological components. In principle, the complexity of such arrangements is irreducible to their distinct 'social' and 'technical', 'natural' and 'cultural' elements. (Barry 2001: 9, original emphasis)

In fact, the so called actor-network theory, popularised by Bruno Latour and Michel Callon, dispenses altogether with the distinction between human and non-human actors, between the social and the technical.

The task of grasping the nature of various technologies beyond their technical properties is, therefore, far from clear cut. In order to clarify the matter Eriksen (2000: 29), for example, uses the term *medium* to reach beyond the technical qualities of various technical objects and to refer to their social context. He defines media as all tools that are used for storing and transporting information, including speech, writing, print, etc. Eriksen points out that a technical object becomes a medium in a social network and through certain social functions that are organised around it. Barry (2001) suggests that a distinction should be made between *technical devices* (ie, material and immaterial artefacts) and *technology*. Barry's description of technology is particularly relevant for the purpose of this book. He describes technology as 'a concept which refers not just to a device in isolation but also to the *forms of knowledge, skill, diagrams, charts, calculations* and energy which makes its use possible' (2001: 9, emphasis added). Similarly, Nikolas Rose (2000) points out that technology should not be seen as 'antithetical to the domain of human being', but rather as mediating people's experiences of themselves as certain sorts of persons. 'Human technologies are hybrid assemblages of knowledges, instruments, persons, systems of judgment, buildings and spaces, underpinned at the programmatic level by certain presuppositions about, and objectives for, human beings' (2000: 313).

Bolter (2001) argues that the technical and cultural dimensions are so related that there is no point in trying to separate them. Together they constitute a technology. He takes writing as an example:

> The technology of ancient writing is not only the papyrus, the ink, and the techniques of making book rolls; it is also the styles and genres of ancient writing and the social and political practices of ancient rhetoric. The technology of modern writing includes not only the techniques of printing, but also the practices of modern science and bureaucracy and the economic and social consequences of print literacy. (Bolter 2001: 19)

Our concern in this book will be, therefore, not only to look at the practical use of information technology in contemporary sentencing reforms, that is deployment of computers as technical devices, but rather to look at computers as connected to certain forms of knowledge, skills, bureaucratic practices and types of thinking and calculation. The purpose is further to explore whether and how technological change can be seen as contributing to a transformation in penal culture to the extent that social mentalities and sensibilities regarding knowledge, truth and justness come to be redefined. It will be argued that various technologies can change cultural contexts and the life of social institutions, and that they are in turn also shaped by these institutions, and receive their specific forms and meanings in them. In the previous chapter, I indicated the practical importance of information technology for sentencing reforms. Now, I would like to explore the impact of computers *beyond* the practical. In the case of information technology, the nature of technology as being both a practical object and an object of symbolic exchange becomes particularly clear. What we are dealing with here are not simply practical devices but, foremost, devices for the creation and transmission of meanings. The question is, therefore, what kind of meanings are they?

## Media – extensions of the senses

The first question one may need to address when dealing with computers' cultural effects is, of course, why should changes occur in the first place? Why is the computer more than just another tool that increases our knowledge about the social world – brings better informed police and social services, enables more informed decisions and quicker dissemination of information through various agencies? When it comes to sentencing, a computer simply provides us with more information concerning sentencing practice, about individual courts' decisions, the various activities of criminal justice agencies, etc. Looked at in this way, computers may be just another tool that increase the efficiency of penal systems while adjusting to their existing objectives.

However, research into the effects of other media suggests that 'media are not simply channels for conveying information between two or more environments, but are *cultural environments* in and of themselves' (Meyrowitz 1986: 16, emphasis added). The form in which people communicate has an impact beyond the mere content of specific messages. Perhaps this can be seen as the continuation of the dispute about the classical division between form and content. We can never get in touch with the 'essence' of things that surround us, with their pure content. They are always presented through a certain form (pictures, sounds, symbols, etc). The point here is that forms are not just neutral channels for the transmission of content, but rather active participants in its creation. In the following pages, I will therefore argue that the computer is not only a medium that provides us with more information. It also provides us with a different *type* of information, a different type of knowledge and social experience.

In his book *Technopoly: The Surrender of Culture to Technology*, Postman writes that:

> new technologies change what we mean by 'knowing' and 'truth'; they alter those deeply embedded habits of thought which give to a culture its sense of what the world is like – a sense of what is the natural order of things, of what is reasonable, of what is necessary, of what is inevitable, of what is real. (1993: 12)

Postman suggests that information technology, as every other communication technology before, alters our understanding of reality. He makes an important contention that: 'embedded in every tool is an ideological bias, a predisposition to construct the world as one thing rather than another, to value one thing over another, to amplify one sense of skill or attitude more loudly than another' (1993: 13). A similar point has also been made by Bøhme (1992: 40), who suggests that technology is not relevant only as a means to an end, as a means to increased efficiency of social structures and social action. The point is that *what is counted as experience* is changed by technological inventions.

The thought has perhaps most famously been framed by Marshall McLuhan's phrase: 'the medium is the message' – meaning that the form in which information is transported can have greater social consequences than the content of the information itself. Communication systems thus promote their own values and effects that go beyond the messages they carry. McLuhan (1998) considers the ways in which different media engage our mentality. How and why is reading the news different from hearing it on the radio, and yet again different from watching the news on television? According to McLuhan, media are extensions of the senses. An introduction of a new medium to a culture changes the 'sensory balance' of the people in that culture, and thereby changes their consciousness. The difference between written and oral cultures, for example, is also partly reflected through the different use of the senses (ear and eye). Oral cultures simplify their stories in order to make them easier to remember – they adjust them to the ear. Similarly, Walter Ong, in his work *Orality and Literacy: The Technologizing of the World* (1988), contends that thought and expression in oral cultures, despite what is commonly believed, is often highly organised but requires a social organisation often unfamiliar to the literate mind. This organisation is basically formulaic, structured in proverbs and other set expressions. It is participatory rather than distanced, and situational rather than abstract. Literacy, on the other hand, transforms consciousness, producing patterns of thought which, to literates, seem perfectly natural, but which are possible only when the mind has internalised the technology of writing.

Postman's, McLuhan's and Ong's theories are, of course, open to the criticism of technological determinism (Bolter 2001). Critics have asked if formal properties of certain media determine their use and their messages, what is left there for the users to do? How can social actors imprint their meaning on technologically-mediated relations? Consequently, cultural theorists have pointed out various ways in which people appropriate technologies; how, for example, commercial forces shape the design of the World Wide Web and television today. However, while acknowledging the critique, Bolter (2001) concludes that we also need to acknowledge the material properties of various technologies:

> Individuals and whole cultures do mold techniques and devices to their own purposes, but the material properties of such techniques and devices also impose limitations on their possible uses. ... It also seems that a technique or a device can render certain social constructions easier and or even possible. (Bolter 2001: 20)

Bolter argues that the various technologies of writing (handwriting, print and digital writing) all favour certain types of expression and impede others. Print, for example encourages and makes 'natural' linear writing, while computer writing encourages associative linking. The users can appropriate different styles of writing, but by doing that they 'work against the grain' of their medium (Bolter 2001: 21).

Similarly, Meyrowitz's book *No Sense of Place: The Impact of Electronic Media on Social Behaviour* (1986) argues that the social impact of television should not be ascribed foremost to the power of its messages, but rather to the fact that it reorganises social settings in which people interact. To put it simply, new communication technologies do not necessarily bring about social change through *what* people say to each other, but rather through *how* they say it. Media change people's 'patterns of access to each other'. This access is determined not only by physical settings and places, but also by the 'patterns of information flow' and 'barriers to perception' (1986: 33, 36). It may be important to note that, here, information means *social information* – ie, all that people are capable of knowing about the behaviour of others. This definition of information differs from the common use of the term, which refers to 'facts', 'technical information', 'objective facts' – that supposedly exist beyond the subjectivities of social interaction. According to Meyrowitz, when talking about information, the concern is with the social, not the natural order, with 'social experience' rather than with general 'knowledge' (1986: 37). This is an important distinction that can be of great relevance when analysing the effects of information technology on contemporary penality. Consequently, one should be concerned not only with the amount of facts and 'objective information' that contemporary penal systems operate with, but also the type and amount of *social* information that people in the systems are able to communicate to each other (personal information, gestures, movements, facial expressions, etc). Therefore, the question is not only how computers increase our factual knowledge, the amount of 'objective information', but also how they affect the amount and types of social information and people's subjective experience of each other.

For example, television as a medium conveys a different *type* of information than printed media. Meyrowitz argues that the shift from printed media to television represents a shift from formal 'onstage' information to informal 'backstage' information, and also, therefore, a shift from abstract impersonal messages to concrete personal ones. This shift is 'not related directly to what "subjects" are discussed or to which particular people are placed in front of microphones or cameras, but to *basic difference in the form of the information presented'* (1986: 93, emphasis added). Similarly, Postman (1985) suggests that the institution of book as a dominant form brought with it respect for order, objectivity and consistency of thought. In short, the book presented thoughts, while television presents effects and sensations. A political debate may therefore produce quite different messages about the candidates, depending on whether it takes place on television or in the newspapers.[1]

## Goffman in the electronic world

Meyrowitz illustrates the differences between forms of information by building on Goffman's distinction between 'expression' and 'communication'. 'Expression' refers to:

> gestures, signs, vocalizations, marks, and movements produced by the *mere presence* of a person in an environment. The expressions exuded by the individual do not present any explicit 'statement' or 'argument' about things in general, but they do provide information about the expressing organism. (Meyrowitz 1986: 94)

In contrast, 'communication' refers to the:

> use of language, or language-like symbols, for the intentional transmission of a 'message'. In this special sense, 'communication' involves purposeful symbolic utterances or written statements about things, events, and ideas. Unlike expression, communication can be abstract … In terms of this distinction, one can start and stop communicating at will, but one cannot stop expressing. Communications are consciously given, but expressions are unconsciously 'given off' … (1986: 94)

One of the major differences between print and television is that print contains only communication, while the latter also conveys personal expression. Therefore, television is a personal medium to the extent that it provides personal information about the speaker even when speaking about impersonal matters. Only when non-verbal communication is weak does verbal communication become dominant. Meyrowitz contends that this, and other differences between the types of information provided by the various media, have had an important impact on the nature of group identities, on socialisation processes and conceptions of authority and status in modern societies.

Meyrowitz's study can be also a useful starting point for exploring the possible effects that information technology may have on penal culture. It leads us to ask the questions: what type of information do computers provide us with, and, furthermore, how does the computer change 'patterns of access to each other' in contemporary punishment? How do they change the 'sensory balance' in penal culture and in the experiences of the various actors within the penal apparatus? What senses do they encourage them to use, and what are the experiences that cannot be represented in a computerised form? Information technologies have

1 Perhaps one of the most well-known examples is the first televised US presidential debate between John F Kennedy and Richard Nixon. According to some commentators, the debate, and consequently also the election, was won by Kennedy because of his personal charisma and ability to communicate through television (Meyrowitz 1986). Thus, it is argued that the result of the election could have been different had the political arguments been communicated only through newspapers and radio.

established a new range of frames of interaction and possibilities for presentation of the self. These new frames, such as e-mail and the internet, differ in important respects from the richness of the face-to-face interaction. A person may exercise greater control over the communicating process, and the amount of information that is 'given off' during interaction is significantly reduced. For example, Rasmussen describes personal web pages as media for pre-presentation of the self:

> It is *not* a projection, *not* an extension of the self. It is a mask in front of something and someone, with a complex relationship to what's behind. The web page as a writing tool for autography is designed for the shaping and structuring of a pre-presented self. History and the past are wiped out, the mistakes and the disappointments of life disappear. The pure Self remains on the scene in an almost parodic position. (2004: 11)

Similarly, communication by e-mail offers new possibilities for self pre-presentation as well as detachment. The other person cannot see my facial expression, cannot see if I am tired or bored with the messages, or realise that I am focusing on other things while communicating. I cannot see people's reactions to my homepage or e-mail. I cannot read their faces and, for that reason, the extent to which I adjust my behaviour to theirs is limited. The pressure of potential embarrassment is therefore much less in electronic life – which can be experienced as both a problem and a relief. The fact that computer-mediated communication takes place in a 'disembodied' world can be felt as a considerable relief for those who are socially or functionally disadvantaged. Later, we shall see that this dual nature of disembodiment is also a dilemma for contemporary sentencing reforms. On the one hand, it is desirable that justice is colour- and status-blind. On the other hand, such impersonality could become an impetus to feel less and punish more. At the same time, starting an interaction always carries a risk concerning what the interaction will lead to. However, compared with face-to-face interaction, computer-mediated communication greatly reduces these difficulties. One can, to some extent, initiate interaction without risking becoming more involved than one would wish. We can ask ourselves whether this means that computer-mediated communication can also be used as a means for segregation of experiences. Can it enable its users to dispense with unpleasant and unplanned consequences of personal interaction? Not only does this type of communication spare me the experience of bad breath of my conversation partners, their unexpected visits and other unpleasantness of physical interaction; it also enables me to stop talking when the topic becomes too personal or too inappropriate for my liking.

Nevertheless, the fact that I can know what the interaction will lead to, and that I can always remain safe and detached, may somehow leave cause for concern. What could the consequence be if courts and other penal institutions started to interact within these parameters? What kind of possibilities for institutional self-presentation and pre-presentation, what kind of accounts of institutional activities are being created in the new media landscape? Detached and abstract rationality has long been an inherent part of penal bureaucracy. Would a penal decision-maker who turns from an oral to a computer communicator merely continue this old trend? We can ask ourselves: what kind of judicial decisions would result from disembodied communication where physical presence and distance do not really matter? To put it simply: do we need to see each other's faces in order to create justice? Or better still, what kind of judicial decisions would be created in a 'faceless' world? Human identity, our 'selves', is developed for the purpose of interacting with others, and maintained through such interactions. A question which will be explored throughout this text is: what kind of identities of offenders and decision-makers is developed within computer-mediated communication? If social interactions and decision-making can be 'lifted-out', beyond physical presence, one has to use other 'clues' to create a picture of the other. What kind of clues would they be and how then would these pictures differ from previous ones?

## The computer

A computer can be described in simplistic terms as an apparatus that performs routine calculations automatically. The term 'computer' usually refers to an electronic device that can perform a series of tasks according to a precise set of instructions. The set of instructions is called a *program*, and the tasks may include making arithmetical calculations, storing, retrieving and processing data, controlling another device, interacting with another person, etc (Encyclopaedia Britannica Online 2002). Today, enumerating the tasks that computers can perform would be a futile exercise. It is probably easier to find the ones that they cannot.[2]

Computer programs consist of *data structures* and *algorithms*. Data structures represent the information that the programs process. Algorithms are the sequences of steps that a program follows to process the information. For example, a payroll application program has data structures that represent personnel information, such as the number of hours that each employee has worked and their pay rates. The program's algorithms include instructions on how to compute each employee's pay and how to print paycheques (Encyclopaedia Britannica Online 2002). According to Finnemann (1999a), any symbolic content that is to be represented by a computer has to follow three main criteria:

- representation in a mechanical (binary) alphabet, consisting of a finite set of letters, each of which is void of semantic content. If there is a computational process, there will always be a sequentialised series of bits;
- algorithmic syntax/formalisms;
- interface, determining the semantic content of the algorithmic (or syntactical) processes as well as the semantic content processed.

Finnemann also points out that a fundamental requirement for both algorithmic procedures and data structures is that they must be available in the form of *mono-semantic values* (having only one meaning). Algorithmic procedures have to be

2 When it comes to the structural changes that computers introduce the organisation of *knowledge*, Finnemann makes three main points:

> The computer is both a medium for *producing, editing, processing, storing, copying, distributing, searching* and *retrieving* knowledge. It integrates the production of knowledge, the production of books, bookselling and library into a single medium.
>
> It is both a medium for presenting linguistically (spoken and written) formally, pictorially and auditively expressed knowledge. It provides the possibility for integrating writing, pictures and auditive forms.
>
> It is a medium for communication. It integrates the most important previous forms of communication, such as mail, telegraph, radio, telephone, television, etc. (1999b)

unambiguous. They do not permit 'the cumulative acquisition of new dimensions of meaning' which is a characteristic feature of linguistic expressions (Finnemann 1999b: 8, p 15).

We will see later that this vital role of algorithms in the functioning of a computer, and their mono-semantic nature, are also the traits that should be taken into account when examining the computer as a cultural medium. Finnemann (1999b) points out that the number of algorithms has virtually exploded since the 1950s, causing something which could be called an 'algorithmic revolution'. It includes the development of algorithms for old as well as new purposes and in new areas. While algorithmic procedures until the 1950s only occupied a central place in mathematics, logic, physics and economics, they then began to occupy a central position in biology, psychology and linguistics and a wider range of social sciences. Consequently, algorithms brought with them a growing clarification, structuring and abstraction of the areas which they covered. In short, they brought with them a certain view of reality and a system of beliefs about what is knowledge and how it should be organised.[3]

## The human mind as an information processor

Throughout history, technologies have provided the models by which people imagine the mind. From the clock, steam engines and now computers, various technologies have redefined man's relationship to nature, to other people and to himself. However, the paradigms were not necessarily provided by the technologies themselves, but often by the theories behind them. This also seems to be the case with computers. As Manovich argues:

> cognitive psychology, born in the 1950s and gaining prominence ever since, approaches the *mind as an information-processing system*, as software which runs on the hardware of the brain. But what gave cognitive psychology its epistemological basis was not the new technology itself (computers), but the information theory accompanying it. It was this paradigm which substituted the discussions of the mind and brain by the notion of 'human information processing'. (2001a: 5, emphasis added)

With the rise of computers and information theory, the human mind often began to be defined as an 'information processor', and the world surrounding us as 'information to be processed' (Bolter 1984).

In *The Cult of Information*, Theodore Roszak (1994) calls this kind of thought the '*data processing model of thought*'. It is characterised by a belief in predictable rules for thought and a search for formal procedures. As Roszak suggests, in the data processing model of thought, thinking is reduced to a process of connecting data points in formal sequences:

> Computers can be taken apart, scrutinized and put back together. Their activities can be tracked, analyzed, measured, and thus *clearly understood* – which is far from possible

---

3 Information technology is a large phenomenon, including a number of different technologies and their uses. Therefore, when I refer to computers and information technology in this text, I refer primarily to the aspects outlined above, rather than alternative forms such as the internet, multimedia, etc. These are forms that have been to some extent less relevant when it comes to judicial decision-making.

> with the brain. That gives rise to the tempting assumption ... that the computer can serve as a model of the mind, which then comes to be seen as some manner of information processing machine ... (1994: xv, emphasis added)

In the next chapter we shall see that the image of a human mind as an information processor has had an impact on penal thinking as well. There has been a tendency, for example, to imagine the penal process as exact and predictable, with clearly defined inputs and outputs. Furthermore, there has been a shift in the ways in which we imagine judges and other decision-makers think and should think. The discussion about whether sentencing is an art or science, and the argument that sentencing in fact is a science, reflect some of these tendencies.

Computers are based on specific rules and the idea of representation. They function according to the so called 'effective procedures', which are sets of rules that unambiguously and with mathematical precision specify certain processes. The symbols in the procedures must be clearly defined and have unambiguous meaning. They are arbitrary – they mean only what the programmer and the machine define them to mean in the context of a particular programme. The focus is therefore on a closely defined process or programme, rather than on people defining and redefining the meaning of the process. Furthermore, computer symbols are not literary devices that point to a higher reality. There is no reality behind the symbols (Bolter 1984). Their meaning is rigidly defined and reduced to the binary scheme of true and false. Bolter writes that ambiguity, so important in human communication, is fatal to the computer because it simply means a failure of a program. Spoken language often 'fails' to make our intentions clear. Ambiguity often concerns emotions and intuition, concepts that computer language is simply not capable of representing. 'Computer language consists of strings of arbitrary symbols; computer thought is nothing more than the manipulation of these strings according to the rules of logic' (Bolter 1984: 132). Or, as John S Brown and Paul Duguid (2000: 1) argue, to live on a strict information-only diet is like being driven by someone with *tunnel vision* who sees only where he wants to go and who has cut off the peripheral visual field ('the fuzzy stuff around the edges – context, background, history, common knowledge, social resources' (2000: 1)).

A computer program, therefore, embodies a totally logical mode of communication. Symbols and thoughts are drained of wider connotations. Thus, text is always understood only as a text, without a context or a subtext. The program cannot read between the lines, understand insinuations, moods, feelings and irony, or have a sense of humour. It cannot handle words and thoughts with several meanings and explanations. If I, for example, used the word 'fag' in an e-mail to an American friend ('fag' in Norwegian means an academic subject or a profession), I would be warned by a computer program about indecent use of language and that I may get my keyboard washed out with soap'. The fact that so many e-mails today end up being eliminated by various highly efficient spam programmes reflects the inability of these programs to grasp the semantic meaning of the messages. The word 'offer' is simply seen as an indication that a message needs to be eliminated, regardless of whether the message contains an offer by an eBay company to buy the latest style of make up, or an offer by a colleague to write an article in a book.

Metaphors are a similar example. In *Metaphors We Live By*, George Lakoff and Mark Johnson (1980) persuasively suggest that metaphors are not simply poetical or rhetorical ornaments, but rather a vital aspect of language. Metaphors define the ways in which we perceive, think and act in the world. For example, the metaphor that 'argument is war', can be seen in a number of expressions: 'Your claims are indefensible'; 'I demolished his argument'; 'His criticisms were right on target'. Not only do we talk of losing or winning arguments, but we in fact *do* lose or win them. We see persons we argue with as opponents, and we attack their positions and defend our own. Metaphors are thus an essential part of our acting and perception. In addition, as metaphors change from culture to culture, so too do the realities they define. Computer programs, on the other hand, simply expect people to say precisely what they mean. As Bolter points out, there is no such thing as thought that cannot be expressed in computer language, because thought and language always coincide – thought descends to the level of language. '[D]reamy imaginings, feelings, ambiguities, and contradictions have no meaning in the central processor of a von Neumann machine. The anomaly of half-completed thoughts, which come sometimes as we are falling asleep, also cannot be computed' (1984: 75).

The project of cybernetics has always been to develop a language that would enable control, organisation and a totally logical mode of communication. However, the computer itself is not enough. What is required is the encoding of language. The *code* is a language of sign systems that is characteristic of electronic communication (Poster 1990). Computer codes, as codes in general, are designed to restrict the meaning of words. Codes are, therefore, quite different from written and spoken language. As Poster puts it:

> Written language, however, relies on connotative meanings that are embedded in cultural contexts. Consequently the capacity of writing to 'encode' cultural material is infinite ... Writing accomplishes the infinite expansion of its encoding capacity by the ability of one word to have many meanings. In digital encoding no such capacity exists. In fact digital encoding derives its peculiar strength from the degree to which it restricts meaning and eliminates ambiguity or 'noise'. (1990: 94)

In contrast to coded language, natural language is in constant flux. The meanings and sub-contexts of words constantly change. The meaning of words is open, while the meaning of computer words is rigidly closed and prescribed in advance.

David Bolter (1984) argues, in fact, that the computer represents 'the triumph of structure over content', or more precisely, reinterpretation of content in terms of structure:

> The processes are far removed from conscious human reasoning in their regularity and repetitiveness, as well as in their abstract structural beauty. Rules of logic concern form not content; a computer manipulates pure symbols that are devoid of content. (1984: 169–72)

The task of a computer programmer, therefore, is to mediate between two worlds and between two kinds of thinking: one imprecise, complex, ambiguous, filled with connotations and metaphors, the other coldly precise and formal, without ambiguity and therefore capable of perfect clarity. One might ask whether contemporary sentencing reforms are not striving for precisely the same 'rigidity' and clarity that is characteristic of computer language. Are they too not striving to close the semantic field of sentencing and striving for abstract logic and structural beauty, while excluding alternative meanings of words and thoughts that cannot be expressed in this language of logical precision? Furthermore, one needs to ask what the consequences of a penal system that loses its sense of the social and historical context could be. After all, as Lewis Mumford writes:

> Since the computer is limited to handling only so much experience as can be abstracted in symbolic or numerical form, it is incapable of dealing directly, as organisms must, with the steady influx of concrete, unprogrammable experience. (1963: 6)

Can a judicial system operate without such contextual and non-verbal clues? In the discussions regarding sentencing reforms, an objective system was seen by many as an ideal of impartiality – a justice blind to the colour, sex, age, history and social status of its subjects. One could, of course, ask whose objectivity this is: human or machine's?

## What kind of information?

Use of the data processing model of thought in decision-making and social research may have important consequences for the ways in which people experience the social world. The computer is of no use without formalisation (and without the computer there would be one reason less to formalise observations) (Dahlbom and Mathiassen 1993). In fact, the word 'information' stems from the Latin verb *informare*, which meant to impose a form on something, particularly on the mind, in order to instruct and improve it (Borgman 1999).

Therefore, it is important that we distinguish between the meanings of information and knowledge. Rasmussen (2000: 95) understands the meaning of information as 'the storing, retrieval and processing (objectivation) of *knowledge*'. He sees knowledge as mental (not yet objectivated) facts and ideas. Knowledge is individual, while information is social, and usually collective:

> In contrast to knowledge, information can be commodified. The transformation/objectivation of knowledge into information is a condition of modern commodification in 'information society'. Increasingly, information means commodification of knowledge, which of course is one of the main reasons for the application of information technology, and the explosion of information in rich nations over the last 50 years … Although information should be distinguished from knowledge, which is a personal, non-symbolic, non-materialised quality, use of information requires knowledge. Increasing information does not necessarily increase (or decrease) knowledge, but tends to change knowledge. (Rasmussen 2000: 95)

Rasmussen asserts that communication technologies usually involve three processes that transform knowledge into information:

- *Objectivation* is a process in which knowledge acquires an external form outside its authors, and thus becomes information. Objectivation is present in speech, print, writing, databases, etc.[4]
- *Distanciation* is a process in which information moves, multiplies and extends over time and space. Information thus becomes an autonomous object, independent of its authors and of the context of its creation.

4 Communication among people also involves subjectivation (interpretation) of information by its recipients.

- *Conservation* refers to flexibility of information in time. It means that 'information is "frozen", and can be delivered or traced at a later point in time' (Rasmussen 2000: 114).[5]

Brown and Duguid distinguish knowledge from information with regard to the fact that knowledge usually entails a knower, while information is usually treated as an independent and self-sufficient entity:

> [G]iven this personal attachment, knowledge appears harder to detach than information. People treat information as a self-contained substance. It is something that people pick up, possess, pass around, put in a database, lose, find, write down, accumulate, count, compare, and so forth. Knowledge, by contrast, doesn't take as kindly to ideas of shipping, receiving, and quantification. It is hard to pick up and hard to transfer. (Brown and Duguid 2000: 120)

Brown and Duguid further suggest that a shift of focus from knowledge to information is a shift away from people to disembodied processes. Knowledge requires a certain degree of commitment and understanding from the people. Someone has to 'make sense' of it. Information, on the other hand, is often viewed as a disembodied entity – independent of meaning and interpretation. However, Brown and Duguid argue that interpretation and the process of sense making are a vital part of knowing. The same information directed at different people does not produce the same knowledge in them, the reason being that people have different practical experiences and therefore interpret differently. Knowledge is thus tightly connected to practice. It not only has *explicit* dimensions written, for example, in manuals, dictionaries and guidelines but also has, to use Michael Polanyi's (1966) distinction, *tacit* or *implicit* dimensions that arise from practical living in the world.[6] Barry (2001) points out that this tight connection of knowledge and practice and the enormous amounts of tacit knowledge represent a considerable problem in contemporary highly technological societies. Even software, although designed in the form of clearly defined packages, can seldom be applied without practical training and experience. 'Skills, techniques or devices that work in one place rarely work in exactly the same ways in another' (Barry 2001: 16).

Grasping the processes described above may be necessary for understanding the changes in the nature of knowledge when it comes to contemporary penality. An issue that I wish to explore further is the overwhelming focus on the *explicit* dimensions of knowledge in contemporary penal culture. Using sentencing as an example, we shall look at how an area of penal knowledge came to be explicated and turned into a decontextualised, information-driven process, increasingly

---

5 Norris (2002) for example, describes how the introduction of CCTV frees surveillance of the constraints of time and space. Surveillance is no longer constrained by the requirements of physical co-presence. With CCTV images of events and people can be lifted out and stored for viewing at a later time or at another place (a CCTV control room in London can be responsible for viewing locations over 200 kms away).

6 Brown and Duguid (2000: 130) refer to research into how children learn vocabulary. By comparing children's learning from dictionaries with learning in everyday practice, researchers have found that learning words from dictionaries is much slower than through practice. By listening, talking and reading, an average 17-year-old learns vocabulary at a rate of 5,000 words per year. He or she knows what these words mean and how to use them in appropriate sentences. On the other hand, learning words from abstract definitions in dictionaries is much slower (between 100 and 200 words a year), as well as much less useful for practical purposes (producing sentences such as 'Mrs Morrow stimulated the soup').

independent of interpretations by the various social actors. The argument will be made that what accompanied technological change (for example, introduction of sentencing information systems (SISs)) is precisely the process of objectivation and externalisation of available knowledge and its subsequent conservation in time for later use and further processing.

Therefore, it is important to point out that when studying technological change, one also witnesses a change in the nature of knowledge. While, in previous times, penal systems also relied on objectivated and stored information, a substantial amount of knowledge was still undocumented and unexplicated, existing only in people's heads. With the introduction of information technologies, the extent of such internalised knowledge came to be substantially reduced. Obviously, it is an illusion to expect that knowledge can ever be completely explicated. However, the tendency in penal decision-making has been to create decision-making systems that operate with as much explicated knowledge or information as possible, without having to deal with the influx of 'unformatted' and unpredictable input. The project of technological and communicational change has been connected to a process of organisational and decision-making reform that introduced new control mechanisms, precisely through preferring certain types of knowledge and precluding others.

## Governance through information

Another issue that needs to be addressed is the persistent need, or better, imperative, to be informed. Contemporary highly technological societies have been described as both being 'flooded' by all kinds of information as well as being 'addicted' to it (Hylland Eriksen 2001). The slogan 'all information at all places at all times' (Poster 1990: 70) can be seen both as a normative imperative as well as an actual description of contemporary life. The process takes place on several levels: from individuals, who as free-market agents need to take responsibility and make informed decisions, to government agencies which collect increasing amounts of information about the external world as well as their own internal activities. Information is, therefore, tightly 'linked to practices of government and self-government' (Barry 2001: 153). The fervour to be informed can be situated in the context of consumerism, risk thinking and the so called 'responsibilization strategy' (O'Malley 1992, Garland 2001) within crime control (involving, among others, the creation of active and responsible citizens and communities, inter-agency co-operation, information sharing, etc). A further point of reference for the 'information imperative' can be found in Giddens's analysis of reflexivity, connected to the specific type of governance (governance-at-a-distance), based on stretched social relations and communication of standardised items of information and standardised modes of reporting, of which sentencing guidelines and sentencing information systems are a part. The issue will be further addressed in Chapter 3 and Chapter 5, below.

What is important at this point is that, in the context of contemporary penal systems, information is not simply, not even primarily an objectivated piece of scientific knowledge, but rather a tool for governance. Contemporary governmental strategies are intricately connected with various knowledge systems. In order to govern, one needs to know the objects that are being governed. 'In turn, knowledges produced about the objects of governance shape the types of strategies that are imaginable, as new knowledges open up unique sites of intervention' (Haggerty 2004: 214). Therefore, information, as a number of authors suggest (Strathern 1999, Barry 2001, Hylland Eriksen 2001), has deeply *regulatory effects*:

> Its [information's] existence is thought to imply a transformation in the conduct of those who are, or who should be, informed. Information does not merely exist; it *demands* (immediate) attention. Ignoring information which is made available is reckoned to be either misjudged or willful. Information is practical and technical in its form and performative in its function ... It is a moral as well as a technical concept. (Barry 2001: 153, original emphasis)

The regulatory effects of information are plainly visible in the case of sentencing information systems, where the duty to be informed imposed on judges has clearly normative connotations. Judges not only have to be informed about past sentencing practice; they are also required to act according to the objectives with which this information is being collected. What kind of information is being collected is a question of political choice about what issues and problems need to be illuminated and addressed in a society. The issue of consistency/disparity of sentencing decisions is therefore a political choice, which implies an act of choosing certain types of information, and also an act of not choosing information about other aspects of judicial reasoning. Furthermore, as Barry (2001) points out, not only the selection of objects of information, but also the 'survival' of information is an inherently political act. Information needs to be produced and circulated; it needs a technological, organisational and economic infrastructure that enables its survival.

Ironically, Barry (2001: 172) argues that these clearly political choices can often have an *anti-political* effect, shifting focus from other problems and displacing demands for other forms of action and other forms of telling the truth. Political issues in technological societies tend to be framed as technical problems which call for technological solutions. Consequently, Barry argues that 'specific technologies dominate our sense of the kinds of problems that government and politics must address, and the solutions that we must adopt' (2001: 2). In *Political Machines* he describes how, in the case of air pollution, the preoccupation with daily air-quality monitoring across Europe, the collection and comparison of increasing amounts of technical information, has displaced other ethical and scientific concerns that have traditionally been present in the discussions about air pollution:

> [A] concern to produce continuous and *precise* information on the part of the public authorities displaces the concern of scientists to tell the *imprecise* truth about pollution. In effect, the contemporary preoccupation with the importance of information production overrides an (older) ethical scientific order ... Critical reflection is not necessarily enhanced by more information than by a more nuanced sense of the strengths and weaknesses of different ways of telling the truth. (Barry 2001: 32)

The passage has particular salience in the case of contemporary penal institutions. As will be argued later, in Chapter 3, the incessant and routine measurement of 'what works' aspects of criminal justice agencies increasingly tends to override other types of concerns and discourses, which cannot as easily be translated into precise information flows. The goal of producing precise streams of information about criminal justice activities thus overrides other discourses which would produce less precise, but perhaps more ethically relevant, results.

What I want to point out here is the alliance between the technical development (proliferation of information technologies), the creation of certain norms and imperatives (such as the duty to be informed) and specific forms of governance in a society. Governance is, therefore, intimately connected with technical issues, as well as with the deployment of various discourses, arrangements, skills, etc, that enable the measurement and analysis of these issues. Rather than talking about government and technology as two separate issues, it may be useful to follow Rose (1999), and talk about *technologies of government*. He describes them as 'human technologies', since it is human conduct that is being shaped by technical means.

> A technology of government, then, is an assemblage of forms of practical knowledge, with modes of perception, practices of calculation, vocabularies, types of authority, forms of judgment, architectural forms, human capacities, non-human objects and devices, inscription techniques and so forth, traversed and transacted by aspirations to achieve certain outcomes in terms of the conduct of the governed … (Rose 1999: 52)

Rose's (1999) writing, here, takes up the discussion that has been framed by Foucault and the post-Foucaultian field of governmentality studies, as well as a number of books within the sociology of technology and the so called actor network theory. In this account, government is essentially a technical practice, which demands a study of material practices as well as a study of 'the political mentality of rule' (Barry 2001).

Therefore, the development of new modes of governance relies crucially not only on the production of information and the technical means to produce it, but also on the realisation of individuals and institutions that it is their duty to be informed. Furthermore, as we shall see in the next section, this new style of governance not only implies constant collection and analysis of information, but also a certain view of social processes as something that can be externalised and thereby standardised. As Barry argues:

> Necessarily, the production of information involves the manipulation of an object into more or less standardised form in which its properties can be measured, recorded and made visible. It entails placing the object in calibrated grid with which it may be compared to an ideal or normative standard, giving it a *new* reality. (2001: 154, original emphasis)

It will be argued later that contemporary sentencing reforms have to a varying extent included the subjection of sentencing to this type of governance: collection of information about disparity/consistency, the externalisation of judicial thinking into so called sentencing factors and, finally, standardisation and creation of measuring grids. The point here is that the process of creation of information is a creative process with possible political consequences. Information is not simply data about pre-existing objective conditions, but rather, as Barry (2001: 155) suggests, a result of a practical and technical intervention in the world which 'forges something new, with more or less inventive consequences. It multiplies realities'. Furthermore, the demand to be informed is not simply a question of a quantity of information, but also a question of the qualitative nature of information and a question of further forms of social action.

## Externalisation and standardisation of the mind

> What before was a mental process, a uniquely individual state, now became part of a public sphere. Unobservable and interior processes and representations were taken out of individual heads and put outside … Now they could be discussed in public, employed in teaching and propaganda, standardized, and mass-distributed. What was private became public. What was unique became mass-produced. What was hidden in an individual's mind became shared. (Manovich 2001a: 4)

An essential part of what we might call 'computer ontology' is the process of externalisation of the mind. Knowledge and ideas need to be externalised in order to be translatable into computer language. Each part of the thinking process needs to become visible, and thereby, external to the subject. Externalisation of thinking is therefore a first, necessary step in standardisation. Scott Lash (2002) argues that externalisation is a necessary part of living in contemporary 'culture-at-a-distance', where so much of social life in fact takes place between people who are physically far apart, and where even nature can be externalised and stored in various DNA databases.

Similarly, an important aspect of sentencing reforms, as described previously, is to make decision-making processes explicit and predictable, thus dissociating decision-making from its reliance on the expertise of individual decision-makers. Contemporary sentencing reforms are characterised by the same wish to 'externalise the mind' and to make the sentencing process rational and consistent. Judges now need to rely on explicit, written materials only, rather than on their years of experience (the 'craft' aspect) that are in their heads. Sentencing guidelines have probably gone furthest in this attempt. The number of pages in the US Federal Sentencing Guidelines Manual has increased from 325 at the time of their introduction in 1987 to 1,579 pages in 2003, including amendments. The average number of Federal Guidelines amendments is 60 every year.[7] These numbers illustrate the US Federal Sentencing Commission's extraordinary eagerness to control the minutiae of judicial reasoning, and its belief that it is possible to make the process of sentencing truly transparent and externalised.

What we are witnessing in sentencing reforms is an attempt to externalise the idea of justice, or at least to externalise judicial thinking and create an ideal sentencing process. As Manovich (2001a) describes in his illuminating essay, the attempts to externalise abstract ideas are nothing new in modern history. As early as 1877, Sir Francis Galton, a statistician and founder of eugenics, pioneered a procedure for making composite photographs. By successively exposing portraits onto a single plate, Galton thought that he created photographs that represented true statistical averages – a criminal, a Jew, a prostitute, etc. Manovich suggests that Galton's belief that *abstract ideas* could be *objectified* and materialised is only one example of a general trend that has been taken much further with modern technologies for visualising data sets, increasingly precise imaging of brain activity, etc.

Manovich suggests that the trend towards externalisation of the mind is a process characteristic of modern mass society and related to its demand for standardisation. What we may be seeing in sentencing is that, just as our idea of

7 Source: www.sentencing.org/facts.htm.

beauty is externalised and then standardised on a movie screen or in a Barbie doll, so can the idea of justice be externalised and then (massively) reproduced in a guideline design or a computer graph. The thinking process, previously uniquely individual, becomes externalised and then, at the next step, standardised:

> The subjects have to be standardized, and the means by which they are standardized need to be standardized as well. Hence the objectification of internal, private mental processes, and their equation with external visual forms which can be easily manipulated, mass produced, and standardized on its own. *The private and individual is translated into the public and becomes regulated*. (Manovich 2001a: 1, emphasis added)

Barry (2001) points to an interesting fact that while for a long time standardisation used to be considered a problem just for engineers, now, standardisation plays a crucial role in political and economic life. Standardisation is not only a technical but also a political project.[8] In the contemporary, increasingly interconnected and global world, objects and processes need to be standardised in order to be compared, communicated about and traded.

Once externalised and standardised, knowledge and processes can, in a way, be lifted out and dissociated from particular individuals. It is no longer necessary that a thinking process is something that, by its very nature, happens in a subject's *interior*. As Lash (2002) argues, in a technological culture, reflexivity no longer takes place inside a subject:

> There is an outsourcing of the flux of inner experience onto the flows of images, media and information in the external world. The unconscious itself is outsourced into the world ... Even reflexivity is outsourced, is externalized. It is no longer a *reflection from the interior* in an effective conversation within the self, but an externalized gloss on activities and events to others. Reflexivity becomes *communicational*. (Lash 2002: 208, emphasis added)

In the case of judicial thinking, this means that thoughts concerning sentencing need to be *communicated* further in the system. The thoughts that are not, or cannot, be communicated are, in a way, rendered irrelevant or at least viewed with suspicion. They are in some aspects an anomaly in a cultural landscape where communication of information is of primary importance. Penal knowledge, therefore, needs to be able to travel.

## Knowledge that travels and knowledge that does not

The idea that human thought can be externalised is not unproblematic. Judges, for example, have been one group that has traditionally shown strong opposition to this concept. As mentioned previously, the argument has been that sentencing is a *craft* or an *art*, rather than a science, and, as such, cannot be reduced to a rigid computer program or a sentencing table. Here, judges point to a central distinction between two types of knowledge and two types of thinking that are at stake: *craft*

8 Barry (2001) points out that the reason for the extraordinary technicality of the issues that are usually addressed by EU institutions is that these institutions basically do not function as traditional state institutions. The primary job of the European Union's institutions is to set forth the conditions within which a certain degree of standardisation (or harmonisation) can take place.

*knowledge* is largely inductive and 'in the world' with the objects of knowledge, and tends to be tacit rather than explicit. Craft knowledge is fundamentally different from *discursive knowledge* which forms the basis of the information society and its production. Discursive knowledge is analytic, based on abstraction, selection and reduction of complexity. It is highly codified knowledge which requires distanced reflection, rather than more immediate and habitual, 'hands-on familiarity' (Lash 2002: 141).

Knowledge among craftsmen is transmitted through 'being in the world' and through years of experience. We should keep in mind that, until not very long ago, most knowledge was transmitted in this way, from one generation of tailors or bakers to another. In a number of societies this is still the case. People learned primarily from practice rather than texts. With computerisation, these activities became verbalised and codified, and thus, knowledge became transmitted through words rather than practice. As Lyotard writes about the impact of computers:

> We may thus expect a thorough exteriorization of knowledge with respect to the 'knower', at whatever point he or she may occupy in the knowledge process. The old principle that the acquisition of knowledge is indissociable from the training (*Bildung*) of minds, or even of individuals, is becoming obsolete and will become even more so. (1999: 4)

The craft aspect of sentencing, insisted upon by judges, is therefore increasingly at odds with the abstract and analytic nature of knowledge in the information order.

The central question here is whether knowledge can simply be externalised and transmitted, independent of the experience of the knower. The issue is connected to the distinction between *knowledge that travels* and knowledge that does not (Hanners 1992). Some knowledge cannot travel because people who have it simply see it as inalienable. Some indigenous groups, for example, see their cultural capital as inalienable, unable to be given away or sold. On the other hand, some knowledge cannot travel because of its nature. It is no surprise that German culture has a smaller commercial potential than Hollywood films. Knowledge that does not travel is often also knowledge that one acquires with years of experience or maturity or that needs to be learned with one's body, like learning a sport.[9] The insistence of many judges today that sentencing is still partly a craft/art rather than science bears the residue of this past tradition. They maintain that the legal and personal knowledge that they have obtained with years of experience simply cannot be externalised and transmitted independently of the people who possess the knowledge.

At the same time, the fears of the judges also resonate with Lyotard's (1999) argument that what does not travel often simply tends to be reduced to what travels. 'What travels' can be digitalised and takes less time to learn and understand than the embodied knowledge of craftsmen. Lyotard suggests that information technology brings with it a 'certain logic' and a 'certain set of prescriptions determining which statements are accepted as "knowledge' statements"':

9 I am grateful to Thomas Hylland Eriksen for bringing the issue to my attention.

> It can fit into the new channels, and become operational, only if learning is translated into quantities of information. We can predict that anything in the constituted body of knowledge that is not translatable in this way will be abandoned and that the direction of new research will be directed by the possibility of its eventual results being translatable into computer language (Lyotard 1984: 4).

A question to be asked when it comes to contemporary penality is, therefore: to what extent is penal knowledge today being transformed from knowledge that does not travel to knowledge that does? Decisions made on the basis of reasoning such as 'He is a good lad' may seem uninformed and even ignorant. It is, in any case, the type of reasoning that today is viewed with suspicion due to its lack of explicitness, transparency and scientific basis. However, such decisions may be supported by non-verbalised knowledge, based on years of experience; experience that suddenly becomes irrelevant compared with reasoning such as 'He scored low on a risk assessment instrument'. This, of course, is also of central importance when it comes to sentencing.[10]

Throughout the past 30 years, sentencing has been a controversial issue due to the amount of discretion that judges exercise in the process. Looking at the nature of discretionary judgment, we can see that it is founded on a certain type of knowledge that seems to be at odds with the 'logic' of the computer. As political philosopher Michael Oakeshott has argued: judgment and discretion are not learned by the acquisition of facts and rules, but through social relations and participation in human activities. He describes judgment as:

> the tacit or implicit component of knowledge, the ingredient which is not merely unspecified in propositions, but which is *unspecifiable* in propositions. It is the component of knowledge which does not appear in the form of rules and which, therefore, cannot be resolved into information or itemized in the manner characteristic of information. (1967: 167, emphasis added)

The contemporary 'suspicion' of judgment and the lack of acknowledgment of experience, particularly visible in the case of penal institutions, can therefore partly be caused by the fact that judgment and experience cannot be 'resolved into information'. As Stith and Cabranes emphasise, in their analysis of the US Federal Sentencing Guidelines, judgment is an 'irreducibly human capacity' (1997: 1,254) which eludes explication into objective categories:

> By replacing the case-by-case exercise of human judgment with a mechanical calculus, we do not judge better or more objectively, nor do we judge worse. Instead we cease to judge at all. We *process* individuals according to a variety of purportedly objective criteria. (1997: 1,253, original emphasis)

## Working with simulations

In order to develop information, the same model needs to be used for everything. Scattered knowledge in diverse forms is thereby transformed into a generalised

10 Later, an argument will be made that sentencing knowledge and theory had to be 'made *translatable* into computer language'. In a way, the eventual omission of social context and personal circumstances from sentencing can be also seen as 'coding' of sentencing knowledge, as we know that translation of messages into codes requires the elimination of ambiguities.

medium for processing and exchange by a global system. Experiences that cannot be described in words, like sensual contact, intuition, etc, have difficulties being represented by the computer. Sensations are replaced by *referential* concepts as the primary source of information. Referential in this context means containing a reference (a mention, an allusion or a direction) to something else. The 'something else' that computers' referential concepts refer to would then be something other than the concrete physical reality of sensory experiences.

Of course, one can ask whether it is at all possible for us to gain direct access to the physical reality. Do we not always experience the world through some referent or another? Nevertheless, the fact that we always wear 'glasses' when observing the world does not need to preclude us from asking what kind of glasses computers provide us with. What kind of senses do we use and what do we mean when we speak about information, knowledge and truth? When it comes to the penal system, the vital questions concerning information are, of course: whose information is this? Who has the right of interpretation? Information is not neutral. It takes on meaning in the context of an organisation and the various roles people have in it. Various penal strategies and ideologies also shape the meaning of information.

Furthermore, we can ask: does having a great deal of information necessarily make me a better informed person? We have mentioned previously how information theory has, in a way, dissociated information from meaning, the form from its content. Information is therefore more often associated with a quantity of bits of information, rather than the quality or meaning of signs. The question is therefore: is having information the same as knowing? Albert Borgmann (1999) distinguishes two kinds of knowledge: *direct* knowledge and *indirect* knowledge, and only indirect knowledge is the same as having information about something. 'I know *of* Toni Morrison; I know *that* she wrote *Tar Baby* and received the Nobel Prize. But, I regret to say, I do not know *her*' (Borgmann 1999: 14). Bertrand Russell characterised this distinction as one of *knowledge by acquaintance* vs *knowledge by description*. In fact, French and German language have separate terms for direct knowledge (*connaître* and *kennen*) and indirect knowledge (*savoir* and *wissen*) (Borgmann 1999). The fact that information is objectified, can travel across long distances and can be 'frozen' in time implies a certain distance between signs and the objects behind them; distance between addresser and addressee and distance between a message and its context. As a consequence, the basic 'sense of reality' that one gains through sensory contact and direct knowledge may become elusive in computer-mediated communication:

> In the mode of information, it becomes increasingly difficult, or even pointless, for the subject to distinguish a 'real' existing 'behind' the flow of signifiers, and as a consequence social life in part becomes a practice of positioning subjects to receive and interpret messages. (Poster 1990: 15)

As an example of how information technology changes the sensory nature of work, Shoshana Zuboff (1988) studied how workers in a pulp mill experienced computerisation. Zuboff points out that before the factory was computer-automated, the use of the senses was an essential component of work. Workers listened to the sounds of the boilers, looked at the colour of the flames and noted the smells to acquire information about how the production process was proceeding. Following automation, however, they visually monitor the process on a computer terminal and use the information to make adjustments via a keyboard. Working through the medium of 'data interface', workers can no longer feel and touch their work. As one worker put it: 'As if one's job had vanished into a two-dimensional space of abstractions, where digital symbols replace a concrete reality' (Zuboff 1988: 63). Zuboff points out that the introduction of information technology in industrial production changes the 'action-centred' nature of work and skill. Action-centredness comprises four qualities: sentience, action-dependence, context-dependence and personalism. Understanding how work loses these qualities may also be useful for grasping the changes in progress in sentencing. Although far from offering a completely adequate description, the similarities between Zuboff's findings and sentencing reforms are quite salient:

(a) Sentience. In the pre-computerised working environments, workers' knowledge of the working process was essentially connected to sensory experience. They relied on their sense of concrete objects to obtain knowledge regarding production. 'Instead of Descartes' "I think, therefore I am," these workers might say, "I see, I touch, I smell, I hear; therefore, I know"' (Zuboff 1988: 62). Computerisation, on the other hand, disturbs this unity of knowledge and experience. Instead of using their bodies and senses, workers now rely on the use of computerised knowledge to perform their work. This, in turn, also means that workers cease to develop and rely on their own expertise, because all the know-how that was once diffused is now accumulated in the system. This forces them to ask a crucial question: 'If you don't have the experience you have to believe everything the computer says. You can't stand up to it ... How will anyone be able to confront the computer information?' (Zuboff 1988: 65).

In *The Corrosion of Character: The Personal Consequences of Work in New Capitalism*, Richard Sennett (1998) similarly describes the transformation of work in a bakery. Computerisation has changed the nature of the work in a sense that bakers no longer make physical contact with the materials or the bread. They monitor the baking process via on-screen icons, depicting colour, types of bread, etc. Few bakers actually see the loaves of bread they make: 'Bread has become a screen representation' (Sennett 1998: 68). As a result, the bakers no longer actually know how to make bread or how to take over if something goes wrong:

> [W]hat they can't do is fix the machines, or more important, actually bake bread by manual control when the machines all too often go down. Program-dependent laborers, they can have no hands-on knowledge. The work is no longer legible to them, in the sense of understanding what they are doing. (Sennett 1998: 68)

Moving to the judicial situation, the question could be how important is it for judges to *know* the people behind the worried faces in front of them, if all the information they can refer to is provided by other sources than direct, face-to-face contact?

(b) *Action-dependence.* Zuboff points out that with the introduction of the computer, work is removed from action. Physical responses must be replaced by an abstract thought process, actions translated into the terms of an information system. Intuition becomes replaced by theory and procedural reasoning (a systematic correlation of data elements). As a consequence, thinking can exist independently of physical context. It is distant and remote, and the emphasis, of course, is on intellectual rather than action skills.

(c) *Context-dependence* means that the meaning of information can only be discerned within the context in which it occurs. Meaning is therefore not given in advance, but is rather something that must be constructed each time. However, the introduction of computers reduces the contextual nature of work. Data symbols are abstractions that are remote from rich sensory reality. Consequently, Zuboff observes, workers often distrust electronic data's ability to represent the concrete world and establish trust. Since they have lost crucial contextual information, they express a feeling of 'losing touch with reality'. They feel discomfort in having to trust remote symbols.[11] The emphasis is on systematic reasoning and theoretical knowledge.

(d) *Personalism* stresses the linkage between the knower and the known. With the introduction of computers, this linkage is fundamentally weakened. Interestingly, the changes in sentencing described in the previous chapter are characterised by a similar development. The abstract, non-sensory and decontextualised knowledge of sentencing patterns has gained primacy over contextualised and personal knowledge of concrete offenders and events.

Ironically, Zuboff reports, top management has managed to retain all the qualities taken away from blue-collar and middle-management workers with the introduction of computers. Top management knowledge is still implicit and has not been explicated into the computer programs. It is often intuitive, contextualised, based on face-to-face communication, verbal rather than written, relationship-intensive and based on a 'feel' for people and situations. Top management is characterised precisely by the fact that their work is based on privileged, personalised information that evades explication and rationalisation. The strength of judicial resentment against (almost any) attempts to formalise their work may indicate their awareness of the fact that explication and standardisation of work may be accompanied by a potential loss of professional power and status. As we have seen in the previous chapter, not all penal professions have had to go through the process of formalisation and depersonalisation. Some, most notably prosecutors, have retained and even increased their possibilities to exercise discretion and to 'cut corners'.

In scientific research too, some argue that computerisation is accompanied by increased emphasis on referential symbols. Couch (1996: 219) points out that computerisation has increased the distance between researches and the phenomena under investigation. Instead of examining the real phenomena, scientists are more likely to examine computerised *simulations* of these phenomena. Instead of examining the flow of fluids through organic tissue, a modern biological scientist, for example, is likely to examine simulations of the phenomenon. In sociological research, the computerisation of record keeping procedures has made bureaucratic records more readily available to sociologists. The ease with which such records can be processed with computers has enticed many social scientists to accept the

11 Zuboff points to an interesting fact that, historically, the same mistrust was also expressed when writing was established.

categories developed by bureaucrats as sociological concepts, which can have some problematic implications. As Nils Christie argues:

> [G]enerally, the problem is that we are given too easy access; not to raw data, but to data already processed by authorities, data already given their certified meaning … By taking state categories as our point of departure, we are captured by the meanings given by the official system of registration. We are therefore in danger of losing the myriad of alternative possible meanings. (1997: 19, 20)

Use of information technology, therefore, influences the types of information with which researchers as well as decision-makers operate. Penal systems, as other systems, have not been spared computer-generated graphic charts, 'tunnel of justice' visions, etc. However, the question is whether the information presented in the form of a guideline or a graph is the same but merely easier to grasp, or have there been changes in its very nature?

The answer may lie partly in the fact that an essential part of computers' use is the creation of *formats* for thought. In order to create formatted information, computers rationalise and standardise the activities and phenomena in question. However, what is important is that computers not only formalise individual phenomena, but they also shape our *future* perception of these phenomena. They produce new streams of data about the processes in question. Zuboff (1988) calls this the 'informating' capacity of information technology. It means that information technology has an important dimension of reflexivity – it produces data accessible for analytical purposes in the future:

> It not only imposes information (in the form of programmed instructions) but also produces information. It both accomplishes tasks and translates them into information … Information technology not only produces action but also produces a voice that symbolically renders events, objects and processes so that they become visible, knowable and shareable in a new way. (Zuboff 1988: 9)

When it comes to SISs for example, their effect is not only the increased uniformity of sentencing decisions, but also the fact that they produce information about these decisions. They render them transparent and visible in a new way – a dimension that, as we shall see later, can function as surveillance of decision-makers.

Further questions need to be asked, therefore, regarding what information we will have in the future. Will sentencing judgments, for example, be considered according to any other standards than those that computer systems can provide information about? Will we still bother about the experiences that fall outside the computer formats? Will these experiences be considered at all credible? One of the computer pioneers, Joseph Weizenbaum, went so far as to describe, somewhat dramatically, the computer as 'an instrument for the destruction of history':

> For when society legitimates only those 'data' that are 'in one standard format' and that 'can easily be told to the machine', then history, memory itself, is annihilated. *The New York Times* has already begun to build a 'data bank' of current events. Of course, only those data that are easily derivable by-products of typesetting machines are admissible to the system. As the number of subscribers to this system grows (…) how long will it be before what counts as fact is determined by the system, before all other knowledge, all memory, is simply declared illegitimate? (1976: 238)

Information technology therefore, as with every medium, carries with it a 'hidden theory' (Turkle 1995), hidden assumptions about what it means to communicate, to think and, furthermore, what is considered legitimate knowledge. Technologies force their users to develop new skills, as well as make them forget old ones. They bring about changes in the nature of the knowledge and experience required for work and social interaction. Now, with a computer, a scientist or an industrial worker no longer needs to rely on his or her senses to be able to perform a certain task. Similarly, people no longer need to use paper and pencil to multiply numbers manually. As a consequence, our ability mentally to compute information is reduced. This is a loss of skill, comparable to the loss of the ability to memorise large quantities of information in poetic form that occurred when written language replaced orality (Couch 1996):

> Technology designates for the users the mechanical, linguistical and conceptual parameters in which they must develop and execute strategies of social interaction and articulation. (…) [T]he user becomes 'servomechanism of the apparatus, substituting a language of codes of processed information for 'natural experience'(McLuhan 1964), which is internalized by the individual in order to successfully utilize the device. (McCormick and Visano 1992: 339)

Technological change is, therefore, never value-neutral. Furthermore, the meaning of the word 'information' should not be seen as value-neutral either. When referring to modern societies as information societies, one usually refers to the amount of information with which these societies and their members operate. However, information cannot simply be discussed as a quantity, devoid of meaning; as something that exists as such, which can be measured in bits without discussing its nature.

## Disembodiment

Lyon writes that: '[d]isappearing bodies is a basic problem of modernity that has been accentuated with growth and pervasiveness of communication and information technologies' (2001: 15). Bodies disappear because of the ability of modern technologies to do things 'at a distance'. However, the fact that culture can live at a distance, the fact that information can travel across time and space, is not unproblematic. Behind it lies an assumption that information can be regarded as an entity without a body and material context. In *How We Became Posthuman,* Katherine Hayles (1999) contests this materiality/information separation and the assumption that information and its material context can be seen as two distinct entities, with information as the important one. Hayles calls this *disembodiment*, a process in which information loses its body.

Disembodiment separates the mind from the body, believing that human identity and intelligence can be reproduced in a pure form and represented in an information pattern. This view has a number of advantages. Disembodied information is free to travel across time and space. It becomes 'free-floating, unaffected by changes in context' (Hayles 1999: 19). In the next chapter, it will be suggested that sentencing guidelines and SISs are characterised by a similar process of disembodiment. They are abstract information structures aiming to operate regardless of their social context and the individuals using them. Their focus is, therefore, on information itself, 'lifted up' from its day-to-day embodiments. Sentencing guidelines and SISs share the belief that we can deal directly with patterns of information, while disregarding the body and the material world of the unpredictable:

> Technical artefacts help to make an information theoretic view a part of everyday life … [I]nformation is increasingly perceived as interpenetrating material forms. Especially for users who may not know the material processes involved, the impression is created that pattern is predominant over presence. From here it is a small step to perceiving information as more mobile, more important, more *essential* than material forms. (Hayles 1999: 19, original emphasis)

However, Hayles argues that this leap from embodied reality to abstract information should be more closely examined and problematic. We should 'make clear how much had to be erased to arrive at such abstractions'. In the case of sentencing, one can ask what happens when a penal system makes the leap from an embodied system to an abstract, information driven entity where *'pattern is predominant over presence'*. What are the gains and where are the erasures? If form can be captured in a 'non-biological medium' (for example, a computer or a guideline), 'why do we need the flesh'? (Hayles 1999: 13). Indeed, why do we need the flesh? Why should abstract patterns not take precedence over concrete material events and individuals?

Hayles points out that regarding information as 'a free-floating, decontextualized, quantifiable entity' carries some important assumptions about human mind and identity: it changes the nature of what we define as human. The process of disembodiment is based on a belief that the mind can be separated from the body and that human identity and intelligence can be reproduced as an information pattern.[12] For Hayles, this is an incentive to ask what is distinctly human, and whether we can draw a line between the human and the technological worlds. 'When information loses its body, equating humans and computers is especially easy, for the materiality in which the thinking mind is instantiated appears incidental to its essential nature' (Hayles 1999: 2). Is human life and intelligence then essentially an informational code? Can it be reproduced at will? This has been the assumption behind DNA and the human genome project, as well as the many attempts to create artificial intelligence.

Similarly, the assumption behind sentencing guidelines and SISs has been that the sentencing process should be an objective process with a clearly visible information pattern that can be reproduced, regardless of its context and the nature of individual decision-makers. The central focus of a decision-making process thus becomes information itself, rather than the thinking individual using the information in various contexts. Guideline grids and computer-generated charts of sentencing patterns are the pictures of sentencing that have gained prominence over individual cases. As we shall see in the next chapter, these systems also produce information which is used by system managers for better budget and resource planning such as adjusting sentencing trends to prison capacities. The spheres of information, technology and management thus become indistinguishable, forming a unified new order of governance.

12 We shall see later that the objective behind guidelines and SISs has been precisely to create an information system that could capture the essence of judicial decision-making and reproduce it whenever needed. The extent to which judicial expertise can be reproduced varies from system to system; however, the belief that human intelligence can be reified as an information pattern is nevertheless the same.

# Chapter 3
# Computerised Justice as a Trend

## Informating the system

There is no doubt that penal institutions today are adjusting to the demands of the information society. Computers have become a standard tool in research and administrative work in Western penal systems and are often viewed as a 'virility symbol' (Tata 2000). To have an organisational structure and professional culture that is not adjusted to data gathering may simply seem outdated and suspicious, particularly in relation to the contemporary managerial ethos that depends on intensive data analysis.[1] Information technology has enabled the creation of knowledge related to institutional and individual activities, and such systematic knowledgeability is a precondition for successful management, budget allocation, etc. System management relies on the management of information and the ability of central administrative authorities to devise monitoring devices and maintain an overview of practitioners' activities. Electronic data processing has created new possibilities for assessing the effectiveness of various government agencies, as well as their monitoring routines. Consequently, Tata suggests that:

> As managerialist pressure builds on officials who administer the courts (Bottoms 1995) to provide evidence of efficiency, effectiveness and economy (Jones 1993), so there is perceived to be an imperative to invest in computers to perform a variety of tasks ... The question is likely to develop from 'could we introduce aggregate information systems?' to 'if other jurisdictions are introducing information systems then why isn't ours?' (Tata 2000: 302)

According to Kling and Allen (1996) we should, however, distinguish between two aspects when looking at the adoption of information technology in penal systems:

- environmental explanations (ie, the rational reasons of, for example, efficiency);[2]
- institutional and cultural explanations (how computerisation reflects the values and interests of specific groups and actors in an organisation).

Computerisation is as much a question of reflecting certain values and images of an organisation, and of gaining legitimacy in a culture where 'computerized information systems have joined factory smokestacks as major symbols of economic power' (Kling and Allen 1996: 107). Computerised information systems and organisational structures that are adjusted to data analysis can thus be regarded as symbols of health and legitimacy, an aspect that should not be overlooked when studying the 'informatisation' of modern penality.

---

1 Kling and Allen use the term *information entrepreneurialism*, which is embedded in the larger system of information capitalism, and which describes all the 'organizational practices involving the use of data-intensive techniques (including computerization) as key strategic resources for corporate production' (1996: 107).

2 Here, it could be argued that criminal justice has often been slow when it comes to information sharing and exploiting the potential of new information and communication technologies, especially when compared with the private sector.

When discussing the effects of information technology on criminal justice agencies, most commentators predictably point to the increased efficiency and effectiveness which IT brings. What also tends to be mentioned is the tendency of information technology to increase *routine* operations, limit the discretion of individual decision-makers and enhance the focus on *accountability* (Chan 2001, Ericson and Haggerty 1997). In Chan's (2001) Australian survey on the effects of IT on the work of police officers, the majority of police officers questioned agreed that information technology has required them to report on their work more frequently, and has led to closer scrutiny of their work by their supervisors. Some officers see this development as an 'overemphasis on accountability' and even describe information technology as leading to 'a less trusting or more paranoid organizational atmosphere'. As one officer put it:

> These days ... the emphasis on accountability has become much higher, and in doing so they introduce 9,321 different registers that's got to be filled out to maintain the accountability. But in doing that, you spend that much time on becoming accountable and spend less time doing the job you're paid for. I think accountability is a good thing, but at the same time it's got to be weighed up between getting the job done. And trusting people too, you get to the point where you're so busy being accountable you feel nobody trusts what you do. (Chan 2001: 155)

This disturbed balance between trust and the drive for accountability is also a vital issue when it comes to sentencing. In some ways the preoccupation with rules and accountability may be in danger of creating hostility and resentment among decision-makers who work in a system where it is increasingly difficult to exercise discretion and 'cut corners'.

Ericson and Haggerty (1997) report a similar development in Canada. They describe a pervasive culture of distrust within the police force, and, consequently, an increased 'surveillance of the police by the police'. A growing number of formats and procedures are designed to ensure that police officers act and think in the required ways.[3] Information technology plays a crucial role in this development:

> The computerized reporting formats for presentation of police knowledge provide classifications that fundamentally influence how the police think and act. Supervision is prospectively embedded in the formats as well as retrospectively in supervisors' checks of field reports, and there is an increased technological capacity to monitor reporting *as it is being done.* (Ericson and Haggerty 1997: 58, original emphasis)

Similarly, Raine (2001) reports that the extensive investment in computerisation in England and Wales has resulted in 'the automation of most of the key administrative functions within court offices and which is now beginning to infiltrate the courtroom too' (Raine 2001: 107). Furthermore, he points to the increasing *proceduralisation* and *standardisation* of the way in which courts work. This has resulted in having to operate with a more tightly defined framework of practice

3 Ericson and Haggerty give an example of a police officer who, after investigating a (relatively uncomplicated) motor vehicle accident, has to fill in no less than 16 separate reports and forms regarding the accident: a motor vehicle accident report, a general occurrence report, an arrest report, two itemized reports of property (including vehicles) seized for safekeeping, etc. While he used one hour to investigate the accident, he used three hours to write about it, to account for it and bureaucratically process it (1997: 23).

rules and regulations, with a consequent narrowing of the scope for discretion by the judiciary and its supporting staff.[4]

Of course, it needs to be stressed that demands for accountability are not fuelled by information technology *per se*, but rather the organisational and political environment in which technology is implemented. The desire to control discretionary powers of penal decision-makers may have been present for a long time, yet the rise of information technology has certainly opened new possibilities for its practical implementation. Computers have become central in installing an institutional framework that is standardised and transparent. Information technology is making it possible to design and institutionalise accountability through forms and reporting procedures which individual decision-makers have to follow in order to get their work done. Ericson and Haggerty write that databases, rather than individual bureaucrats, have become 'the basis for governance through knowledge' (1997: 13) – or what in the previous chapter I described as 'governance through information'. In what follows, I shall look more closely at forms, databases, and, later, algorithms, as phenomena that are of central importance for knowledge production and decision-making in contemporary computer-mediated penal culture. The objective is to look at these phenomena first and foremost as *cultural innovations* which are tightly connected to the issues of identity and the constitution of the subject. I will follow Poster's (1996) suggestion that computerised databases function as *discourses*, in Foucault's sense of the term. They are linguistic configurations which constitute individuals according to their 'rules of formation'. In what follows, a question will be asked regarding what kind of impact do these 'rules of formation' of the database have on the nature of penal knowledge and control, in general? How do forms differ from the previous ways of producing and organising knowledge? What can the consequences be for our knowledge about crime and punishment? And finally, what effects do these knowledge configurations have on the ways in which we construct offenders' and decision-makers' identities?

---

4 Raine (2001) also points out that the increasing focus on so called 'performance management accountability' is partly connected to the greater availability of statistics on administrative efficiency and other performance measures. One such example in England is the magistrates' courts' management information system (MIS), which provides information on costs, delays, quality of service, fines, etc. At first, the government argued that the purpose of the system was purely to help the courts in allocating their resources better. However, the information collected by the system soon became a weapon in the hands of the government to assure tighter accountability of individual courts to central government. Furthermore, Raine expresses a concern that:

> [O]ver time, the pursuit of increased accountability to the executive for court administrative performance has 'shifted the goal posts' somewhat so that the scope of performance monitoring has widened steadily to encompass aspects of judicial performance as well. Certainly it is a short step between the measurement of, say, aggregate case processing times for a court and the average speed and productivity of individual members of the judiciary. Moreover, it is a step that is all too easily facilitated by the automated monitoring capabilities of today's and tomorrow's computer systems. (2001: 122)

## Formatted vs personal

In *The Great War and Modern Memory* (1975), historian Paul Fussel traces one of the first examples of the use of forms: the British 'Field Service Post Cards' in the First World War. To control public anxiety at home, these cards were given to soldiers wounded in battle. They were instructed to circle the appropriate phrase and send them back home (without any additional writing on them).

| I have been admitted into hospital | |
|---|---|
| Sick | and am doing well. |
| Wounded | and hope to be discharged soon. |

According to Fussel:

> The Field Service Post Card has the honor of being the first wide-spread exemplar of that kind of document which uniquely characterizes the modern world: the 'Form'. It is the progenitor of all modern forms on which you fill in things or cross out things or check off things, from police traffic summonses to 'questionnaires' and income-tax blanks. When the Field Service Post Card was devised, the novelty of its brassy self-sufficiency, as well as its implications about the uniform identity of human creatures, amused the sophisticated and the gentle alike. (1975: 185)

Needless to say, British soldiers soon developed techniques of underlining that ironicised and undermined the one-dimensionality of the cards.[5]

The growth of *forms* is one of the main characteristics of contemporary risk thinking, and formalisation is also strongly present in sentencing reforms. It has been argued that one of the main characteristics of contemporary risk societies is that they are constantly refining the rules regarding how knowledge is communicated (Ericson and Haggerty 1997). One example can be found in the British Youth Justice Board ASSET assessment form, presented in the Appendix. Knowledge formats define how professionals within the system should think and act. There is a pervasive sense of *distrust* of alternative forms of knowledge (Ericson and Haggerty 1997, Giddens 1990). For example, instead of relying on unstructured narratives about accidents and other events, Ericson and Haggerty report that Canadian police officers now have to fill out increasing numbers of forms and questionnaires where the circumstances of interest are prescribed in advance. 'In risk society all occupations are subject to surveillance out of fear that their unique, informal cultures will violate procedural propriety' (Ericson and Haggerty 1997: 57):

> Computers allow the development of new formats of risk communication, as well as instant dispersal of knowledge of risk to interested institutions ... The databases rather than the individual bureaucrat become the basis for governance through knowledge. Knowledgeability becomes systematic, operating at collective and institutional more than individual level. (Ericson and Haggerty 1997: 13)

5 Reference reported in Simon (1995).

If in the past, penal professionals and their knowledge were viewed as the main resource of the system, now, by contrast, this same knowledge is viewed with suspicion, as a possible source of disorder and unpredictability that needs constant monitoring. On the following pages, I outline a similar development with regard to sentencing, where judicial knowledge, too, is being scrutinised in order to achieve greater order and predictability. The point that needs to be made here, is that the nature of professional knowledge itself is being transformed. Knowledge itself (or rather, its content) becomes, in many ways, *secondary* to the format (Ericson and Haggerty 1997). Formats simplify choices, they create transparency and predictability, they ease the classification and processing of data, and last but not least, they are the tools of control and surveillance. They can enable a shift of discretion and power from professionals to administrators. Managerial control is based on limiting the access of certain groups to introduce alternative types of knowledge and language that do not correspond with the closed-ended formats and classifications.

I would like to suggest that the shifts of power taking place in contemporary penal systems are, therefore, not only defined by limiting discretion of certain professions, but, even more importantly, by limiting the opportunities that these groups have in the production of knowledge (Garland 2001). The struggles over the exercise of sentencing discretion are closely connected to the struggles over legitimacy of various types of knowledge. The professional power of judges, as well as probation workers and some other occupations, is intimately connected to the understanding of offenders as unique and contextualised. The force of managerialism, on the other hand, is deeply dependent on a structured and formatted view of reality. Therefore, the ideological struggles around the fall of rehabilitation and the rise of competing paradigms are not only struggles about the content of penological knowledge; they are, perhaps even more crucially, struggles about the *format* and nature of knowledge. In the end, these struggles have to a considerable extent legitimised and institutionalised structured and formalised thinking as an ideal of penal professionalism.

Contemporary penal policies are sometimes described as lacking coherent theory, which arguments around rehabilitation previously used to provide. However, unity today may be based not on the existence of a unifying discourse or ideology, but on a uniform *format of knowledge*, on standardisation of procedures for thought and communication about events and individuals in the system. Coherence, therefore, lies in the fact that the ideas and concepts which are, or can be, formatted tend to be given priority. One may say that they need to fit into the 'information processing scenario' and be 'compatible' with the existing communication systems. Bøhme puts it in this way:

> In order for society to be controllable through knowledge, it must itself be organized in terms of knowledge. Social processes must be differentiated according to function and arranged according to models, and social actors must be *disciplined in a way that makes their behaviour amenable to data collection* or makes their social roles and activities relevant only insofar as they produce data. (Bøhme 1992: 46, emphasis added)

What does it actually mean that 'social actors must be disciplined in a way that makes their behaviour amenable to data collection'? Put simply, it means that events and persons need to be understood as data, as objectified, formalised information, and that thinking and decision-making processes need to be envisioned in terms of formal procedures, algorithms and formats rather than open narratives and complex professional discourses. Or, as Ericson and Haggerty describe it:

> Policing … is subject to intensive 'informating' (translating events and objectives into visible information via formats) and 'automating' or 'fordization' (machine appropriation of human skills and labour) (Zuboff 1988). Again, the goal is a simplification of choices in the face of a kaleidoscope of possible interpretations and courses of action – 'taylorization'. (1997: 36)

In a way, we can say that the field of penal knowledge needs to adjust to 'computers ontology'. In this context, it becomes clearer how sentencing guidelines are, in fact, a good example of a 'computer-friendly' decision-making tool.

## Guidelines – a child of the information age

> [T]he assumed 'incoherence' of judicial behaviour stems from a fixation with normative-philosophical justifications for judging, which are also convenient to mechanistic thinking about computerized decision support. (Tata 2000: 297)

Guidelines as well as computers cannot be used without formalisation of language and thinking. The encoding of thinking and language is inherent in the guidelines' design. 'The mechanistic ideas of representation and formalisation are at the very heart of computing' (Dahlbom and Mathiassen 1993: 12). Or, as Alldridge argues:

> If you are going to use computers in legal contexts, the pressure which computers generate is towards a rule-bound framework, because it is what they do best … The link is a contingent one – there is no logical one but a practical one. (Alldridge 1997: 4)

The guidelines system promises predictability and an easy overview and access to judicial decisions, according to clear and unequivocal standards. It makes possible accumulation of great amounts of information concerning criminal justice decisions; the information which, precisely because of its standardised form, is capable of being stored, analysed and communicated in the penal system. We can, therefore, regard the guidelines as a sort of *automata*[6] for information processing. The Canadian Sentencing Commission, for example, wrote in 1987 that 'it is literally unthinkable that such an inherent relationship would not exist between sentencing guidelines, as developed by a sentencing commission, and the establishment of a reliable sentencing information system' (1987: 295).

It needs to be pointed out that in practice, guidelines are still primarily a print-based technology. However, computers do play an increasingly important role in monitoring and assisting their implementation. Already in the 1980s, an expert system named ASSYST (Applied Sentencing System) was designed by the US

6 Some contemporary analysts are re-introducing analogies which indicate the machine-like nature of modern decision-making: 'case processors', 'assembly-line producers' (Simon 1993), 'sentencing machine' (Tonry 1996), 'fordisation' and 'taybrisation' (Ericson and Haggerty 1997).

Sentencing Commission to help in the implementation of the US Federal Sentencing Guidelines. The complexity of the guidelines made them difficult to apply without a 'road map'. The purpose of the system was, therefore, to ensure the correct application of the guidelines, to make them easier to use, as well as to help the Sentencing Commission monitor the guidelines' implementation. ASSYST set up a mechanism for automatic data collection and thereby crucially facilitated the Commission's job of achieving uniformity of sentencing decisions. However, there was also an interesting political force behind the development of ASSYST, namely the desire to increase the *demand* for computers in the penal system and to bring it into the information age (Simon and Gaes 1989). Furthermore, the program had an important heuristic value. It helped to uncover ambiguities and inconsistencies in the design of the guidelines themselves. A computer thus became an integral component in the process of guideline creation and use (Simon and Gaes 1989).

Furthermore, even though the original concern behind the guidelines was to address the problems of sentencing disparity, they later became used as a tool for facilitating managerial planning and the allocation of resources within the penal system. In a number of states a major benefit from the guidelines has been the development of *computer-based population simulation models* which project the amount of money needed to support a state's sentencing policy (Lubitz and Ross 2001). Guidelines make it easier to predict sentencing outcomes and, therefore, also correctional costs. As one company advertisement for a prison population simulation model proclaims, their products:

> mimic the flow of offenders into, through, and out of the state correctional systems, beginning with conviction and continuing with discharge from the correctional system. ARS's simulation models provide the ability to analyze the impact of changes in operating policies, sentencing practices, post release practices, and external system pressures on the system. This includes, for example, the projected impact of different sentencing models (guidelines, determinate, or indeterminate) on institutional bed space, jail backlog, correctional alternatives, resource allocation ... (www.simul8.com/products (viewed 4 February 2004))

Growing prison overcrowding has also caused guidelines to become a tool for channelling non-prison offenders into intermediate and community based sanctions, thus conserving scarce prison resources. Reitz (2001) reports that the above-mentioned prison projections of sentencing policies have sometimes had a sobering effect on legislators, who realised the costs of various sentencing policies. As a result, compromises were made by increasing sentences for certain types of crimes (such as violent crimes), while decreasing them for some other categories that are of lesser public interest. On the other hand, prison projections were used in the federal system simply to predict correctly the amount of resources needed to implement the federal sentencing legislation. The US Sentencing Commission used its ability to predict the impact of sentencing guidelines on prison space to recommend construction of the accurate number of prisons.

Sentencing commissions are thus becoming vital centres of correctional resource management and sentencing data gathering. Judges are required to fill out forms or worksheets, such as the one presented in the Appendix (Table 4), for each sentence they impose. In some states the manual forms are now replaced by electronic worksheet systems. The system helps judges and other users to determine the right guidelines application. The completed forms can then be submitted electronically to the commissions.[7] The Minnesota Sentencing Guidelines Commission, for example, introduced a web-based electronic worksheet system in August 2000. Now, sentencing worksheets are submitted to a statewide database accessible to Minnesota's criminal justice practitioners. The commission states[8] as particular advantages of the electronic system: 'uniformity, accuracy, speed, convenience and security' – thus, adopting in its vocabulary the buzzwords of the information age.

## US Sentencing Commission's Sentencing Worksheet (training worksheet)

Sentencing forms or worksheets in many respects resemble Ericson and Haggerty's (1997: 364) description of 'forms about forms', whose purpose is to regulate and supervise the uses of other forms. If the role of the guidelines is to make the sentencing process uniform, the task of worksheets is further to ensure that the process and the reporting of it are standardised. Sentencing commissions are, thus, becoming important managers of sentencing information and furthermore, controllers of uniform collection of this information, which is increasingly collected and transmitted through electronic systems. The role of sentencing commissions is, first, to make sure that information is reported and, secondly, that it is reported in a standardised manner. Commissions collect information not only on guidelines departures and guidelines scores, but also information on offenders and their characteristics, information on victims, judicial circuits, etc.

However, using guideline software highlights how a sentencing decision basically comes closer to following the right steps in a computer program than finding the ethically or morally adequate answer to a particular act. As one manual for using so called guidelines calculation software instructs its users:

> The steps to creating a guideline report are:
>
> 1) Enter the relevant case information, such as defendant name and case number, in the Case Information Screen.
> 2) Enter each offense of conviction (or anticipated conviction), in the Offense Information Screen. The program will select the appropriate guideline for each offense entered.
>
> If an offense is associated with more than one guideline, the program will provide the user with a list of applicable guidelines and their scope in the guidelines Narrowing Screen. Select an applicable guideline from this list.
>
> 3) If more than one offense is entered, the program will group the offenses into preliminary groups. Review the recommended groups and over-ride the selections as necessary in the Offence Grouping Screen.
> 4) Answer each guideline question. Guideline questions are presented in different screens, depending on the nature of the question. The three main screens are as follows:

---

7 However, we shall see later that the purpose of sentencing worksheets is not only (perhaps not even primarily) data gathering, but also to ensure accountability and compliance of the judiciary (see the discussion on judicial transparency, below).

8 Information from the Minnesota Sentencing Guidelines Commission's web page: www.msgc.state.mn.us/Guidelines (viewed 31 May 2004).

> a) Guideline question screen. This screen presents a single guidelines question. Answer the Question by selecting a response in the answer grid.
>
> b) Relevant conduct screen. Enter the relevant conduct amount, such as the amount of loss in fraud cases, or the controlled substances quantity in drug cases ...
>
> (Federal Sentencing Guidelines Research Center 1999: 6)

The title of a recent US Senior District Judge Jenkins's speech is, therefore, not surprising: '*For thinking press 1, for compassion press 2, for judgment press 3.*' Jenkins (2002) compares the federal sentencing process to 'talking to a pre-programmed computer chip', quite like computer chips that we encounter in other spheres of our lives:

> In the field of sentencing, it is almost like pressing one for thinking and finding that pre-thinking is all that is available, that compassion is not available at all, and that local hands-on judgment is not wanted ... It appears to me that in this computer age there is a subtle change in the manner in which we think and act. We forget that the computer is just a tool. It is supposed to help – not substitute for – thought ... It can add up figures, but can't evaluate the assumptions for which the figures stand. Its judgment is no judgment at all. *There is no algorithm for human judgment.* Press one. Press two. Press three. Contexts are dynamic. Human beings are infinitely variable. Differences do make a difference. Categories are suspect. (Jenkins 2002, emphasis added)

Judge Jenkins's impassioned observations highlight the dichotomy between two distinct approaches to sentencing and judicial thinking: one that focuses on concrete cases and relies on 'hands-on' experience, and, on the other hand, there is the type of thought, embodied in the guidelines and sentencing information systems (SISs), that sees rules and categorisation as its primary point of reference and justification. In the latter case, the compatibility of this type of judicial reasoning with computers is not simply a matter of literary comparisons, but increasingly also of practical necessity.

## The ideal (type of) bureaucrat

The use of computers fits into a certain understanding of sentencing, and punishment in general, as a rational process, governed by rules.[9] A quest for universal procedures, for achieving mathematical certainty, consistency and clarity of thought, is embedded both in computers' and guidelines' design. We could perhaps say that they share a certain '*structural likeness*'.[10] Judge Frankel, one of the ideological fathers of the US Federal Sentencing Guidelines, had already in 1972 envisioned a possible role for computers in sentencing:

> It is not necessary, or desirable, to imagine that sentencing can be completely computerized. At the same time, the possibility of using computers as an aid toward orderly thought in sentencing need not be discounted in advance. (Frankel 1972: 115)

Perhaps we can say that both guidelines and computers employ what is in Chapter 2 described as the 'data processing model of thought'. This mode of thought is

---

9 The compatibility of guidelines and computers has also been pointed out by Christie (1993: 149).

10 I would like to thank Jonathan Simon for the suggestion.

characterised by a belief in predictable rules for thought, and a search for formal procedures. Thinking is reduced to a process of connecting data points in formal sequences (Roszak 1994). As presented above, thinking in the guideline model is characterised by the same mechanical process of connecting objective categories in already prescribed ways. Therefore, guidelines are in a sense an information-processing medium, which, in essence, bears similarity to computer-mediated thought and communication.

In a way, creators of sentencing guidelines, as well as sentencing information systems, decision-making worksheets and risk assessment forms, appear to share the same philosophy as computer programmers: the creation of a predictable and self-contained world. They are trying to keep the 'rules of the game' as clear as possible. Surprises and ambiguities are not welcome. The success of the idea of proportionality may therefore just as easily be found in its timelessness and disembeddedness – its insistence that concrete offences can be turned into *objects of information*, independent of the subjects that give them meaning. The concept of proportionality is quite convenient for handling by a computer because it indicates a certain sense of mathematical equation, of numerical equivalence and precision. However, this is true only under the condition that social and personal factors which enter the equation are predictable, explicated and kept to a minimum. By doing that, even though not consciously, contemporary sentencing reforms appear to accept the data processing model of thought. They share the same demand, that sentencing goals need to be made explicit and that the purpose of punishment has to be clear, even though this is seldom the case in real life. While there are so many, often contradictory, intentions behind a real-life sentence – protection of society, rehabilitation of the offender, the needs of the victim and the offender's family, etc – the purpose of proportionality seems to make all this 'messiness' clear, and the computer is a perfect tool for its implementation. The guidelines explicate ideals of justness and formulate it as a set of computer instructions. They insist that there is no 'mystery' behind judicial thinking and that all information contained in decisions could and should be prescribed in advance.

It needs to be pointed out, however, that the insistence on the rational, rule-governed administration of justice is far from new. Originating in Weber's analysis of bureaucracy, the notion of modern institutions as depersonalised, calculable, predictable and adhering to rules, has had major influence on modern social thought. Weber points to the importance of governance based on calculable rules and objective expertise for the functioning of modern state and economy. The identity of the bureaucrats performing various administrative tasks should not matter; similarly, today, the identity of the people installing computer software or reading temperature from thermometers should not matter. The answers should lie in the technology or the rule rather than in the persons performing the tasks. Garland suggests that to some extent 'most accounts of modern institutions speak a Weberian language without feeling the need to acknowledge it as such' (1990: 178). Weber also provides us with one of the earliest descriptions of the modern *judge as automaton*. The idea of the automation of justice, of 'law without gaps', though, was clearly not seen as practically conceivable by Weber and his contemporaries, at the beginning of the 20th century:

> It is perfectly true that *objectivity* (*Sachlicheit*) and *expertness* (*Fachmazigkeit*) are not necessarily identical with the rule of general and abstract norms. Indeed, this does not even hold in the case of the modern administration of justice. The idea of 'law without gaps' is, of course, under vigorous attack. The conception of the modern judge as an automaton into which legal documents and fees are stuffed at the top and in order that it may spill forth the verdict at the bottom along with the reasons, read mechanically from codified paragraphs – this conception is angrily rejected, perhaps because a certain approximation to this type would precisely be implied by a consistent bureaucratization of justice. (Weber 1968: 978–79, emphasis added)

It probably would have come as a great surprise to Weber, if he visited American courtrooms today, to find that judicial 'expertness' and 'objectivity' are coming closer and closer together, and becoming in some cases almost identical.

Some analysts (Garland 1990, Dreyfus and Rabinow 1983) have pointed out how Foucault's monumental *Discipline and Punish* continues Weber's themes of rationalisation and objectification, as well as what is essentially reliance on 'ideal types'.[11] Whether disciplinary technology is essentially an expression of an 'ideal type' is a contested issue (Dreyfus and Rabinow 1983: 132), and Foucault himself would probably be the first to disagree. He does not mention Weber in his work. Foucault describes discipline as a *technology* of power, 'a type of power, a modality for its exercise, comprising a whole set of instruments, techniques, procedures, levels of application, targets' (Foucault 1977: 215). Foucault argues that discipline, as a 'technology of power', may not be identified and is not reducible to any particular institutions, although it may be appropriated by them in different ways (1977: 215).

The essential component of disciplinary technology is the creation of a *field of visibility*, epitomised in the panopticon, and the establishment of norms which enable constant evaluation and control of the individuals caught in this design of power. I would like to suggest that similarly to the panopticon, the forms, the matrix design and the computer-generated charts described in this book are technologies of power which, through the creation of fields of visibility, monitor and govern human behaviour, as well establish clear standards according to which the behaviour can be monitored. Judge Jack B Weinstein actually describes the Federal Sentencing Guidelines as the fulfilment of Bentham's dream of 'a fully rationalized algebra of criminology and penology' (Luna 2002: 13).

In fact, the matrix design, the form and the computer-generated chart constitute a decision-maker that is in a way a crossing between the 'ideal' bureaucrat in the Weberian sense and the panoptical design. The forms encourage decision-makers to become bureaucrats who apply rules with unvarying precision. However, in this case, the bureaucrats themselves are also caught in the panoptical field of visibility. Now, they – the bureaucrats – have to fill out reports and forms about their own work, thus making their (rather than offenders') 'biography' visible with the help of a few computer clicks. Of course, we should be cautious in presuming that this position of visibility is always in conflict with judges' wishes or that it is necessarily something new. Decisions of judges working in smaller, particularly rural, communities have always been more visible to the public, thus becoming a part of

11 Weber's ideal type is a methodological device which is used to provide clarifying models of complex social phenomena and historic developments by accentuating their 'essences' (for further discussion see, for example, Hekman 1983).

judges' 'personal biography'. However, instruments such as sentencing guidelines create possibilities for increased visibility of judicial decisions, not only within the system but also to the public. For example, Virginia is one of the jurisdictions which has released judges' specific information to newspapers, including judges' names, overall compliance rates with the guidelines, aggravation rates, mitigation rates and number of cases (Kern 1999). A number of other US guideline jurisdictions are considering the same policy. Finally, a recent law amendment requires the federal judiciary to report sentencing records of individual judges to the Justice Department (Bazelon 2003).

## Algorithms vs ideas

An interesting aspect of sentencing guidelines is that their form has been able to adapt to a variety of goals and philosophies (Lubitz and Ross 2001), while preserving the same structural framework. While some may point to the contrast between the Weberian, rule-governed rationalism on one hand, and the emotional nature of contemporary penal populism on the other hand (Garland 1990), sentencing guidelines are being used to implement both the populist policies as well as the goals of more efficient system management and, to some extent, limitation of prison growth. As mentioned before, Minnesota Sentencing Commission added public safety and more severe punishment of violent offenders as the number one priority of the guidelines system, even though the guidelines were originally designed as a just deserts system.

While the discourses and objectives behind the guidelines vary widely, the technique (or rather the format) largely remains the same. Perhaps guidelines can best be described as tools for *administrative communication* – for information gathering, auditing and accountability – rather than instruments for *symbolic exchange* discourses about punishment. Their role and the role of sentencing commissions is to gather information for the purposes of further analysis, to supervise compliance rates, to make budgetary calculations, prison population forecasts etc, rather than address the issues of why and how one should punish. Stith and Cabranes put it this way:

> [T]he sentencing hearing today can be nearly unintelligible to victims, defendants, and observers, and even to the very lawyers and judges involved in the proceeding. Too often, when it is all over, neither the judge nor the lawyers are able to explain coherently, much less justify or defend, the sentence imposed. (1998: 5)

A report about a guideline hearing in *The Washington Post* (6 October 1996)[12] further exemplifies the phenomenon:

> 'The court finds that the base offense level is 20,' the judge began. 'Pursuant to Guidelines 2K2.1(b)(4), the offense level is increased by two levels [to 22] ... The Court notes that the criminal convictions ... result in the total criminal history category score of 18. At the time of the instant [*sic*] offense ... the defendant was serving a parole sentence [*sic*] in two causes of action. And pursuant to Sentencing Guidelines 4A1.1 (D), 2 points are therefore added. The total criminal history points is 20. And according to the

12 Reported in Stith and Cabranes (1997: 1,264).

> Sentencing Guidelines Chapter 5, Part A, 20 criminal history points establish a criminal history category of 6 … [As a result] the guideline range for imprisonment is 84 to 105 months.'

Guidelines clearly have problems justifying sentencing decisions and creating credible discourses about crime and punishment. Therefore, as much as sentencing guidelines (as well as SISs and risk assessment instruments) can be seen as a continuity of the Weberian theme of rationalisation and rule-governed behaviour, a continuation of an essentially modern trend, I would like to suggest that they also have qualities which markedly distinguish them from previous decision-making tools. While the Weberian world of modernity was still focused around discourses and symbolic exchange, the world of information societies, in which guidelines and risk instruments are embedded, is centred around communication of information, and marked by the absence of narratives (Lash 2002). The technological and cultural contexts in which the guidelines and risk assessment forms emerge and are implemented influence the nature of knowledge that these decision-making tools generate. Thus, while there are clear lines of continuity with modernity, there are also clear points of discontinuity.[13]

Guidelines, SISs and risk assessment instruments represent a certain break with traditional modes of judicial thinking, which are essentially connected with written texts and oral communication. While until the 19th century sentencing was primarily an oral event, with the rise of penal modernism it was transformed into an essentially written practice – but still retaining important elements of orality (Simon 1995). However, with the guideline system and the proliferation of forms, penal power is losing its ability to *create a narrative*. The matrix grids and formulae reduce the penal vocabulary to a limited menu of terms and expressions. They produce a uniformity of language, a code of grammar, which is unable to express complex thoughts and ideas to the public and actors in the penal process. As Simon points out, the oral elements of previous epochs helped to 'provide an anchor for punishment in the world outside the penal system' that is now increasingly absent. Guidelines reduce the 'range and quantity of knowledge that can be produced about acts of political significance' (Simon 1995: 20).

In this respect, guidelines share a similarity with computer-based communication. They both share the same project of finally defining the meaning of words, of encoding of language, and they are both marked by abstractness and decontextualisation. Both guidelines and computer programs work independently of people and social contexts.[14] 'A computer program works in a context-

---

13 I refrain from using the term postmodernity, following Lash's (2002) argument that the terms 'informational' and 'information society' provide a more suitable description than the term postmodern. Lash argues that while postmodernism provides us with good accounts of contemporary disorder and fragmentation, the notions of information and information society provide us with better accounts of both the emerging new social order and disorder (Lash 2002: 1).

14 Bottoms (1995) reports that guidelines are resisted in particular local areas in the US because they are seen as insensitive to local context. This may be particularly marked in areas that are distant from the main locus of power (remote rural communities, ethnic minorities, women victimised by serious violent and sexual crimes, etc). Bottoms points out that:

> [W]e live in an increasingly pluralist world … and the demands generated by this pluralism do not always fit well with the rationalizing impulses created both by the 'fairness' critique of the rights approach, and by managerialism. (1995: 37)

independent and person-independent way: it is indifferent to the identity of those who operate, benefit or suffer from its operations' (Barglow 1994: 205). Poster points out that the effectiveness of the database, and one could say the same for sentencing guidelines and various risk assessment forms, lies in their non-ambiguous structure and the elimination of cultural context. A database relies upon the reduction of information and elimination of ambiguity in language:

> It imposes a new, impoverished language ... A database arranges information in rigidly defined categories – speed and efficiency of the database vary directly with the fixity of the form in which information appears in it – the agency constitutes individuals according to these parameters ... It constitutes individuals by manipulating relationships between bits of information. (Poster 1990: 96)

Writing and speech, on the other hand, are highly *contextual* modes of communication, which encode rich cultural materials. The difference has important implications for the types of knowledge and subjectivity that are promoted by information technology and, consequently, also by the guidelines and forms.

According to Poster (1990), individuals are constituted in a different manner in electronic writing and communication than in speech and traditional writing. Speech constitutes individuals primarily as members of a community, based on face-to-face interaction. Written communication is based on rational and autonomous individuals who are able to give meaning to words and texts of great complexity. By contrast, electronic writing tends to be depersonalised, removed from contexts and individuals. Consequently, the subject of communication is weakened and decentred. In electronic communication, Poster writes that words lose their connection to real things and contexts: they tend to become part of a *self-referential* language code which is removed from the face-to-face context of daily life. Therefore, a rational, autonomous individual who gives meaning to a text is, in electronic writing, replaced by a flow of signs which are separated from their senders, and which have no stable meaning. Computer writing, therefore, seems to be challenging the authority of the centred subject (Poster 1990, Barglow 1994).

One might ask whether sentencing guidelines represent a similar transformation in a judge's position: a move from a rational (typically white male) individual who is autonomously giving meaning to a legal text, to a state where a judge's individuality becomes almost irrelevant in the light of objective systems. Furthermore, one might ask how much space formal structures, such as the guidelines, which, to a large extent, exclude the narrative, leave for the practice of interpretation and creation of meaning. The guidelines' self-referential and machine-like nature has distanced them, not only from the communities in which they are applied, but furthermore, from the individuals who are supposed to give meaning to their content – the judges. Do guidelines then still function as a text, which needs to be read and interpreted, or have they come closer to becoming a computer program – which functions automatically?

One could say that sentencing guidelines reduce the sentencing process to an algorithmic procedure. 'Formalistic positivism' is based on the type of reasoning that, in common with the 'data processing model of thought', assumes that there is no 'mystery' behind human decision-making – 'that there is nothing more to thought than a conventional mechanistic analysis will discover: data points shuffled through a small repertory of algorithms' (Roszak 1994: 244). The 'data processing model of thought' has been criticised by Roszak (1994), who argues that the human mind does not work by way of *algorithmic procedures*, but rather by way of *gestalts*; that it consists of thinking with ideas and not only processing of information. Accordingly, he asserts that some aspects of thinking are closer to being an art than a science; they are instinctive and creative and defy capture and analysis. We can remember that those were also the arguments of some judges when discussing sentencing reforms.[15] They argued that sentencing is more of an art than a science and that it is instinctive, based on experience and cannot be predicted.

Roszak (1994) points out that there is a fundamental difference between thinking with ideas and thinking with information. Ideas are 'integrating patterns meant to declare the meaning of things as human beings have discovered it by way of revelation, sudden insight, or the slow growth of wisdom over a lifetime' (1994: 93).[16] Unlike information, which is acquired simply by being told, ideas are created from experience and thinking. They have the potential to be original and creative and are therefore beyond prediction. Roszak suggests that this unpredictability of mind 'saves human society from the changeless rigidity of other social animals' and is a source of unlimited cultural creativity (1994: 99). What can one say, then, about a legal system that makes predictability and uniformity one of the primary parameters of justness? Already in 1966, Julius Stone argued for the recognition of the 'historical truth that most legal change springs precisely from deviance, tentativeness, afterthought and even indecision in judgment'. At the same time, Roszak (1994) argues, one should bear in mind that every fact and every item of information grows from an idea. *Ideas create information*, not the other way around. Furthermore, the computer itself is also an idea about numbers and classification (Roszak 1994). By assuming that information processing is the basis of thought, one blurs the distinction between ideas and information, thus hiding the underlying structures of ideas upon which information rests, placing them further from critical reflection. Facts are, after all, 'human creations, each capable of being questioned, doubted, altered' (Roszak 1994: 106). Roszak draws our attention to the fact that information is never neutral, that it is political through and through. It is not facts that determine policy, it is rather the other way around – it is policy that determines facts (1994: 161).

These are also the issues that should be of relevance for sentencing guidelines and SISs. The concepts that SISs operate with are not objective (Tata, Wilson and Hutton 1996), even though they are being treated as if they were. They are human and social creations, results of social interaction and subjectively defined. Therefore, it may be impossible to create an objective system – penal systems are, after all, not 'game worlds'. They are not self-contained, even though they may sometimes strive to be so, and people working in them are instructed to exclude considerations that

15 In *Intuition and its Role in Strategic Thinking*, Henden (2004) interviewed 105 Norwegian business leaders about the types of thinking they employ in their work. Most of the respondents described intuition as more important than analytic thinking, particularly when facing new and unknown situations.

16 Roszak (1994) points to a number of 'master ideas' living at the heart of every culture, certain basic assumptions about life and human nature (for example, the idea about human dignity) which need no proof. Rehabilitation could probably be seen as one such organising idea in the past, and contemporary penal systems seem to be unable to replace it with a new one.

are not explicitly predicted, instructed to stop the influx of contextual information in order to maintain the consistency of the program. Furthermore, the computer, as a medium, and databases may often strengthen the perceived objectivity of information with which they operate, thus never problematising, for example, the concept of the criminal act itself, whose meaning is far from objective (Christie 1993, 2004). Just as the written and the printed text may seem more truthful and carry greater authority than the spoken word, the database gives an even stronger impression of objectivity. To discern its human origins, and thus its fallibility, may demand considerable effort.

## Storytelling in the courtroom

Some proponents of computer-supported sentencing regard the fact that law already operates with formalised knowledge as an advantage when introducing information systems. 'The law has the advantage of offering a consolidated framework of a systematic structure' (JURIX 1992: 72). In this way, the system has to analyse fewer unknown terms than those occurring in natural language. Strictness of language is important for efficient knowledge retrieval. As pointed out above, the effectiveness of a database depends on its non-ambiguous structure and the elimination of a cultural context (Poster 1990: 96).

Computerised representations of sentencing consistency are, therefore, as with sentencing guidelines, based on formalistic thinking. However, some proponents of SISs have questioned the adequacy of this way of thinking. Tata, Wilson and Hutton (1996) have argued that judges do not, in reality, see cases as similar in terms of official offence categories such as robbery, theft, rape, etc, because these provide little information concerning the seriousness of the offence. All criminal convictions are themselves typologies. As Nils Christie argues:

> Acts are not, they *become*. So also with crime. Crime does not exist. Crime is created. First there are acts. Then follows a long process of giving meaning to these acts. Social distance is of particular importance. Distance increases the tendency to give certain acts the meaning of being crimes, and the persons the simplified meaning of being criminals. In other settings – family life is only one of several examples – the social conditions are of a sort which creates resistance against perceiving acts as crimes and persons as criminals. (1993: 21)

Therefore, categories of criminal convictions do not, and cannot, reflect the full and precise occurrence of 'what happened' during an incident. On the contrary, the criminal conviction, for which a person may be sentenced is necessarily the result of a simplified and normalised representation of events.

The information with which a sentencer is presented has therefore already been pragmatically negotiated and refracted through a series of legal and organisational lenses (police, prosecution). It is never an objective and factual representation of behaviour, but a pragmatic representation of it (Tata, Wilson and Hutton 1996). To refer to the official legal categories as objective facts of a case would therefore be illusory and inadequate. This might also explain judicial reluctance to use SISs. Administrative data seems to be inadequate for the purpose of judicial sentencing, because judges see similarity differently to the creators of SISs. However, as Tata (1998) reports, there is pressure by officials on research developers to accept available data. Until now, only the Scottish SIS project has managed to resist the official pressure and managed to *collect its own data*. The system contains relatively small data sets and is more expensive than using the official administrative data (Tata 1998).

At the same time, it has also been pointed out that computerised systems, and one could say the same about sentencing guidelines and risk assessment instruments, are based on analytical and linear models of thought which can seldom be found in reality. The *analytical* model assumes that sentencing decisions can be partitioned into discrete elements – factors or 'reasons' – which are independent of each other. These factors are then added and brought together in accordance with rational standards and rules. The usual view among the advocates of sentencing guidelines and SISs is that there is, and should be, a clear relationship between the facts and the sentence. The relevant facts are thus specified in advance and the sentence varies according to how strongly represented these facts (factors) are in a particular case. However, it has been argued that the judicial thinking in concrete cases does not necessarily confirm the analytical model. Tata (1998), Hutton (1995) and Tata, Wilson and Hutton (1996) have suggested that judges use a *holistic* approach, where information (or 'factors') does not have an independent but a *relational* meaning (Tata 1997). Often, judges may look at a case and construct a *story* or a narrative about it, and then choose the relevant facts according to that particular story.[17] The list of phenomena that are incorporated into a narrative is much wider and more open, compared to those prescribed in advance. Therefore, the relationship between facts and a sentence is not as clear-cut and predictable, which makes the measurement of consistency much more difficult. Judges may build on a single image which brings all the information together; they come to a solution and then later justify that solution to the public with the official reasons of deterrence, justness, protection of the public, etc.

In fact, in their 1981 study, *Reconstructing Reality in the Courtroom*, Bennett and Feldman persuasively argue that storytelling and the construction of stories about criminal cases are vital aspects of legal judgments. Law and legal judgments involve more than merely formal procedures, but also 'social judgment that anchors legal questions in everyday understandings' (Bennett and Feldman 1981: 4). In order to take part in a criminal trial, both the professionals and lay participants transform the information presented into stories about crime. The stories provide the facts of a case with an interpretative context which makes certain actions meaningful, as well as providing a framework for evaluating the credibility of facts. Therefore, the involved parties in trials not only introduce new evidence and new facts in order to argue their case. They also have to provide a meaningful framework – a credible story:[18]

---

17 There is no doubt, of course, that this approach can result in a number of unfortunate outcomes with regard to what judges may consider to be relevant factors. For example, does the fact that a rape victim was wearing a revealing dress justify a more lenient sentence for the offender (as in a recent Norwegian case), or does it simply reflect a judge's biased perception of women?

18 Bennett and Feldman (1981) also point out that the vital role of storytelling also has a potential for creating bias in criminal trials. Not all social groups and social actors have the same ability to present a credible story, either because they do not share the same language and reasoning traditions as the other participants, or because they do not share the same normative assumptions about what makes a plausible story.

> What makes a particular fact or a bit of evidence take on meaning in a case is not its physical form, the credibility of the witness who introduced it ... What makes a fact or piece of evidence meaningful in a particular case is its contextual role in the stories that make up the case. (Bennett and Feldman 1981: 117)

We may all remember the famous 'glove that did not fit' in the OJ Simpson trial, or other seemingly insignificant circumstances such as Conan Doyle's 'dog that did not bark' – seemingly irrelevant facts which introduced doubt into the existing stories about events and provided radically new interpretations of the known facts.

The point here is that there is more to legal reasoning and sentencing than formal procedures and rationalistic discourse. Law is a socially embedded activity. The current rational-analytical approach in sentencing guidelines and SISs represent, therefore, only one aspect of what occurs in a sentencing process. The approach focuses on the formal, while side-stepping the substantive aspects of justice. A number of authors (Braithwaite 1989, Tait 2002) have pointed out that criminal trials are based on more than just rational discourse. They are also *symbolic rituals* that function as public performances through which a crime is explained, verbally re-enacted and then publicly denounced. The offender is publicly shamed as well as reintegrated into society. These ritualistic and dramatic aspects come closer to religious performances, dealing with some fundamental existential questions of good and evil, guilt, pain, social inclusion and exclusion, than they do to rational calculation (Tait 2002). They are also the aspects that are badly suited for later reproduction. A fundamental aspect of a dramatic performance is that it takes place in a particular historic moment. It is a 'happening', which makes it blatantly at odds with the 'timeless' nature of sentencing guidelines and information systems. The previously mentioned description of a sentencing guidelines proceeding obviously shows that guidelines 'score low' when it comes to drama and symbolism, and 'score high' when it comes to timelessness and ease of reproduction.

This may force us to focus our attention on the limitations of the newer sentencing tools as a means of legal memory. What aspects of law and sentencing are preserved and recorded in the sentencing databases and what disappears at the moment when the particular event is over?

## Computer-friendly tunes

What are the tunes which court computers are programmed to play (Tait 1998: 174)?

The purpose of both computer systems and sentencing guidelines has been to transform sentencing into a formal, rational and standardised process – to introduce 'tariff' sentencing at the expense of individualised justice, and to minimise the role of non-legal factors. Therefore, one can say that, from the deontological point of view, computer systems and sentencing guidelines share important similarities. As Hutton contends, they can be seen as 'occupying different points on a continuum' (1995: 564). Their normative basis is the same, although their political and cultural contexts are different. Can we then separate the spheres of technology and ideology? Are judges in Scotland and Australia today accepting systems that are essentially similar to sentencing guidelines – only that they get the illusion of choice and the 'good name' of technology? One needs to ask whether technological solutions really offer choice and neutrality, or do they, while maintaining the image of objectivity, prioritise certain ideologies? As Tait (1998) suggests, the crucial question is: which *narratives are privileged* by the design of sentencing information systems? '[W]hat are the tunes which court computers are programmed to play?' (Tait 1998: 174).

According to Tait, when judges are assisted by computers, their choice of stories (narratives) becomes much more limited. The stories that guide computer thinking are, first of all, overly simplified and shallower, as well as fewer. They are not the stories that represent how judges think in the courtroom, but rather how judges and academics think in committees. The point is that what happens in a courtroom is a social event – a performance. The narrative of a performance is not the same and cannot be reduced to a written record. However, only some styles and narratives of this performance are singled out for official registration and accepted into the 'cannon of statistical discourse' (Tait 1998). A computerised system prioritises narratives of sentence calculation, proportionality and just deserts, while others are silenced by the way information is recorded. Tait (1998) points out that sentencing information systems exclude both more punitive narratives (showing public anger, punishing disrespect) and more liberal narratives that exist in the courtroom, at the expense of just deserts. In their work, judges often use the narratives of minimising harm, pronouncing forgiveness, resolving conflicts and doing justice despite the law. However, these narratives are silenced by the information systems.

An example given by Tait (1998) is that magistrates often consider a period in custody awaiting trial as an adequate sentence – in line with the minimising harm narrative – even though an appropriate sentence otherwise considered would, for example, be a fine. The problem arises when this information is fed into a computer, where it is not recorded as an appropriate sentence (a fine), but as a prison sentence. This makes prison a typical sentence and gives greater encouragement to sentencers, in the future, to use prison because they want to pass similar sentences to their predecessors (Tait 1998). The examples point to the computer's limitations as an instrument of information storage and 'legal memory'. There is always the danger of loss, not the least, according to Stone (1966), the loss of the emotive component of judicial discourse. Similarly, Christie argues that now, courts may be in danger of being even less suited as arenas of expressive behaviour:

> Detailed instructions for sentencing, particularly computerized ones, may be as foreign to the sentencing process as they would be in the interaction between a sinner and a priest. Vengeance regulated by a table or by pressing a button represents one step further away from a situation where anger and grief are given legitimate outlets. The system has moved from expressive ritualism to managerial efficiency. (1993: 151)

Courts' narratives are also in a similar way silenced when it comes to conflict resolution (Tait 1998). The main objective behind the concept of conflict resolution is precisely to solve a conflict between two parties, rather than to punish one of them. If the court computer presents resolved conflicts as cases of no penalty, or even as fines, it provides irrelevant information, because the main issue was that conflicts were settled, not that penalties were found. 'The assumption that sentencing means punishment, underlying most sentencing information systems, effectively silences one of the narratives judges use' (Tait 1998: 182). Tait contends that the use of computer systems might result in a 'jukebox-like judiciary', playing only a limited number of 'tunes' in a standard manner. Similarly, Lubitz and Ross (2001) point out that, despite the ability of sentencing guidelines to incorporate varied philosophies and goals, they are essentially at odds with the concept of restorative justice. While sentencing guidelines rely on rules and order to achieve standardised and objective punishments, the narratives of restorative justice, on the other hand, emphasise individualised justice, the needs of the offender, the victim and the community. The number of 'tunes' or narratives that the concept of restorative justice is able to produce is, therefore, far greater than the consistency paradigm is able to accommodate. In what follows, I will further explore the conflict between computers and narratives. We shall see that the dilemma is not exclusive to sentencing only, but has rather been described by some as a pervasive cultural trait of computer-mediated communication and culture in contemporary information societies.

## Database vs narrative

In *The Language of New Media* (2001b), Lev Manovich suggests that in the contemporary, computer-mediated cultural landscape, the *database*, although originally a computer's method of organising and accessing data, has now become the new privileged form of cultural expression. As a *cultural form*, a database represents the world as a collection of items upon which a user can perform various operations. This collection of items is not governed by cause and effect logic, does not tell stories and does not have a beginning and an end, or any thematical development at all. As such, a database is a strong contrast to the narrative – which has, until now, been the privileged form of cultural expression.

Manovich represents the database and the narrative as two 'enemy' ontologies 'fighting' for their turf, and he leaves no doubt as to who is winning. Manovich suggests that, today, the database has become the centre of the creative process. The database form obviously dominates the new media, such as the internet, CD-ROMs, multimedia encyclopaedias, virtual museums, etc. The internet itself as a medium has an anti-narrative logic, because it can always change over time and new elements are constantly added. The result, therefore, is a collection, not a story with a beginning and an end. Every page of the internet can, in fact, be page 1. The user can decide how elements shall be put together, which parts should be included, which windows and files should be opened and in what order. Even though some media do not explicitly follow database logic, while others do, beneath the surface, many of them are databases. Here, the narrative becomes just one of several ways of assessing data.

To avoid technological determinism, Manovich suggests that one should not equate databases and narratives with specific types of technologies, but rather regard them as 'two competing imaginations, two basic creative impulses, two essential responses to the world' (Manovich 2001b: 233). In short, they are cultural expressions that exist, to a certain extent independent of technology. The ancient Greeks, for example, produced both long narratives such as *The Iliad* as well as encyclopaedias. However, the database is the cultural form most characteristic of the computer. According to Manovich, the logic of the computer – eg, the ability of a computer to produce endless variations – can become the logic of culture at large

(Manovich 2001b: 236).[19] Analysing the so called 'logic of the computer', Manovich suggests that computer programming encapsulates the world into two types of objects, *data structures* and *algorithms*:

> The world is reduced to two kinds of software objects that are complementary to each other – data structures and algorithms. Any process or task is reduced to an algorithm, a final sequence of simple operations that a computer can execute to accomplish a given task. And any object in the world – be it the population of a city, or the weather over the course of a century ... – is modelled as a data structure, that is data organized in a particular way for efficient search and retrieval ... The computerization of culture involves the projection of these two fundamental parts of computer software – and of the computer's unique ontology – onto the cultural sphere. (Manovich 2001b: 223)

Moving to penal systems, we can see a number of examples where the 'computer's unique ontology' is being projected on to the penal cultural sphere as well. Crime mapping is certainly one obvious example that springs to mind. Exemplified in the New York City police so called Compstat (ie, computer statistics) program, computers are used to create a detailed map of all city streets and types of crimes committed in them. For each crime presented on the map, computers hold databases regarding victims, facts about suspects, *modus operandi*, etc. While, before, collecting this type of information and creating patterns was a time consuming task, now, crime can be immediately visualised on a computer screen. Similar crime mapping programs have also been adopted in a number of other American and European cities.[20]

The database and algorithmic design seem also to be increasingly relevant in contemporary sentencing reforms. Sentencing guidelines are one case of redefining the sentencing process into an algorithmic procedure while sentencing information systems, on the other hand, have a database structure. In both cases, the traditional judicial narrative, although far from disappearing, may in some ways be losing its privileged place with regard to the database and algorithmic thinking. Risk assessment instruments can also be regarded as yet another example of narrative losing ground as the privileged form of cultural expression. If we look at the British Youth Justice Board's ASSET instrument, presented in Table 3 in the Appendix, we can see that its focus is on the numerical score and binary either/or answers. However, designers of the instrument explicitly wanted to overcome the narrow binary logic and have included sometimes quite large boxes that can be filled with narrative analysis and evaluations.[21] Nevertheless, the narrative part *does not change the final score* (*sic*!).

## Power without narrative

The fact that sentencing may be gradually leaving the traditional narrative form and accepting the database ontology is bound to have a number of consequences. The obvious one is, of course, that with the establishment of sentencing databases, the

---

19 Manovich's analysis is characterised by the fact that he is first and foremost an analyst of cinema and new media forms, such as CD-ROMs. However, he does not hide the fact that he also considers his analysis relevant to the cultural sphere at large.

20 Source: http://tectonic.nationalgeographic.com/2000/exploration/crimemaps/tect.html.

21 Source: private conversation.

amount of information regarding sentencing decisions becomes greater and easier to disseminate. Judicial decisions can thus adopt the buzzwords of the information age: 'All information in all places at all times' (Poster 1990: 70). However, a closer look at the nature of this information, which is so easily spread and reproduced, is required. A database is a linguistic situation, which is distinctly different from the spoken, as well as the written word. Poster (1990: 76) points to a vital question: 'What are the ways by which electronic language (in this case databases), as distinct from speech and writing, enable and limit the transmission or storage of meaning?'

The issue becomes exceedingly relevant in the case of sentencing. The 'databasing' of sentencing may lead, not only to a more documented and transparent judicial practice, but moreover it may also transform the practice and adjust it in accordance with the parameters of electronic writing. If the narrative and the database are two opposing ontologies, the traditional practice of judicial narration may be forced to adjust itself to the database in order to be available and reproduced 'in all places at all times'. Furthermore, the new cultural and linguistic situation transforms the process of creating offenders' identities. The stories of violence, pain, social deprivation and frustration now need to be told within the new parameters. Are they, then, still the same stories?

A database is a medium for storing and organising information, and as mentioned before in Chapter 2, information has certain qualities that distinguish it from knowledge. Information is objectivated; it is 'byte-like' and compressed (Lash 2002). It is different from discourse or the narrative because it is produced in a much shorter time span and, therefore, leaves little time for reflection. As Lash argues:

> Narrative as in the novel works from a beginning, middle and end. The subjective intentions of the protagonist are the motor of the plot and events follow from one another as causes and effects. Discourse – as in say philosophic or social scientific texts – is comprised in conceptual frameworks, of serious speech acts, of propositional logic, of speech acts backed up by legitimating arguments. *Information is none of these.* (Lash 2002: 2, emphasis added)

Lash argues that information is, in a sense, 'indexical' – 'it has its effect on you without the sort of legitimating argument that you are presented with in discourse' (Lash 2002: 3).

This is also the point that we have made about sentencing guidelines. They are not characterised by their theoretical consistency, by following a certain scientific narrative. In fact, they are characterised by their lack of narration. They are what Jonathan Simon (1995) calls *power without narrative*. Both sentencing guidelines and sentencing information systems are organised in such a way that they have no beginning, middle or end. Thematically, they have no development that organises them into a sequence. They are marked by what Manovich (2001a) calls the 'database logic'. They appear as collections of items upon which the user can perform various operations.

| Narrative | Database |
| --- | --- |
| Beginning, middle and end | Compressed information |
| Linear causality | Additive, 'stacking' |
| Text | Hypertext |
| Rational argument | Action |
| Order designed by author | Order up to the user |
| Creation | Selection |

Consequently, the new penal instruments, such as guidelines and risk instruments, are not driven by linear cause and effect logic, but rather by the logic of additivity. A does not follow B *because* of some reason; rather, A can be connected or added to B haphazardly. This phenomenon has been described by Thomas Hylland Eriksen (2001) as *stacking* of information.[22] Stacking means that one can increasingly combine various items of information according to whim, without any sense of internal development or progression and direction. One is 'not heading anywhere'. '[T]here are layers upon layers on top of each other, every vacant spot is filled, and there is little by way of internal integration' (Hylland Eriksen 2001: 111). A similar phenomenon is also the so called 'PowerPoint epistemology', which has become the predominant modus of presenting information on meetings and conferences today (Apollon 2004). In PowerPoint the meaning of words is immediately available and does not require complex reasoning and analysis from the audience. Words are marked by their self-sufficiency and independence from other words, exemplified by the boxes, circles and points surrounding them. Hylland Eriksen makes a similar point as Sherry Turkle (1995): in the information-driven culture, one does not strive (or have time) for in-depth understanding. With a Macintosh, 'there is nowhere visible to dive'; one stays on the surface:

> More and more of every kind of information is stacked, like gigantic Lego towers where the bricks have nothing in common but the fact that they fit (but they also fit with any other brick) … [W]e no longer have space for building blocks that can only be used for one or a few configurations with other blocks. Everything must be interchangeable with everything else *now*. (Hylland Eriksen 2001: 119, original emphasis)

According to McLuhan (1998), electronic cultures privilege the visual sense rather than linear cause and effect logic.[23] Although not dispensing with the concept of causality, McLuhan maintains that in electronic cultures linear causality (the cornerstone of the print culture) is replaced by structural 'pattern recognition'. Visual 'pattern recognition', thus, becomes a privileged form of knowledge. It is less logical than analogical (Lash 2002). Here, we notice that a focus on the visual, rather

22 In *Tyranny of the Moment: Fast and Slow Time in the Information Age* (2001), Hylland Eriksen describes stacking as a general cultural phenomenon transforming a number of spheres such as rhythmic dance music, journalism, World Wide Web, multi-channel TV, etc.

23 Just as the Gutenberg age gave us the book, consumed in distanciated contemplation, the electronic age, McLuhan argues, gives us the ad – which consists neither of discourse nor narrative, but a graphic 'condensed and displaced form' (Lash 2002: 184).

than on the causal, and a sense of structure, are also an important characteristic of sentencing guidelines and sentencing statistics graphs displayed by SISs. In fact, these sentencing instruments encourage us to see the structure (or the lack of it) in judicial decisions and *see* a decision-making process in visual terms, just as the Compstat program encourages the New York police officers to see crime patterns in their city. The focus is not primarily on causality, but rather on visual perception and consequent action.

Sentencing guidelines and sentencing information systems, as well as crime mapping programs and risk assessment instruments, are, therefore, penal instruments which do not primarily attempt to answer the question 'why' (a certain act was committed, or why it should be reacted to in a certain way). They are not instruments for understanding, but rather instruments for *action*. In a way, they can be regarded as instruments that make it possible to act without needing to understand. They often do not really relate to one particular theory (narrative) and often are not consistent in a philosophical sense. They can include quite contradictory principles, such as just deserts as well as incapacitation and deterrence considerations. Their success, therefore, lies not so much at the theoretical (narrative) level as in their operationality. The question with sentencing guidelines and risk instruments is, to paraphrase Lash, not so much 'what does it mean but how does it work'.[24] They are an embodiment of a 'logic of sense, a *sens practique* that owes perhaps less to meaning than to operationality' (Lash 2002: 216). This practical logic filters out 'the noise of the world' (Lash 2002: 216) and makes a penal system into a smoothly running machine, well tuned to its environment.

I would like to suggest that sentencing guidelines, SISs as well as risk assessment forms and various crime mapping programs, belong to a culture that Lash calls technological culture where:

> Reflexivity is no longer about distanciated decision-making or life-narrative organizing (Beck, Giddens and Lash 1994). Instead it is about the reflexive tying of knowledge to action, so that there is no distance at all between knowledge and action. Now action is knowledge and knowledge is action. Social knowledge becomes immanent in the technological culture. (Lash 2002: 156)

Lash points to the loss of transcendental thought in a technological culture – a move away from the dualism of universal and particular, and furthermore, a move away from the possibilities for judgment. Technological culture is characterised by a certain playful quality rather than by judgment:

> To play is to *suspend* judgement. It is to be so immediately involved that there is no space for the wise reflection of judgement. Play and cultural activities more generally in the information society presume a suspension of judgement. (Lash 2002: 160)

Similarly, both sentencing guidelines and SISs, to a large extent, limit or suspend judgment. They circumvent the figure of a judge[25] as a person who navigates

24 Therefore, it is perhaps no coincidence that it was Robert Martinson's (1974) question: 'What works?' that became the buzzword of contemporary penal systems. For 'what *works*' is a question of operationality. Those asking 'Is there a meaning to it?' never got to be heard to the same extent as Martinson.

25 There are, of course, important differences in the extent to which sentencing guidelines and SISs limit judicial discretion, just as there are important differences between the guideline systems themselves.

between the particular circumstances of a case and the universal legal rules and who, in order to act, needs to understand and construct narratives.[26] What we see in the guidelines and SISs is the primacy of knowledge itself, rather than the primacy of the thinking and judging *subject*. Action is therefore, as suggested by Lash, tied to knowledge. There is little space or need left for reflection.[27]

## The self-contained world of the system

The penal 'power without narrative', described here, is therefore not focused on providing a story about criminal events, nor an education or communication with an offender and the public. The formal structures and procedures of sentencing guidelines and risk assessment instruments constitute in many aspects a self-contained system. David Garland describes self-referentiality as a general trait of contemporary penal culture:

> Systems of crime-control have become increasingly self-referential and self-serving, increasingly 'autopoietic'. The aim is no longer to respond to external social demands for the control of crime and the reform of offenders. Instead the aim is to develop an immunity from outside demands of this kind by setting up internal aims and self-generated criteria of success. (1999: 525)

The concept of self-reference and autopoiesis has been most notably argued by Niklas Luhmann (1995). Luhmann envisions society as a self-producing or autopoietic system of communication. He argues that self-referentiality is the indispensable device structuring society in a large number of areas, including law. Caplow and Simon (1999) point out that in the case of the US penal system, the recent reforms of discretion have made the system more reflexive and thus also more accountable internally. The focus moves from the goals of rehabilitation and normalisation to smooth running of the system.[28]

Thus, when it comes to sentencing, the focus of contemporary penal policy has mainly been on the sentencing *process* itself, rather than on its social *outcome*:

> When sentencing becomes merely the application of pre-existing penalty tariffs it loses much of its former social purpose. It shifts away from the older framework in which sentencers aimed at bringing about a social outcome – the reduction of crime through

---

26 My point here is not to present technology as the problem and as a tool for the exercise of control and limitation of narratives. It has been pointed out that one could try to expand the narratives and change the architecture of the system. Hypertext-based information systems, for example, could provide the possibility of expanding the range of narratives and the 'tunes' the courts could play (Tait 1998). The various uses of technology are always a result of human choice and social action. Therefore, what I have tried to shed light on are the social forces that have been prioritising the use of certain types of technological designs.

27 The guidelines could perhaps be described as what Lash terms 'the elsewhere-extensions of the situation' (2002: 180), or as supplements. They are not, as with the text of a narrative, logically *representing* reality, but rather *supplementing* it as a new field of social practice. (Traditionally, a legal text contains universal principles that are applied to the myriad of concrete social relations. In the guidelines, on the other hand, the act of sentencing is removed to a different sphere, namely that of guidelines calculation.)

28 Caplow and Simon (1999) suggest that the cost of increased formality and reflexivity is also increased incarceration. In a system focused on formal rules, police and other correctional agents more often choose to process cases forward, rather than exercise their discretion and drop the charges.

> individualized sentencing – to one where the key objective (fitting the punishment to the offence) is well within the capacity of the courts, and much less likely to 'fail'. (Garland 2001: 120)

Brown and Duguid (2000) point out that focusing on the process itself, rather than on the practice and the people involved, has been an important trait of information management. In the 'process view', processes can be clearly defined, their inputs and outputs measured, and people simply 'inserted' into them:

> Opportunities for them to craft, change, own, or take charge of a process in any meaningful way are limited. While lip service is paid to them, improvisation and 'local' knowledge have little place in these schema, particularly if they challenge co-ordination of processes. (Brown and Duguid 2000: 98)

Due to their abstract nature and decontextualisation, the new sentencing instruments seem to be turning into a monologue of self-referential systems. Here, they resemble electronic communication where language, because of its distance from the face-to-face context of daily life, has to be reproduced from within itself (Poster 1990). Because of its capacity to travel across space and have a meaning that is independent of local contexts, electronic systems (and the same could be said about sentencing guidelines) seem to lose their connection to things/individuals/events and, instead, seem to replace them. Or, as Poster says, they appear to be losing the referent. They become free-floating and autonomous. No wonder then that the comparison between playing games, computer programs and sentencing guidelines somehow keeps cropping up throughout this text. Games are a restricted, self-referential universe with an explicit set of rules. For this reason, computers come closest to imitating humans when playing games, when all the rules of the game are prescribed in advance:

> The computer programmer, however, is a creator of universes for which he alone is the lawgiver. So, of course, is the designer of any game ... [Computer programs] compliantly obey their laws and vividly exhibit their obedient behavior. No playwright, no stage director, no emperor, however powerful, has ever exercised such absolute authority to arrange a stage or field of battle and to command such unswervingly dutiful actors or troops. (Weizenbaum 1976: 115)

With their precise definitions of rules and processes, and with their abstract and decontextualised nature, sentencing guidelines strongly resemble game activities. However, punishment is a field that is filled with controversy and lacks clear-cut definitions and rules. By choosing to see punishment as clear-cut and predictable, contemporary sentencing reforms have had to adjust their view of the social world and of offenders to this assumption. The view of sentencing as predictable is, in fact, a political choice (rather than a scientific observation of a fact) which has a number of ethical consequences for our understanding of the concept of justness.

With the focus on the systematic and predictable aspects of punishment, contemporary penalty has been brought closer to the technological culture. According to philosopher Peter Kemp (1996), technology is well suited to universalistic ethics, but is, however, less suited to interpersonal ethics. Technology 'obscures the face of the other'. Therefore, the focus on the system (and the technological artefacts that help us create and understand the system) seems to sideline the concept and awareness of responsibility for 'the other'. A penal system focused on technological solutions can, therefore, be extremely universalistic. It can bring universalism to its full potential, but it has, on the other hand, problems dealing with the concept of closeness,[29] resolution of concrete conflicts, concepts of reconciliation, forgiveness, etc.

As Simon writes, 'alternative solutions require a narrative and explanations' (1995). They tend to come into conflict with the ideals of predictability and consistency that sentencing guidelines hold so high. The concept of power without narrative, of punishment without a story, impedes the ability to negotiate and to find alternative solutions to conflicts. With their rigidity (which is especially true for the US Federal Sentencing Guidelines) and striving for rules, contemporary sentencing reforms minimise the space for negotiation in the courtroom. In this way, sentencing guidelines, in particular, resemble, in a vital aspect, technological systems as described by Michalis Lianos and Mary Douglas (2000b). Lianos and Douglas's analysis of the so called 'Automated Socio-Technical Environments' (ASTEs) shows that technological systems minimise the possibilities for their users to *negotiate* with the system. These are the systems that, for example, monitor our ability to enter a building with an entrance card or our access to a bank account or to a computer with a PIN code. Just as with the guidelines, they are driven by a clear-cut, binary, either/or logic that either accepts or denies my password, with no possibility for me to negotiate that 'my attempt was very close'. Just as I have no possibility of arguing with an ASTE system that I have lost my ticket, so too do the guidelines minimise the scope of judges to transcend the binary logic of categorisation. As Judge Jenkins writes about computers, and implicitly also about the guidelines:

> It [the computer] is a creature of previously-determined categories. You have five choices, or six, or seven, and that is it. Often similar things are bunched into one category pretending that they are identical. They are treated as if they are identical, and eventually, in our laziness or in our apathy, we regard them as identical. We forget the differences. They are similar, but they are not identical. (Jenkins 2002: 199)

According to Lianos and Douglas, this denial of the possibilities for negotiation and transcending the categories has profound cultural implications. They argue that the eschewing of negotiation leads to 'a transformation of culture so radical that it amounts to denial':

> Negotiation is the prime constituent of culture. The cultural process involves essentially the mutual understanding of communication and the development of mental skills that promote it ... Automated environments transform the reproduction of values ... The space which was before open to doubt, this major value incubator, is now merely experienced and judged as loss of time. (2000b: 106–07)

One could say that, traditionally, the courts have been seen as one such 'value incubator' *par excellence*. However, the striving of contemporary sentencing for rules and predictability may indicate contours of a profound cultural change in the meaning of punishment and the role of the judiciary.

---

29 One should bear in mind that the universal ethics of just deserts is not the only possible view of justness – not even in an ideal world. Joseph Fletcher's *Situation Ethics: The New Morality* emphasises the importance of doing right in a *particular case* over rigidly following universal rules – setting them aside in the situation if 'love seems better served by doing so' (1966: 210).

Traditionally, the judiciary has had the task of producing decisions 'in exactly those cases in which the facts, the rules, or how they fit together are *controversial* ... Many of the central concepts in the judicial application of the law – such as "justice", "reasonable care", and "intent" – are deeply enmeshed in the fabric of human life' (Sartor, Sartor and Branting 1998: 105). They are the terms that are strongly embedded in a particular social and historical context. However, the focus on the rule-driven aspects of judicial tasks is at odds with these controversial and creative aspects of judicial behaviour. The imposition of formal structures upon procedures and knowledge 'detracts from the social elements (particularly discretion) which are essential requirements of certain judicial tasks' (Leith 1998: 298). Legal rules are only created by the agents of the legal process. Sentencing is a *social* process, characterised by negotiation between those agents. As focus on the predictable aspects of the process increases, the space for the social – for controversy, creativity and negotiation – gradually decreases. This forces Leith to raise an interesting question of whether:

> when a criminal activity is the subject of highly formalised sentencing and strict liability, is it actually necessary to use magistrates' justice at all? In effect, *when the situation becomes ripe for computerisation, it is no longer a properly judicial activity.* (Leith 1998: 300, emphasis added)

## Losing the subject

The discussion above indicates a well-documented antagonism between the technological culture and the changing role for human subjectivity.[30] A question can be raised as to what space people have left in an autopoietic and self-referential world. From this perspective, the diminishing role of the judiciary in sentencing can be seen as part of the attempt to strengthen the system at the expense of the individual. It has been argued that contemporary risk societies are characterised by a *culture of distrust*.[31] Due to the growing inability to establish trust, the 'system's solution is to turn surveillance back on itself, to develop new communication rules, formats, and technologies' that will watch over decision-makers (Ericson and Haggerty 1997: 56). Protection from uncertainty and risk is sought in the apparent security of objective knowledge systems:

> In risk society all occupations are subject to surveillance out of fear that their unique, informal cultures will violate procedural propriety. While craft knowledge in occupational cultures is crucial for fair and efficient social organization (Manning 1992a), it is subject to increasing administrative scrutiny and intervention in all social institutions because it is seen as too arbitrary (unsystematic) and as allowing craft practitioners to escape accountability (Ericson and Haggerty 1997: 57)

30 See, for example, Poster (1990, 2001b), Barglow (1994), Turkle (1995).

31 However, it may be even more interesting to note that the developments described here are not restricted to penal systems alone. In *Strangers at the Bedside* (1991), Rothman describes a similar development taking place in medicine. Bringing formality and collective judgment into medicine – distrusting doctors, reducing individual discretion, increasing accountability. The result has been: more sovereign patients, but more bureaucratic medicine, enmeshed in forms and procedures – yet one more social encounter now tends to be disinterested, neutral and remote.

The self-referentiality of the system is, therefore, a result of the mistrust of professional judgment. The technological knowledge systems thus offer the promise of rationality and safety which human experts cannot provide (or have become perceived as unable to do so). The story of sentencing reforms is, therefore, also a story about the changing patterns of control and power in penal systems, as well as a part of the story of the changing patterns of trust in modern societies. In this context, human experts and decision-makers are replaced by supra-individual (objective) solutions. Obviously, it needs to be pointed out that such striving for objective expertise is nothing new. On the contrary, it has been a central trait of modernity (Giddens 1991, Christie 1993). In fact, Giddens (1991) points out that increased surveillance, observation and information gathering were the necessary preconditions for the complex level of social organisation and co-ordination found in modern societies. The diminishing trust in judiciary and the increasing demands for transparency of their decisions can be viewed as part of a more general move towards what Giddens terms a 'post-traditional' society, where everything is questionable. The judicial arguments about life-long experience and tradition are contested and viewed with suspicion as a reluctance to change. Sentencing guidelines, computerised information systems and risk instruments, on the other hand, carry a promise of improvement, reliability and the possibility of permanent accountability. They are seen not only as a guarantee that sentencing decisions will be made in required ways, but also as a promise of increased reflexivity – the opportunity for constant information gathering and surveillance, and thus, change and improvement too.

According to Bauman (1992), modern societies are sites of *mediated action*: the skills needed for the effective performance of a task are enclosed in artefacts or in step-by-step instructions. 'The skills the individuals deploy on their own serve the need of locating and getting access to artefacts or instruction' (Bauman 1992: 90). Judging, and law in general, was in fact created as one such set of 'instructions' for solving conflicts. However, what seems to be novel now is that the know-how question is split even further. Judges now appear to need an additional set of instructions in addition to their own expertise. They are, in a way, 'construed as inherently non-self-sufficient entities' (Bauman 1992: 90) which require additional help in order to judge. In fact, the US Sentencing Commission operates two 'hotlines', one accessible to judges and probation officers and another for prosecutors and defence attorneys, in order to help them with correct guideline application. The Commission has also created a number of training materials, exercises and visual aids which help practitioners with correct guideline application (Stith and Cabranes 1997: 1258). Bauman describes the process as 'Taylorization' and 'Fordization' of the life world. It is a process in which choices are simplified and human skills are then removed and transplanted into the machinery:

> Reduction is experienced as liberation from cumbersome necessities of life and feels like freedom. What it hides is growing *incompleteness and insufficiency of the individual* and the ever more complex structure of dependency without which the life process is not any more possible. (Bauman 1992: 91, emphasis added)

The expert systems offer certainty instead of doubt and anxiety. They are certificates of the rationality that is of such crucial value to modernity:

> Need to be rational is grounded, as it were, in the apparently incredible 'messiness' of the life-world. The latter inevitably entails contradictory messages, drives which point in opposite directions ... Most importantly, it is pregnant with a constant threat of error. ... The enshrinement of rationality of choice and conduct is itself a choice, a preference for order against muddiness, security against surprise, constancy of results against a variety of gains and losses ... But in such a world, however dazzling and full of temptation, variety will be tamed, and its sting will be pulled out. (Bauman 1992: 99)

The informational vision of justice is therefore a tool against the 'evil empire' of randomness; the random thus being equated with the chaotic and uncontrolled. The informational vision of justice, embodied in sentencing information systems and numerical sentencing guidelines, promises a world that is 'free from overlapping categories, mixed messages and semiotic unclarity rebounding in behavioural ambiguity' (Bauman 1992: 100).

Looking at the discourse concerning sentencing, we see that rulelessness, unproportionality and unpredictability are considered to be just as much at the core of the 'sentencing problem' as unfairness. In fact, unproportionality has come to be synonymous with unfairness, or better yet, has come to be seen as the 'privileged' form of unfairness. A question can be asked why irrational (or unsystematic) forms of judicial behaviour are considered to be so much graver than rational forms of unfairness. There is no doubt that over the years sentencing guidelines have produced a great number of openly unfair judicial decisions, which in a number of cases have been strongly objected to by the judges themselves. However, it seems as if the guidelines are here to stay. In fact, their perceived rationality acts as an incentive for other countries to try, if not the same, then at least similar solutions. The point here is that, in contemporary penal systems, rationality seems to have an additional political dimension that needs to be addressed. The changing role of the judge is by no means a technologically determined event. It is a cultural shift that has its political authors and is encouraged by certain organisational objectives:

> To act rationally ... is to subordinate one's spontaneity and creativity to the rationality of the technologically based environment. In this way, rationality has become a form of domination whose political character is obscured by the fact that it appears as reasonable. (Silver 2000: 125)

The increasingly limited extent to which sentencing guidelines and SISs leave the judges to create alternative solutions is closely connected with the changing context of penal culture, which in Garland's (2001) words is becoming a 'culture of control'.

## Taming the system

> Criminal justice actors and agencies are now less capable of directing their own fate and shaping their own policies and decisions. (Garland 2001: 172)

The limiting of judicial sentencing discretion is not an isolated phenomenon; rather it is a part of a general shift towards limiting the discretionary powers of penal decision-makers. The movement to control discretion has been one of the dominant themes in penal reforms in the past 30 years, and 'one of the most successful representations of crime and punishment that was produced in the 1960s and 1970s' (Simon and Feeley 1995: 162). While the old treatment model was built around experts' authority and their exercise of discretion, the 1970s were marked by a growing anxiety about discretionary judgments of all sorts. However, as Walker (1993) points out, discretion has not always been regarded as a problem in criminal justice. 'Before you can address a problem, you have to know that it exists' (Walker 1993: 6) and prior to the late 1950s, most experts barely acknowledged its existence. The movement, if we may call it that, to control discretion gained prominence in the 1960s. One of the most influential contributions came in 1969 from Kenneth C Davis. His *Discretionary Justice* provided a salient description of the 'rulelessness' in penal decision-making. One result was, to borrow Walker's (1993) potent motto, a massive effort to 'tame' the system.[32]

It is important to keep in mind that critique of the 'old' discretionary system was twofold, focusing both on its potential for the abuse of power and on its inefficiency and ineffectiveness. Criticism came from both liberals and conservatives alike.[33] Liberals exposed the class and racial bias in the discretionary decisions of judges, parole boards and the police. They argued for equal treatment based on human rights and the rule of law. Bringing penal professionals under control would eventually lead to a less discriminatory and punitive penal system. Conservative critics, on the other hand, argued that the rehabilitation system was ineffective in combating crime. Consequently, as a result of such vigorous critique, criminal justice professionals and agencies became the subject of detailed regulation and government. The tasks of professionals increasingly became submitted to strict procedural standards which guaranteed consistency of decisions as well as enabling the central authorities to exert control over them.

In 1974, Robert Martinson's article 'What Works in Prison Reform?' represented something of a landmark in mainstream criminology. Martinson examined the empirical research about the effectiveness of various rehabilitation programs and came up with the pessimistic conclusion that, basically, 'nothing works'. Martinson's question 'what works?' eventually became the new buzzword of criminal justice. From then on, penal measures came to be evaluated based on their efficiency and effectiveness. As Raine describes:

> Martinson's question – 'what works?' – has come to haunt the practice of criminal justice, not as a critique of rehabilitative treatment, but as a routine feature of every aspect of criminal justice practice. Throughout the 1980s its most important impact was upon the control of criminal justice staff, who were subject to increased levels of monitoring, assessment, and accountability. (2001: 115)

Consequently, penal systems became more than just a group of agencies with specific tasks. They became a unitary entity that could and should be regulated and directed toward a certain *goal*. By borrowing the vocabulary of the private sector, penal systems came to think of themselves as systems and in terms of *systems management* (Feeley and Simon 1994). In fact, as Raine (2001) points out, the

32 *Webster's Dictionary of the English Language* provides several possible definitions of the word '*tame*', a number of which can be more or less relevant in our context: changed from the wild or savage state; domesticated ... tractable, docile or submissive ... lacking in excitement; dull; insipid ... spiritless or pusillanimous ... not to be taken very seriously; without real power, importance, etc ... brought into service; rendered useful and manageable; under control as natural resources, a source of power, etc.

33 For an overview and summary of the central literature, see, for example, Garland (2001) and Rothman (1994).

metaphor of the 'system' has become so powerful that it is hard to imagine things ever having been otherwise.

However, the concept of a 'criminal justice system' is in fact of quite recent origin. Only in the late 1970s and early 1980s did the term gain its prominence. Feeley and Simon (1994) point out that system theory evolved from mathematics, physics and electrical engineering during the 1950s and 60s. In the US, the vision of criminal justice as a system was first popularised through the 'funnel of justice' flow chart in the report of the President's Commission on Law Enforcement and Administration of Justice, *The Task Force Report on Science and Technology* (1967). According to Feeley and Simon (1994: 187), the chart became 'the most frequently reprinted and distributed "chart" in modern American Criminology', thus capturing 'the essence of the new criminology, a shift away from concern with individual-focused justice to a concern with the efficient management of danger'.

The main purpose behind the system metaphor has been to direct focus towards achieving greater efficiency in criminal courts and other penal institutions: to reduce bottlenecks, establish clear definitions of judicial and administrative processes and encourage inter-agency co-operation, which also includes information sharing. The objective was to predict and control the flow of cases in penal institutions, thereby making them more cost and time-efficient. In order to achieve this, the tasks of criminal justice practitioners had to be clearly defined. Previously, criminal justice had been perceived as a group of loosely connected agencies. Now, they became an entity, which could be known and managed – with the help of various monitoring devices and decision-making guidelines. They were subjected to increased managerial control by the use of various *government-at-a-distance techniques* (budgetary limits, national standards, 'gate keeping' guidelines, etc) (Garland 1997).

According to Garland (2001), this new focus on the system itself marks a vital shift in the official perception of criminal justice. One can see the contours of a new approach that, rather than focusing on the individual tasks at hand, focuses on the system:

> not primarily as an embodiment of justice, or a solution to the crime problem, but instead as a *problem in and of itself*. From this point onwards, one can trace a settled perception that the criminal justice process is characterized by arbitrariness and injustice, with a tendency to generate uncontrolled costs and unplanned outcomes, and to create risks and dangers for the public it should be protecting. 'Taming the system' – its costs, its discretionary powers, its liability to expose the public to dangers – came to be part of the project of government in this field. (Garland 2001: 115, emphasis added)

A result of this increased focus on the system as a whole has been that, throughout the past 20 years, the system seems to have become much more homogenised and transparent, while the discretionary powers of the various professionals, from the judiciary to parole officers and social workers, have been limited.

Sentencing reforms, therefore, need to be placed in this context of increasing demands for system transparency and efficiency. As Clarkson and Morgan point out, the ethos of system management demands that:

> all services, including the various agencies that make up the criminal-justice system, state their objectives, devise measuring-rods for their achievement and regularly report on progress. Within this climate the idea that sentencing, the visible pinnacle of

> criminal-justice decision-making, and the progenitor of all penal expenditure, should be subject to broad relatively uncontrolled discretion was managerially anomalous. (1995: 7)

Sentencing guidelines can thus be partly regarded as an expression of the managerialist ethos, partly embracing human rights principles but also offering instrumental possibilities to, for example, manipulate the overall state costs of imprisonment,[34] control the judiciary and make sure that it performs according to the centrally defined standards. Therefore, as much as there seems to exist a discontinuity between the philosophical sentencing discourse, which tends to be moralistic, appealing to the arguments of deservedness and justness, and penal practice, which is planned and managerial, the dichotomy may be a false one. It may be useful to look at the demands for consistency, transparency, predictability and rationality of punishment made in the sentencing discourse, as natural elements (or even preconditions) in a well managed system.

In fact, Tait (1998) argues that the demands for 'consistency in sentencing' are, to a large extent, driven by the desire to 'ensuring that judges (and parole authorities) were extracting sufficient penal pain'. They provide judges with a 'constant daily reminder that they are under surveillance' (Tait 1998: 178). It is probably not a coincidence that one of the circumstances that led to the establishment of the Judicial Commission of New South Wales, and subsequently their SIS, was an allegation that a District Court judge was too lenient when sentencing a number of offenders who were represented by a particular solicitor (Schmatt 2001). The themes of disparity and excessive leniency are thus often intertwined. This is plainly visible when it comes to sentencing guidelines. Furthermore, sentencing worksheets, completed by judges for each sentence, enable detailed judge-specific data gathering regarding guideline departure rates. A number of US jurisdictions have released judge-specific information to the media and the public. In addition, some SISs contain judge-specific information (eg, Scotland). Such instruments place sentencers in a state of increased *visibility*, which, as Foucault has pointed out, results in the constitution of a power relation over the one made visible. As Foucault puts it:

> He who is subject to a field of visibility, and knows it, assumes responsibility for the constraints of power, he makes them play spontaneously upon himself; he inscribes in himself the power relation in which he simultaneously plays both roles; he becomes the principle of his own subjection. (1977: 202–03)

## Transparency and visibility

The perpetual focus on transparency in contemporary government agencies is also a defining trait of another related field, namely, auditing. Some observers even talk of an 'audit culture' (Jones 1993, Strathern 2000b, Power 1999). As with decision-making guidelines and forms, the objective of auditing is also to open up the previously closed world of professional and bureaucratic decision-making. Not

---

34 In Oregon, the primary objective behind the guidelines was to link sentencing policy to correctional resources, such as prison capacity (Tonry 1992), and to allow for rational allocation of individuals in the prison system (Bottoms 1995: 30).

surprisingly, the audit culture has given rise to new comparisons with Foucault's analysis of Benthams's panopticon, since auditing is based on the creation of a new field of visibility, which then helps to control and organise individuals according to certain standards. Auditing practices are what Rose terms 'calculative technologies' which:

> make it possible to render visible both the near and the distant activities of individuals, to calculate the extent to which they depart from a norm of performance, and to accumulate such calculations in computers and files and compare them. (Rose 1999: 153)

The term audit was originally used in financial accounting. However, in the 1980s and 1990s, the term proliferated into a number of new domains (from schools and academia to health and welfare). Strathern (2000b) suggests that the cultural change which occurred due to the transfer of audit technologies from the financial to the public sectors is so fundamental that it justifies talking about an *audit culture.* McLaughlin, Muncie and Hughes (2001), for example, describe the British Government's constant striving for development and refinement of evaluation procedures within the justice system, as 'the permanent revolution' seeking to institutionalise the 'managerialized state form'.

One of the key attributes of audit culture is a perpetual state of *mistrust*, and thus a constant requirement for surveillance and evaluation of organisations and their activities. Audit technologies are based on evaluative grids and measurements, such as performance charts, which constantly compare institutions and individuals against each other. For this reason, audit has been named by a number of commentators as a 'technology of mistrust' (Power 1999, Rose 1999). It is often promoted by its proponents as a tool which will reinstate trust in organisations and professionals by enhancing their efficiency. However, it has been argued that by doing that audit may have quite the opposite effect – it multiplies 'the points at which doubt and suspicion can be generated' (Rose 1999). A system which was based on trust and belief in the judgment of professionals is thus displaced by a system which is based on constant evaluation and visibility. Audit procedures 'order the whole system while ranking everyone within it. Every individual is made acutely aware that their conduct and performance is under constant scrutiny' (Shore and Wright 2000: 77). However, this spirit of 'submitting to scrutiny' and 'rendering visible' has been also one of the main drives behind the implementation of a number of sentencing reforms, thus promoting a new ethic of governance based on 'a particular style of formalised accountability' and abstract 'rituals of verification' (Power 1999).

Since 'rituals of verification' are, in effect, relations of power between the scrutiniser and the observed (Shore and Wright 2000), the question of applying these procedures to the judiciary inevitably also raises the issue of *judicial independence*. Can the courts be seen as merely another public service which needs to be monitored in the same way as schools, hospitals and social services? Although in danger of simplifying the complex ongoing debate concerning judicial independence, I suggest that part of the problem might lie in the nature of language that has been adopted in the accountability debate. This is a language which focuses on aggregate information and systematic performance parameters which have traditionally been the prerogative of the executive branch. Therefore, even though the judiciary may in some cases take the driving seat and control of the reforms promoting accountability, as was the case with some SISs, the danger may still be that the judiciary will adopt the technologies and language of the executive, rather than traditional legal reasoning. The discomfort which judges often express in connection with various accountability reforms is, therefore, not simply a dislike of 'being made visible', but also discomfort with a new analytical language and a different perception of their own field. Creation of a state of transparency not only means that things which used to be secret now become visible; it also implies a new perceptual apparatus. Therefore, rather than saying that processes and organisations become visible or audited, one should say that they *are made* visible and auditable. Power points out that in order to be audited, organisations have to be 'made auditable': 'audit demands the environment, in the form of systems, and performance measures, which make a certain style of verification possible' (1999: 91). In other words, organisations have to be structured around *measurable outputs*.[35] What sentencing reforms provide today are precisely those measurable outputs or objective standards which make judicial activity auditable by external experts rather than by judicial professionals only. A sentencing statistic in SISs can be understood by almost anyone.

Furthermore, it needs to be pointed out that these evaluative practices do not simply describe a somehow pre-existing domain of facts. Rather, auditing constitutes and changes the domain that it audits. 'A certain kind of administrative objectivity is created whose logic is to standardize, which prefers rules over unfettered judgment and which hides its processes of selection' (Power 1999: 95). Standardisation is thus one of the vital preconditions for evaluation, because only standardised activities can be compared and rated against each other. In order to audit and evaluate universities, for example, academic degrees need to be of comparable level and nature (BA, MA, PhD). Only in that way can the various institutions be compared according to their output (Shore and Wright 2000). In a similar way, in order to compare sentencing decisions, they need to share some common traits that make them comparable and auditable. Therefore, sentencing decisions that are based on offender characteristics and a myriad of social circumstances are much more difficult to compare because of their natural versatility. However, sentencing decisions that are based strictly on (legal) offence definitions make comparison and evaluation easier. As Power points out, auditing procedures not only monitor the quality of various organisational activities, but even more importantly, they construct *new definitions of quality*:

> Audit becomes possible in complex environments by abstracting from that complexity and by operating upon a systems surface which in some cases has been designed with auditability in mind. (Power 1999: 88)

---

35 Numbers are, according to Nikolas Rose, a crucial technique for modern government; they make modern forms of government both possible and judgable:

> Numbers, like other 'inscription devices' actually constitute the domains they appear to represent; they render them representable in a docile form – a form amenable to the application of calculation and deliberation. (1999: 198)

Rose points out that numbers have an intrinsic 'ordering capacity' and capability for the *reduction of complexity* – myriad and varied social conditions, experiences and characteristics of people can be reduced to a single number, such as a score on an IQ test or a recidivism rate.

Proportionality and consistency that have in the past 30 years become the privileged 'definitions of quality' of sentencing decisions, can therefore be seen as concepts of justice which, to some extent, have been designed with auditability and transparency in mind. They define the world in objective terms that a database can store and administrators and researchers evaluate and compare *ad infinitum*.

Marilyn Strathern points to the inherent similarity of audit procedures and information technology – their inability to tolerate loose ends. 'As a descriptive practice, audit cannot afford to tolerate loose ends, unpredictability or disconnections' (Strathern 2000a). Similarly, as we have mentioned above, both computer programming, SISs and sentencing guidelines are all guided by the belief in predictability of human thought and decisions. Strathern describes information technology as a 'highly visible ally of audit practices' (Strathern 2000a), not only by practically facilitating the production of audit reports, but also as a 'self-evidently good practice', which elicits a similar view of institutions, organisations and society in general. Strathern points out that auditing is based on an essentially different conception of society from, for example, sociology or ethnography.

> Itself a system, audit elicits a view of an institution or organisation as a system – as system, not as a 'society'. Ethnographic practice, on the other hand … elicits the open-endedness of institutions and organisations as 'society'. What characterises people's behaviour in 'society' is precisely their capacity to tolerate loose ends, to deal with unpredictability and revel in the disconnections which mean that they live in multiple worlds, traverse different domains. (Strathern 2000a)

While the loose ends may mean failure for computer programmers and auditors, they are an essential part of our everyday thinking and conversations. To submit what has been open-ended and unpredictable to a procedure that makes it into a predictable and closed system means that a practice has to go through a process of abstraction and restructuring that essentially changes the nature of the practice. Striving for transparency and structure is therefore essentially also a process of restructuring.

## The various faces of transparency

It needs to be pointed out, however, that the techniques used to achieve transparency of sentencing and other criminal justice decisions vary greatly from jurisdiction to jurisdiction. A great number of Western countries have gone through debates, if not reforms, regarding transparency and accountability of sentencing decisions (Tonry and Frase 2001). However, numerical sentencing guidelines seem to be almost exclusively a US phenomenon. Similarly, the spread of computerised SISs has been until now limited only to a handful of jurisdictions and a number of more or less active enthusiasts in others. The spread of 'computer-friendly' sentencing tools, therefore, seems to be quite limited at present, in spite of the fact that computers are becoming standard items of criminal justice work. However, in order to look at the impact of information technology in sentencing, one may also have to look beyond the official discourses and academics' and criminal justice officials' views about sentencing discretion. Computers may have an impact even though this may not be visible on the level of official and academic discourse. Norway may be one example at hand.

Norway is a country where sentencing at first glance still appears to be a 'black box' decision. If we use Ronald Dworkin's (1977) famous analogy that discretion is 'like a hole in the doughnut' (Tata 2000: 309), we can say that the doughnuts of Norwegian judges have quite big holes, particularly compared with their American counterparts. When it comes to sentencing, Norwegian judges have fairly broad and unregulated discretionary powers. The Norwegian penal code does not have a general provision or a rule about the principles of sentencing, and about which circumstances should be taken into account when judges determine the appropriate sentence. As long as they move within the prescribed sentencing range, judges can decide quite freely which circumstances will be taken into consideration. There have been discussions about the need for general sentencing principles, but the idea has been rejected (Hennum 2002).[36] Unlike its neighbouring country Sweden, the just deserts 'wave' never really reached Norway in the 1970s and 1980s.[37]

However, a recent study (Hennum 2002) of sentencing patterns of Norwegian lower courts concluded that the sentencing practices are surprisingly similar in similar cases. Surprisingly so if we think of the wide discretion given to the judges by the law, and quite the opposite to the popular belief presented in the newspapers. Naturally, there was some disparity that was unaccounted for, but the extent of disparity was surprisingly small considering that Norway has so little judicial guidance in its legislation. We should, of course, be wary of gaining an impression that the Norwegian justice system is an ideal picture of egalitarianism. There are a number of mechanisms that make the system far from equal for various social groups – from police suspicion, to definitions of criminality, the ability of getting decent legal help, etc (Mathiesen 2001). However, the findings about the relative uniformity of judicial decisions may force us to ask whether sentencing decisions of Norwegian judges perhaps are governed by some kind of rules even though they are not visible at first sight.

Scandinavian countries are among the most, if not the most, technologically developed countries in the world. If the computer is to have a cultural impact, it would surely have to be here and there certainly has been a number of developments. The Norwegian justice system is in the process of introducing a new, integrated electronic case-processing system, as well as establishing a so called 'information highway' between the various actors and agencies in the penal

36 This does not, however, mean that there are no sentencing rules in Norwegian law. First of all, there are a number of specific provisions that permit departure from the minimum or maximum sentence (offender is under 18, repeat offenders, multiple offences, etc). In addition, the Supreme Court cases play a significant role in guiding the lower courts. Norwegian case law has created a number of precedents about which circumstances should be taken into account in sentencing. Norway also has an extensive appeal procedure regarding sentencing. Another important aspect is the general theoretical justifications for punishment, where general prevention and individual prevention have had a particularly strong influence in Norway (Hennum 2002).

37 Retributivism is nevertheless a salient justification of punishment in the everyday functioning of Norwegian courts. A recent study (Stenborre 2003) of cases decided by the Supreme Courts of Sweden and Norway finds that there are surprisingly few differences between the Swedish and Norwegian decisions, even though the two countries appear to be guided by different penal theories (retributivism and preventivism respectively). The study shows that there are only a few differences between the circumstances mentioned in the cases and that these differences cannot be explained by different penal theories. The Swedish and Norwegian courts seem to be motivated by the same combination of general and special prevention with some elements of retribution or just deserts.

process. Norway has also an advantage of having one of the most advanced legal information systems in the world. A system known as Lovdata has been in operation for about 20 years. Established in 1981, Lovdata is a non-profit agency which, among other things, provides online legal information. Its information has been available on the internet since 1995. Lovdata's internet and online databases cover all the Norwegian primary legal sources, including: all statutes and regulations which are in force in Norway and their historical versions, treaties, the European Economic Area (EEA) Agreement and EEA directives, a number of documents by the Parliament, EU legislation, and more. What is important for the purpose of this book is that Lovdata also provides texts and summaries of judicial decisions: of Supreme Court decisions from as far back as 1836, full text appellate court decisions and selected lower court decisions, as well as decisions of a number of administrative tribunals. The decisions can be searched for according to the legal paragraph, the length of the sentence and a number of other factors.

Since Norwegian privacy law protects names and sensitive information about individuals involved in criminal cases, Lovdata must ensure that all such information is removed from their databases. The removal of personal information is a time consuming and expensive job. This is one of the reasons why in most other Scandinavian countries, such as Denmark and Sweden, the access to online full text judgments is not as good (Thorpe 2001). We can see that online information systems, particularly in Norway, make it quite easy to get information about the existing judicial practice. The courts themselves are also beginning to provide information about their activities on the internet. However, the number of full text judgments available through the courts is still limited. Therefore, although Norwegian judges and the Norwegian legal system in general are far from the sentencing reforms occurring in the English-speaking world, they are certainly living in the age of information. In addition, they are certainly informed. Judicial decisions, including sentencing decisions, are becoming increasingly visible and transparent. However, it needs to be pointed out that transparency is not simply something that can be achieved in its 'pure form'. In order to see things, to make them visible, one needs a perceptual apparatus. One needs glasses and these glasses are social creations. They are cultural creations which enable us to see things as we see them. The glasses can tell us something, not only about the phenomena we observe, but also about us – the observers. Therefore, it can be useful to compare the methods, or the 'glasses', which are used to achieve transparency of judicial decisions of American, Australian and Norwegian judges. It might give us some insight into the nature of these penal systems and the position that judges have in them.

Lovdata's databases, which enable availability of legal information about Norwegian sentencing and case law online, obviously greatly increase the visibility of sentencing practices. The fact that certain information becomes immediately available on the internet may have quite different effects from that information simply being available in print or in the form of files. In her research on disparity of Norwegian sentencing decisions, Hennum (2002: 95, 96) concludes that the availability of judgments through Lovdata is probably an important factor behind the existing level of consistency in sentencing practices of Norwegian courts. Today, all the parties involved, including the prosecution and defence lawyers, have the possibility of gaining an overview of existing sentencing practice. Previously, it was extremely time consuming to keep oneself oriented about sentencing practice. It entailed going through a massive quantity of files. Consequently, only a few people with a special interest and time would be able to have access to such information. Now, on the other hand, the information is available in a matter of minutes. There exists no empirical research comparing sentencing before and after the introduction of Lovdata. Sentencing consistency was not an issue nor an explicit justification behind the introduction of the system. However, Hennum (2002) concludes that because of the easy access to information, past sentencing practice is probably more often used as an argument in sentencing decisions, which makes the sentences more uniform. At the same time, the unreasonably disproportionate judicial decisions may be more likely subject to appeal due to the availability of information about the existing practice. Therefore, although Norway has not experienced an explicit change of penal climate towards just deserts, there may be reason to believe that a certain level of change may have taken place. Among the factors reducing disparity of sentencing decisions is not simply legal regulation, but also the availability of information through a new means of communication.

However, it is important to point out that there is a vital difference between SISs, introduced in Scotland and New South Wales, and the Norwegian and other online information systems. The Norwegian system does not provide statistical information about sentencing decisions. It is, therefore, up to the users of the system themselves (defence lawyers, prosecutors, researchers and, of course, judges) if they want to find out the 'tariff' or the average sentence for a certain type of offence. Unlike SISs, the Norwegian online information system was by no means created with the purpose of consolidating sentencing practice. It was guided by no explicit sentencing philosophy at all. Its primary purpose is to provide better information about all kinds of laws and legal practice to the general public and legal practitioners. The legal framework and practice of the state should be as transparent to the public as possible. This is quite a different background from SISs, which were designed with the specific purpose of creating a more uniform sentencing practice and reducing judicial discretion. Furthermore, SISs are meant primarily to be used by judges themselves, rather than other lawyers and the general public. SISs were guided by a clear philosophy about what would be desirable outcomes of judicial sentencing decisions, and they have statistical information as one of their central components.

In his illuminating book *Trust in Numbers*, Theodore Porter (1996) suggests that use of statistical knowledge is closely connected with the social basis of authority. Statistical knowledge is objective, universal knowledge which is detached from the individuality of its makers. Porter argues that reliance on statistical knowledge has a political dimension. When a profession comes under suspicion from powerful outsiders or the public, it abandons a reliance on experts and personal knowledge and replaces it with reliance on objective rules. Trust in numbers is, therefore, an alternative to trust in persons and their professional judgment.

The fact that the Norwegian information system does not provide statistical information may also, therefore, be seen as a sign of a greater level of trust that Norwegian judges enjoy compared with their counterparts in the US or Australia. The primary point of reference for Norwegian judges is still a written text, even though this text appears in electronic form. This text still needs to be read and interpreted. The judge therefore has a position of being in the centre. He or she is an active subject striving for the right interpretation of a kaleidoscope of rules and circumstances. The focus is not only on the quantities of punishments, but rather on the quality of the arguments. On the other hand, in the case of databases with statistical sentencing information, a judge is simply presented with a number or a range of numbers. The job of interpretation is therefore already done for him or her. Judges can still depart from the statistical average, but they are explicitly encouraged not to do so. Their position is one of greater passivity – and consequently also diminished control. When the average sentence is known, an individual judicial decision can always be compared against the average (Tait 1998).

Therefore, an Australian judge using an SIS is not simply more informed – he or she is also supervised (Tait 1998). The political and cultural dimensions of technology thus become more visible. The demands to limit judicial discretion – to fill the hole in the doughnut with rules – thus always first of all depend on the political climate, and not simply on the existence of various technologies which make it possible to fill that hole. The use of the various sentencing technologies is not only, and not primarily, a matter of technological development. It is a matter of a political and cultural climate and the relations of trust in a given society. Technological solutions are a result of human choice and design. The various methods used to control sentencing have different political objectives and different images of a judge and of an offender in mind.

## Responsibility in a transparent system

A further point that needs to be addressed is whether a transparent penal system, open to scrutiny, is in fact a system where it is easy to discuss responsibility. It is not easy, for example, to locate the author in a guideline system, risk assessment instruments or sentencing statistics. Sentencing guidelines are usually created by sentencing commissions, which in some cases leave so little space for judicial discretion that judges, required to pass sentences in which they do not believe, have only one option remaining to them – to resign. A number of American judges indeed have chosen to do so. By prescribing the relevant information in advance and considerable pre-programming of the solutions of conflicts, these systems, to a large extent, prevent individuals from making decisions and putting their personal marks on relationships. In a way, they have created a Kafkaesque world where everything seems to be prescribed, yet where it is impossible to find any authorial authority in the system. This is not to say that judges, before the reforms, did not 'hide' their responsibility behind standardised justifications such as the usual narratives of deterrence, protection of the public and rehabilitation. However, despite that, they were still clearly the authors of their decisions.

Judicial authority and responsibility is considerably diminished in formalised decision-making systems, where abstract, systematic knowledge has greater legitimacy than concrete, case-oriented knowledge and experience. As one federal judge pessimistically put it:

> When we come to see ourselves as judicial accountants, freed from the awful responsibility of imposing a sentence, we will have abdicated our judicial role entirely. (Weinstein 1992 in Rothman 1994: 37)

These systems provide decision-makers with almost all the information they need and leave little space for active participation and creativity – a similarity that they, in many respects, share with computers. As Shoshana Zuboff's study of industrial work shows, with computerisation, 'know-how, once diffused, is accumulated in the system, which has more and more authority' (1988: 69). The industrial workers interviewed by Zuboff raise a question that I perceive to be increasingly relevant for criminal justice today: what will the consequences be of relying exclusively on the knowledge that computers provide us with? As one of Zuboff's interviewees puts it:

> We are losing the context where hands-on experience makes sense. If you don't have the actual experience, you have to believe everything the computer says, and you can't beat it at its own game. You can't stand up to it. And yet who will have the experience to make these kinds of judgments? It will surely be a different world. You lose the checkpoints in reality to know if you are doing it right; therefore, how will anyone be able to confront the computer information? (1988: 65)

Roszak expresses a similar concern. The computer's world of order and logic is asserting superiority over other kinds of experience and is promising to be the only 'correct' line of reasoning. Speaking of contemporary subjects, he asks:

> Will they, themselves products of the Information Age, still know any other reality than the computer's reality? Above all, will they believe they have the right to correct a machine which, they have been told, is rapidly evolving toward 'an intelligence beyond man's'? (1994: 71)

What is at stake here is a power shift with regard to the possession of legitimate knowledge, a shift from individuals to the system. It is also a question about who has the right to the interpretation of social life. When work is transformed into the manipulation of abstract symbols, a question arises as to who has the right to define the meaning of these symbols and the rules for their use. As Neil Hutton points out, the 'data used in information systems is not neutral. It is "pre-digested", a product of the interpretative processes of criminal justice actors' (1995: 564). The data which guidelines and computer systems operate with are not neutral, because they are 'human creations, each capable of being questioned, doubted, altered' (Roszak 1994: 106). '[I]nformation ... is political through and through' (Roszak 1994: 156). However, as Roszak suggests, the information-processing model of thought obscures the social and political nature of information and provides it with a certain (unquestionable) objectivity and neutrality. This mode of thought, also embodied in the guidelines, buries ever deeper 'the substructure of ideas upon which information stands, placing them further from critical reflection' and thus obscures 'basic questions of value, purpose and justice' (Roszak 1994: 106, 107).

As information-processing tools encourage individuals to think according to their procedures and categories, they suppress the unpredictable and the original. They reduce the space available for the mind that does more than follow procedures, a mind that is capable of cultural and social interpretation, able to see and create new meanings in social conflicts. To make a judgment, one needs a position of active, contextualised subjectivity. However, the goal of taming the system has been precisely to reduce the number of judgments (which are unpredictable and often arbitrary) and replace them with objective knowledge systems. What is lost, Roszak argues, is 'the gift of intellectual adventure' and 'the old art of thinking' – 'grounded in the mind's astonishing capacity to create beyond what it intends, beyond what it can foresee' (1994: 244). In a way, one could also regard the new sentencing designs as the power to determine future decisions, to 'compute the future' (Talbott 1995) and reduce it essentially to the present:

> The future is no longer the other of the present – it therefore no longer contains the possibility of unknown encounters and events that would be transformative. Without the unknown in front of us, there can be no human creativity or autonomy. 'Creation', says Castoriadis, 'means the capacity to bring about the emergence of what is not given – not derivable by means of a combinatory or in some other way – starting from the given'. (Robins and Webster 1999: 123)

The introduction of guidelines and SISs, and the surveillance of the judiciary which they, to a lesser or greater extent, entail, lead us to the question of what happens to the subject of punishment in these new penal strategies. We have seen how guidelines and computer communication have challenged the autonomy of a judge's subjectivity. On the one hand, they have made judges' individuality increasingly less relevant and have attempted to create an objective system. On the other hand, however, they have placed judges under greater scrutiny. At the same time, the demand for visibility and accountability of decision-making focuses on the penal organisation and its internal functioning rather than on individual offenders. Consequently, the individual expert–client relationship tends to be made predictable and standardised. One could say that uniformity and consistency of decisions is prioritised, at the expense of individualisation. Garland (1997) points out that this change clashed with the existing penal ideologies that professionals had about the nature and the purpose of their work. It generated resistance from a number of professional groups that prioritised the need to treat each case according to its own merits (Garland 1997).

Simon's study (1993) of parole in California provides an interesting example of this development. Simon reports that a parole system which previously was built around parolees was replaced by one which focused on the organisation itself, conceived as a system. Now the system and its efficiency, not its social objectives (the offender), have come into focus. According to Simon, internally derived procedural standards and performance parameters, rather than social and professional norms, come to guide the work of the parole agents. The project to control discretion has therefore radically transformed the ways in which individuals relate to each other within penal systems. The relationships between a parole officer and a parolee, a judge and an offender, have been thoroughly redefined. As one American ex-probation officer expressed the feeling: 'We were not allowed to think any more. We were more controlled than the offenders.'[38] He felt that their work did not correspond to offenders' needs, but rather to the categories imposed by the government.

38 Source: private conversation.

Numerical sentencing guidelines can be seen as an illustrative example of such a development. As Simon writes, the guidelines represent a significant break with the past and the logic of peno-correctional modernism:

> Then, it was the criminal subject that was embedded in the network of writing and the subject of the legal proceeding. Here, it is the legal agents involved in the case who find themselves caught in that web of writing and it is the official documents themselves, simulacra of previous legal findings, that are the subject of the proceeding. (1995: 18)

Here, we are obviously witnessing a certain change of focus in penal strategies – a certain change of objectives that leads to different perceptions of decision-makers and, as we shall see in the next chapter, also to a certain change in the perception of offenders' identities. Not only can we ask whether the stories about violence and deprivation are still the same stories when they are told through the language of databases; we can also ask whether the people who take part in these stories are still the same people, when their identities are adjusted to computers' categories.

# Chapter 4
# The End of 'Delinquent With a Soul'

## The new objectivity

> If the Enlightenment made legitimate the emergence and the autonomy of the subject, then the much less Faustian, the much more modest enlightenment makes it legitimate to speak of the autonomy, not of the subject but of the object. (Lash 2002: 50)

The ways in which penal systems conceptualise offenders' identities are closely connected with the types and forms of knowledge they are based on. Different forms of knowledge bring with them different forms of control (Foucault 1977, 1980), and give different meanings to the word 'punishment'. In the following two chapters, I explore further what it means for offenders to be punished in a system which increasingly has difficulties creating narratives, and what it means for offenders to be disciplined 'in a way that makes their behaviour amenable to data collection' (Bøhme 1992: 46). The trend opens a number of issues with regard to identity construction and the nature of disciplinary control. It is often easier to get a grasp on the present by comparing it with the past. For that reason, I compare the present notions of the self with some past ones and try to pin down the possible lines of continuity and discontinuity. For a long time, Foucault's *Discipline and Punish: The Birth of the Prison* has provided a potent image of offenders and penal strategies.[1] For Foucault, to punish means to control the 'soul'. The disciplinary state attempts to get hold of the essence of one's inner life and to normalise it. However, it will be suggested that we may now be seeing contours of a different strategy. Control of the 'soul' may no longer be the main objective of contemporary penal strategies. Often, these strategies seem to be eschewing the notion of the individual altogether. They are increasingly able to avoid dealing directly with offenders' individualities.

This development may be partly influenced by the use of information and communication technologies and the changing cultural perceptions that come with it. In the introduction, PIN codes and electronic passwords were mentioned as new methods of identification in contemporary societies. A PIN code such as YWXJ5KEM, Lqtyui87 or 23458, which may seem incomprehensible and banal, has become a vital tool for government agencies, online bookstores, banks, etc, in telling them who we really are. I am the carrier of all of these codes. However, the information that each of these codes contains about me is in various ways limited, perhaps not in its size, but rather in its versatility. One may contain information about my purchases of books in online bookstores, another about my purchases of gardening items, yet another about my cash transactions. They are compartmentalised records of my life, each category separated from the other, and even if they were to be put together, they would not be 'me'. The fact that I am an

---

1 This does not necessarily mean that Foucault's description was historically unflawed (Garland 1990). There is, however, little doubt that the images of modern penality provided in *Discipline and Punish: The Birth of the Prison* have had a great impact on the commonly held perceptions of crime control and punishment, particularly in the academic world.

online gardener may indicate my interest in gardening but, in fact, it is also my escape from the everyday pressures of work – a story which only I, personally, can convey.

My purpose in writing this is not to confess to the sins of self-indulgence, but rather to raise a question: what is the relation between the computer-constructed identities and the self? More precisely, how do computer-generated categories describe 'flesh and blood' individuals in penal systems? The themes of information gathering and information sharing have resonated throughout penal systems. The focus on information patterns has become an obvious and quite unproblematic objective. However, the extent to which information technology has transformed the patterns of identification remains, to some extent, unexplored. Taking sentencing reforms as a starting point, I propose that, as much as computers are tools for expanding human agency, they also appear to be the tools which provide new notions of the self – as well as tools which, in the end, are challenging traditional notions of a unified subjectivity.

## Categorical identity

In the first chapter we saw that standardisation of penalty has been, to a varying extent, an essential objective and a consequence of sentencing guidelines and sentencing information systems. As a consequence, it has been argued, the striving for clear and objective decisions may impede a multiple understanding of offenders' personalities. Tonry (1996: 20), for example, concludes that, in guidelines systems, offenders are not treated as whole people, but rather as 'two-dimensional crime-and-criminal history amalgams'. Three-dimensional human beings have to be reified into two-dimensional abstractions in order to achieve system consistency; consistency, which precisely because of the limited number of factors, is a false one (Tonry 1996). Freed also argues that '[t]he goal of uniformity in sentencing presupposes a uniformity of crime and criminals which simply does not exist' (1992: 1,743). The attempt to abstract the consideration of individual circumstances from the context of sentencing is to assume a *generic offender* (Tonry 1996: 19). Similarly, Stith and Cabranes argue that guidelines transform defendants from persons to '*kinds* of persons, abstract entities to be defined by a chart, their concrete existence systematically ignored and thus nullified' (1997: 1,263, original emphasis).

At this point, Craig Calhoun's description of *categorical identity* may be useful for conceptualising the phenomenon referred to above. Calhoun sees categorical identity as part of a 'pressure towards repressive sameness', as opposed to 'more complex notions of persons or networks of concrete social relations'.[2] He suggests that conceptualising individuals' identities on the basis of their belonging to certain social categories:

> allows a kind of abstraction from the concrete interactions and social relationships within which identities are constantly renegotiated, in which individuals present one identity as more salient than other, and within which individuals achieve some personal

2 Calhoun suggests that the tendency to categorise 'is particularly pronounced where large-scale collectivities and mobilizations have been facilitated by new forms of systematic organization (capitalism, the modern state) and new infrastructures of transport and communication (from paved roads and railroads to telephones, TV and computer networks)' (1995: 220).

> sense of continuity and balance among their various sorts of identities ... The abstractness of categories encourages framing claims about them as though they offered a kind of trump card over the other identities of individuals addressed by them. This encourages an element of repression within the powerful categorical identities. (Calhoun 1995: 220–21)

Categorical thinking[3] is based on the binary either/or logic that puts people or objects into categories, while obscuring the ambiguities. For example, people are seen as either male or female, black or white, etc. A person is seen as 'angry' or 'not angry', not as 'concerned' and 'frustrated' by a given context. Categorical thinking tends to go down a list, choosing between various categories and requiring the choice of one. Each question narrows the focus of the previous one. However, this kind of thinking omits the situational and narrative components of the various data, which explain the context in which data occurs. The fact that anger is situated means that the situation in which anger is felt by a prisoner is different from the situation of a prison guard's anger. The ways of expressing the anger, the reasons, the power relations and the sanctions regarding the feeling are all situated and based on the different contexts and stories behind them. A similar point has also been made by Margaret R Somers (1994), who points out that a woman's identity cannot be adequately represented simply by belonging to the category of women, without taking into consideration the 'categorically destabilizing dimensions of time, space, and relationality' (Somers 1994: 606). Calhoun's comments about the plurality of identities, and Somers's argument about taking the dimensions of *time*, *space* and *relationality* into consideration, are also highly relevant in the case of criminal offenders.[4, 5]

Categorisation has been an essential component of sentencing reforms, based on either sentencing guideline grids or computerised information systems. These reforms have employed what may be described as analytical models of thought. In analytical thinking, a phenomenon, as an entity, is studied through its constituent elements. The objective of the process is to find correlations between different variables or categories. In order to achieve this, the meaning and the boundaries of categories have to be as clear as possible. Categories containing classes of persons or events have to be unified. A process of *objectification* takes place and social phenomena come to be presented as objects, lasting in time. As Dag Østerberg

---

3 Category should be distinguished from a group. Categories and groups are two types of collectivities which differ according to whether their members can or cannot identify themselves with the collectivity, or, in some cases, are not even aware of the existence of the collectivities. Groups, on the one hand, are constituted by their members; while categories, on the other hand, are constituted by outside observers and can be defined arbitrarily, according to any criteria (Jenkins 1996: 82). This does not mean, however, that members of categories, by definition, do not, or cannot, identify themselves with the categories in which they have been placed. Members of certain income tax groups, for example, can identify with each other and have strong social relations. Or they may not. The point is that, for the purposes of income tax authorities, people's subjective feelings of membership are irrelevant. The category was established for the purposes of outside observers rather than its members.

4 The category of a drug user presents perhaps one of the most popular 'trump cards' for explaining individuals' identity and criminality from the point of a singular sign. The fact that drug abuse is usually seen only as a problem of physical addiction (and therefore a distinct and objective factor) strengthens the salience of this category as an explanation of identity.

5 Norris, for example, talks about the *categorical suspicion* of CCTV operators, meaning the suspicion that is 'not based on objective behavioural and individualised criteria, but merely on being categorised as a part of a particular social group' (2002: 26).

(1993: 40) points out, a consequence (or constituent part) of objectification is that social phenomena, which, by their very nature can have more than one meaning, come to be presented as having only one meaning. However, Østerberg's objection is that social processes are *dialectical*. Their meaning is a result of a constant process of rediscovery and renegotiations by social actors. Therefore, he argues, if we take the meaning of social phenomena to be clear and given in time, we are using a method that does not fit its object of research. Furthermore, implicit in the two methods is a different position and self-understanding of the decision-maker. The dialectical understanding of truth implies a judge's conscious participation in the process of defining meaning: it implies an ability to experience, empathise and change one's own views. This is a position of active subjectivity. Analytical method, on the other hand, is characterised by its belief in the existence of regularities in the world. The decision-maker as an individual (as a subject) is irrelevant to the discovery of truth. In a way, sentencing guideline grids can be described as 'knowledge without a subject'. Knowledge regarding criminal events and individuals is seen as an objectivity that can be uncovered in advance; before the resolution of conflicts takes place and without necessarily the participation of the actors involved.

Categorising human identity into axis grids is an act of deconstruction of subjectivity. It is an act of taking individuals apart and then putting them together according to the requirements of the system. The process does not require a narrative or communication with the persons in question. An essential feature of the processes of categorisation is fixing or, as we can call it, '*freezing*' the meaning of identity and criminal events. Due to the distance created by procedural rules, an offender is precluded from participating in the process of defining his or her identity. The offender's (public) identity thus ceases to be his or her personal project and is rather given from above.

## Offence over life, category over narrative

Categorical thinking places greater emphasis on criminal acts than on offenders' biographical and social narratives. In a way, it is assumed that people are their acts. For someone sentenced for burglary, the criminal act itself becomes the primary point of reference, overshadowing, for example, the biographical narratives about frustration, homelessness or drug addiction which may have been the circumstances influencing the act. Nils Christie points out that this tendency to make no differentiation between the act and the person is common when we label people as terrorists, monsters, etc. However, he raises a question:

> But are people their acts? Are thieves stealing all the time, are murderers killing all the time, - or, for that sake, are lovers making love all the time, or painters painting? Some people come close to being their acts. Gandhi and Jesus are supposed to be of that type. But most often we are able to see that most people are multidimensional. A person might have exposed some acts we might deplore, but he has also other sides. (Christie 2002: 24)

It is precisely this awareness of people's multi-dimensionality which makes dialogue and mediation possible.[6]

The ability to transgress categorisation and present a multi-dimensional identity often depends on the possibilities that offenders have to present a life story, and a *narrative* (rather than categorical) identity. According to Giddens (1991), in modern society, 'a person's identity is not to be found in behaviour, nor – important though this is – in the reactions of others, but in the capacity to *keep a particular narrative going*' (Giddens 1991: 54, original emphasis). 'Each of us not only "has", but lives a biography' (Giddens 1991: 14). The autobiographical narratives provide a sense of coherence and shape in people's lives. They help to explain and give meaning to the past, present and the future. However, Jerome Miller (2001) argues that meaning (that a particular action may carry for an individual and society) has become the 'Great Satan of contemporary criminological research and criminal justice practice' (2001: 154). He criticises the view that the facts of the offence should be the sole determinant in sentencing. Paraphrasing Eric Voegelin, he says that 'facts are here for one main purpose – to illuminate meaning' (2001: 155). Miller points to the trend of 'shutting out the narrative – from our theories, our research, and our courts' (2001: 156). Today, researchers as well as a number of treatment providers base their work on mass phenomena without regard to the life histories of individuals. He observes that, in the past 20 years in the US, narrative has been:

> increasingly marginalized in state courts while it has all but disappeared in federal courts – particularly insofar as those proceedings involve poor and minority defendants. Not surprisingly, however, the narrative continues to survive in courts among upper and upper-middle class and for some specific categories of institutionally 'sympathetic' defendants, eg police ... (Miller 2001: 156)

Miller points here to an important fact: that the ability to present a life story[7] and create a multi-dimensional identity often depends on offenders' social status. The poorer individual is less able to buy a thorough life history and a complete diagnostic workup. In a way, we see a reversal of Foucault's 'descending individualisation' – where those on the bottom were the ones most subjected to the curious gaze of psychiatric and penal power. Categorical identity, on the other hand, comes closer to what Lash (2002) describes as *generic* identity – not characteristic of any particular person. It is a result of a sentencing system that focuses mostly on legal categories, lifted up from their social context and in a way turned into a generic activity that could in fact be executed via computers from anywhere in the world.

As argued above, sentencing guidelines are based on the analytical thinking and componential image of human identity. They deconstruct identity into separate

---

6 This is why the principles of proportionality and sentencing consistency, embodied in sentencing guidelines and SISs, are deeply at odds with the principles of *restorative justice*. Restorative justice is an individualised way of solving conflicts, where the *particular* circumstances of the offender, the crime, the victim and the community are in focus. The focus is on the (qualitative) resolution of a conflict, rather than on the appropriate quantity of punishment.

7 Miller refers to the research of Mary Berry, who sees the narrative as a crucial aspect of law: 'I know now that everyone has stories, including lawyers, judges and jurors. Stories provide a frame of reference which determines what each of us believes is true about the law. They also shape law and how it is enforced' (Berry 1999: 80).

factors and then assign values to them in order to achieve a 'score'. A score assigns numerical value to identity. This evaluation is achieved by combining pieces of information in a fundamentally different way to what would be achieved through speech or writing. The fundamental difference lies in the possibilities of interpretation that are present, both in written texts (when the interpretation refers only to written signs) and in speech (when interpretation also includes non-verbal clues).[8]

Numerical identity is, therefore, in sharp contrast with the narrative. Hayles (1999) argues that the narrative can be seen as a form of resistance to the various forms of abstraction and disembodiment, also represented in numbers: it is personified, it is situated and historically specific. However, these are also the qualities that make narratives somewhat at odds with contemporary information-processing culture.[9] As Lash points out, information compresses narratives into short messages:

> Unlike narrative, information compresses beginning, middle and end into a present immediacy of a 'now-here'. Unlike discourse, information does not need legitimating arguments, does not take the form of propositional utterances, but works with an immediate communicational violence. (Lash 2002: x)

However, one should be wary of assuming that contemporary culture is somehow 'prevented' from creating narratives due to its technological workup. Manovich points to the interesting fact that computers enable new forms of narratives which did not exist before. He wonders (2001b: 237) whether 'our new abilities to store vast amounts of data, to classify automatically, index, link, search, and instantly retrieve it, lead to new kinds of narratives?' Bolter (2001), for example, describes how hypertext and the World Wide Web lead to a 'remediation' of print and creation of a new space for writing. The question is, of course, whether and how these possibilities could be used in sentencing. Tata (2000), for example, reports that there have been attempts to create information systems based on case-based reasoning (case story rather than factors). However, none of these has yet become operational. In recent years, the tendency has certainly been to see the (legally defined) offence as the privileged criterion of sentencing. It must be pointed out, of course, that the degree to which the 'offence' is prioritised over 'life' varies from jurisdiction to jurisdiction. The US Federal Sentencing Guidelines can certainly be seen as the extreme end of the spectrum. However, the 'tariff' sentencing embodied in sentencing information systems is driven by a similar logic of categorisation. And as Barbara Hudson (2002) describes in the case of England and Wales, where there are at present no numerical sentencing guidelines or SISs:

> As well as legislation, during the 1980s a series of guideline judgments, the establishment and activities of the Judicial Studies Board; Home Office and Lord Chancellor's Department circulars and booklets directed both judges and magistrates

8 As mentioned previously, Ericson and Haggerty's (1997) analysis of police work provides a similar account of a shift from the blank page and open narrative to, as is the case today, fixed-choice risk classifications. They argue that in the late 1990s, the policing of narratives extended to limiting written accounts of occurrences to a specified small number of characters, circumscribing, and sometimes almost eliminating, the use of abstract and interpretative language.

9 See Chapter 3 on the database/narrative antagonism.

> firmly towards selecting the 'going rate' for the offence category concerned rather than choosing the sentence appropriate to the circumstances of the offender as the socially-situated individual. (Hudson 2002: 567)

It may be important to point out that this striving for categorisation is nothing new. History is full of quests for clear categories, and thus clear boundaries. Categorisation has always been a way of imposing order on chaos. In many ways, the striving for categories is based on a wish (or a perceived necessity) to find simple explanations for complex phenomena. On the other hand, Garland (2001) argues that the standardised view of offenders does represent a shift from earlier periods, and that we are witnessing a new pattern of individualisation in contemporary penal policy. While before, the individualisation effort was focused almost exclusively on the offender, now the victim is at the forefront, while the offender is 'rendered more and more abstract, more and more stereotypical, more and more a projected image rather than an individual person' (Garland 2001: 179).

## Revival of the Enlightenment?

It has been pointed out that the desert theory can be regarded as a return to the Enlightenment project of a responsible individual – that there is a 'direct line of influence from Beccaria to Morris and von Hirsch' (Bottoms 1995: 23). According to Foucault (1977), disciplines subverted the Enlightenment project by achieving social order through mental and corporal training, and through coercion rather than 'symbolic communication' and legal discourse. Are we now, through the renewed emphasis on legalism and the offence, also seeing a revival of the Enlightenment subjectivity? I would like to suggest, however, that the deserts theory and the guidelines systems reinstated only certain aspects of the Enlightenment tradition. The Enlightenment individual is characterised by his free will and universal individuality, free from the constraints of history, locality and tradition. He is rational and calculating, seemingly unaffected by his social class and biography – a quality he shares with his just deserts counterpart. However, the Enlightenment reformers saw legal conflicts and punishment as a part of an ongoing discourse about social norms. Penalty was seen as part of a narrative about moral norms, or, as Foucault puts it, a 'flow of signs' carrying the message to the society. Punishment was to be exercised according to this technique of symbolic communication; it would be a school of morality (Foucault 1977: 105, 111, 112). According to Foucault, Enlightenment saw 'the "mind" as a surface of inscription of power, with semiology as its tool' (1977: 102). Penal power would be exercised through the control of ideas. Disciplines consequently broke with this principle of symbolic communication and reinstated the body and soul as primary objects of penal control.

Through the technique of punitive signs, the subjects who receive these signs (the public) and the subject who emits them (the criminal) are of primary importance for government. An offender participates in the process of symbolic communication as a social member, defined as a subject of law – a 'juridical subject of the social pact'. Consequently, punishment is the process of restoring individuals' subjectivity. What Enlightenment brings is a tradition of *active subjectivity*, emphasising individuals' reasoning capabilities and their ability to participate in the ongoing social discourse. Here, although seemingly similar, the sentencing reforms described in this book are in a number of aspects deeply at odds with the Enlightenment tradition. What is addressed through the new sentencing models is not an active moral subject who is a part of an ongoing communication concerning laws and social norms, but rather a passive standardised individual, whose identity and active thinking capacity are not essential to defining him with regard to the legal system. As argued above, an offender's position in the sentencing process is closer to being an object – with regard to his participation in defining the meaning of his or her acts and with regard to his moral communication and responsibility. Furthermore, it needs to be emphasised that the Enlightenment subject is characterised not only by his independence and activity, but even more importantly by his *moral awareness* – perhaps most emphatically represented by Kant. Contemporary sentencing reforms, on the other hand, have difficulty reflecting the subjective degree of offenders' moral responsibility. They rely primarily on objective *legal* measures of desert. Their notion of responsibility is based on legal rather than moral assessments of blameworthiness – the offender is to be blamed for the offence and not for the moral blameworthiness it expresses (Tonry 1994: 67). They, therefore, promote *objective culpability* rather than a subjective one.

Nevertheless, popular political discourse often still talks about responsibility, as if it were morally communicating with an active subject. The guidelines were and are essentially justified by a deeply moralistic discourse of just deserts – of only punishing offenders according to their desert and only because they deserve it. Furthermore, the guidelines have also been appropriated by those who justify the increasing punitiveness on moral grounds of 'achieving justice through punishment'. However, the reality of a sentencing process tends to turn this position of moral awareness and active subjectivity into passive objective signs – with minimal possibilities of creating a narrative. The moralistic discourse takes place on the level of abstract principles and universalistic ethics rather than in the process of a concrete sentencing proceeding. The architecture of two-dimensional grids seems, therefore, to be much better suited for conveying universal principles than blameworthiness and moral culpability in concrete cases. The interesting question here is, to borrow Bottoms' words:

> why this liberal individualism, which has after all been available as an intellectual resource for a long time, should have become substantially more prominent in the sentencing theory and practice, and the prison law, of the period from the mid 1960s onwards. (1995: 23)

Explanations are obviously manifold. However, the renewed interest in the Enlightenment and its stress on legalism and universal individuality appears to coincide with the present focus on predictability and objectivity. As Feeley and Simon suggest, by eschewing wider social considerations and by neglecting offenders' uniqueness and individuality, the penal process is designed as a cost-effective way for the management of the dangerous rather than as a means for reintegrating offenders into the community (1992: 455–56).

It has been argued that the Enlightenment reformists always punished with the image of society in mind. Although one should not overestimate the moral aspects of disciplination, the mere fact that its objective was to reform the soul or the inner self made it possible for an offender and an institution to share a certain social and moral community:

> Traditional social policies have always respected, even if viewing with suspicion, what might be called a certain *naturalness of the social*: individuals are inscribed within territories, they belong to concrete groups, they have attachments, heritages, roots. (Castel 1991: 295, emphasis added)

The new penal strategies, on the other hand, seem to distrust the social aspects of individuals.[10] The categorical individual is decontextualised – taken out of his web of social and personal narratives, group belongings, personal history and motivation. Bearing these differences in mind, one can question the relevance of Foucault's concept of disciplination for contemporary penal practice and sentencing. Can contemporary sentencing practice still be described as disciplinary, even though it seems to lack the individualising dimensions of disciplination?

## Delinquent with a soul

> This form of power applies itself to immediate everyday life which categorizes the individual, *marks him by his own individuality*, attaches him to his own identity, imposes a law of truth on him which he must recognize and which others have to recognize in him. It is a form of power which makes individuals subjects. (Foucault 1983: 212, emphasis added)

According to Foucault's *Discipline and Punish: The Birth of the Prison* (1977),[11] the end of the 18th century and the first half of the 19th century marked a new period in penal history. Its most obvious sign was the gradual disappearance of torture, typical of the old monarchical power. In feudal societies, every penalty of certain seriousness had to involve corporal punishment, a certain physical infliction of pain. Punishment had to leave marks on the offender's body, and this ritual took place in public. Its objective was to reveal the monarch's unlimited authority. Thus, torture was not only a legal, but also a political ritual that revenged crimes regarded as a personal attack on the king's authority. This physical and personal nature of punishment reflected the physical and personal nature of power relations in feudal societies. Consequently, Foucault argues, in the 19th century, prison became the privileged form of punishment. Accordingly, the objective of punishment shifted from inflicting pain directly on a criminal's body to controlling what Foucault terms 'the soul' – meaning psyche, consciousness, individuality. The purpose of punishment became to reform and discipline the criminal rather than to revenge the crime. Penal systems became disciplinary regimes whose objective was to change individual behaviour and motivation; to change an offender's identity through training, moral education and other correctional techniques in order to achieve obedience and conformity. This is why a prison was called 'a reformatory'.

10 For a further discussion with regard to the changing nature of 'the social' and legal governance, see Sarat and Simon (2003: 2). The authors point out that, while not necessarily endorsing Rose's claim about the 'death of the social', one needs to acknowledge that 'the social' is a historically specific concept, which experienced its peak during the period of welfarism but which, however, increasingly seems to lose its privileged place as primary point of reference of contemporary governance.

11 This will only briefly and partially present Foucault's work, focusing on the topics that are relevant to the discussion in this book. For a more thorough analysis, see, for example, Hubert L Dreyfus and Paul Rabinow (1983).

In fact, Foucault claims that the rise of the sciences, whose task was to normalise 'the soul' (psychiatry, psychology, criminology etc), also established the modern Western notions of individuality. One of the great values of Foucault's work lies in the fact that it drew attention to the fact that the individual itself has a history, a history that is not independent of the broader power relations in society. To put it more clearly, the notion of individuality is constructed within historically specific social structures. This was perhaps most famously expressed in *The Order of Things*:

> Does man really exist? To imagine for an instant, what the world and thought and truth might be if man did not exist, is considered to be merely indulging in paradox. This is because we are so blinded by the recent manifestation of man that we can no longer remember a time – and it is not so long ago – when the world, its order, and human beings existed, but man did not. (Foucault 1970: 322)

Just as there is no such thing as madness as such, but merely a socially and discursively constructed notion of certain people as mad, so too, there is no 'I', no subject, prior to its constitution in certain social discourses and practices. Foucault represents a view that the very notion of individuality (a madman, a criminal, a sexual pervert, a homosexual, etc) is constituted within a certain web of social and discursive relations.

Historians often place the origin of the modern Western notion of individuality in the time of transition from feudalism to industrialism, from tradition to modernity. Then, a person came to be seen as increasingly able to chart the course of his or her own life through the personal choice of profession, a spouse and religion. These choices gradually came to be seen as matters of individual conscience and conviction rather than determined by family or tradition (Bagge 1998: 10). Thus, the metaphors of the 'inner' and the 'outer self' have become of central importance to the modern Western notion of individuality (Meyer 1993). Although probably having its origins in the Christian tradition, the notion of the 'inner self' was particularly emphasised during the Reformation and by Protestantism, professing a man's duty to act according to his conscience rather than external authorities. Foucault's history of modern individuality (1977, 1978) is also, to a large extent, situated in the 19th century. However, he does not see the 'inner self' as a place of individual uniqueness and autonomy, but rather as the result of subtle social manipulation and conformity. In fact, Foucault claims that this control of the inner self occurred to such an extreme that it not only controlled, but also *produced* individuals. In *Discipline and Punish*, the inner self – 'the soul' – is constituted through technologies of correction and normalisation. Individuals are made docile and subjected to habits and order. Later on, in *History of Sexuality*, individuality is described as being formed by medical and psychiatric discourses about sexuality. In both cases, Foucault contends that control of individuality, of the 'inner self', is an essential component of modern state power. He sees the modern state as an entity 'in which individuals can be integrated, under one condition: that this individuality would be shaped in a new form' (1983: 214). He describes the modern Western state as a 'pastoral power', having its origin in the Christian tradition. Pastoral power:

> cannot be exercised without knowing the inside of people's minds, without exploring their souls, without making them reveal their innermost secrets. It implies a knowledge

> of the conscience and an ability to direct it ... [I]t is individualizing (as opposed to legal power); it is coextensive and continuous with life; it is linked with a production of truth – the truth of the individual himself. (Foucault 1983: 214)

Therefore, for Foucault, power relations have a direct, productive effect on people's individuality. Prisons' and penal systems' open objective was to change individuals and turn them into responsible citizens. This is also where Foucault finds essential similarity between prisons, schools and psychiatric hospitals – they all share this personality-forming dimension. They are trying to produce 'normal', docile individuals in accordance with the norms of industrial society. To fight against the state, therefore, meant not only to oppose its violence but also to fight against the individuality it tried to impose (Foucault 1983).

In light of the above, from the beginning of the 19th century, in penal systems, offenders' lives became in fact more important than their actual offences. The objective of punishment became less to revenge the crime and rather to transform the criminal. This historical move from the 'scaffold' to the 'penitentiary' reflects the modern concern 'to know the criminal, to understand the source of his criminality, and to intervene to correct them wherever possible' (Garland 1990: 136). The transformation involved the introduction of experts (psychiatrists, criminologists, social workers, psychologists, etc) into the judicial process in order to identify individuals' abnormalities and bring about their reformation. It was individuals' criminogenic lifestyle that was being examined and punished, rather than their crimes. Through biographical investigation into the causes of his or her acts, about the circumstances of his life, etc, prison examines as well as 'produces' a *delinquent*. 'The delinquent is to be distinguished from the offender by the fact that it is not so much his act as his life that is relevant in characterizing him' (Foucault 1977: 251). The delinquent is submitted to numerous training and examination procedures in order to allow the authorities to know and 'cure' his criminality. Delinquency is a product of:

> a new modality of power in which each individual receives as his status his own individuality, and in which he is linked by his status to the features, the measurements, the gaps, the 'marks' that characterize him and make him a 'case' ... With it are ritualized those disciplines that may be characterized in a word by saying that they are a modality of *power for which individual differences are relevant*. (Foucault 1977: 192, emphasis added)

In a disciplinary society, a criminal's soul is not referred to only in order to explain the crime and to define the appropriate level of responsibility. The soul itself is an object of punishment and penal intervention – an object that needs to be corrected and normalised according to scientific rather than legal norms. Through reference to the soul, penal power intervenes over something other than offences, namely, individuals. This penal strategy is essentially individualising. Its primary intention is not to punish the crime but to supervise the individual. For this purpose, it accumulates large amounts of knowledge about individuals, carefully examines their acts, personalities and social conditions, and seeks recourse in scientific knowledge to find explanations. The point here is that disciplines' approach to offenders was both individualising and *holistic*. They made it their objective to know and control the whole of an individual's life and personality. They provided the penal system with a:

> justifiable hold not only on offences, but also on individuals; not only on what they do, but also on what they are, will be, may be ... [T]he judges have gradually ... taken to judging something other than crimes, namely, the 'soul' of the criminal. (Foucault 1977: 18, 19)

A conversation taking place between a judge and an offender in 1840, reported by Foucault in *Discipline and Punish: The Birth of the Prison*, exemplifies the disciplinary power's incessant interest in people's lifestyles and not simply their offences:

> The judge: One must sleep at home. – Béasse [offender]: Have I got a home? – You live in perpetual vagabondage. – I work to earn my living. – What is your station in life? – My station: to begin with, I'm 36 at least; I don't work for anybody. I've worked for myself for a long time ... – It would be better for you to be put into a good house as an apprentice and learn a trade. – Oh, a good house, an apprenticeship, it's too much trouble. And anyway, the bourgeois ... always grumbling, no freedom. – Does not your father wish to reclaim you? – Haven't got no father. – And your mother? – No mother neither, no parents, no friends, free and independent. (Foucault 1977: 290–91)

As such, the Foucaultian delinquent can be contrasted with our analysis of the categorical individual presented above. While going under the surface, understanding motivation and causation of the 'criminal man' was the essential aspect of disciplinary power, quite the opposite is the case in contemporary sentencing guidelines and risk assessment forms (see the table below).

| **Delinquent** | **Categorical individual** |
|---|---|
| • 'soul' (psyche, consciousness) | • surface |
| • depth | • uniformity (categories, groups) |
| • individuality | • a-biographical (offence over life) |
| • biographical (life over offence) | • componential |
| • holistic | • decontextualised |
| • relations, networks | • system-management, categorisation |
| • transformation | |

## The ghost in the machine

The categorical individual is essentially different from Foucault's delinquent, precisely because of the fact that he or she does not seem to have a soul. A 'soul' is a very elusive concept – and Foucault does not really provide a clear definition of it. He also uses other expressions such as 'the heart, the thoughts, the will, the inclinations' and 'psyche, subjectivity, personality, consciousness' (1977: 16, 29). However, there is no doubt that the soul is central in understanding the concept of a delinquent. In fact, Foucault himself described *Discipline and Punis: The Birth of the Prison* as a 'genealogy of the modern soul' (1977: 29) and leaves no doubt as to the centrality of the soul for the exercise of disciplinary power:

> It would be wrong to say that the soul is an illusion, or an ideological effect. On the contrary, it exists, it has a realty, it is produced permanently around, on, within the body by the functioning of a power that is exercised on those punished – and, in a more general way, on those one supervises, trains and corrects, over madmen, children at home and at school, the colonized, over those who are stuck at a machine for the rest of their lives ... The man ... is already in himself the effect of a subjection much more profound than himself. A 'soul' inhabits him and brings him to existence, which is itself a factor in the mastery that power exercises over the body. The soul is ... the prison of the body. (Foucault 1977: 29, 30)

We can see, then, that the effects of disciplinary power are directed primarily at a man's soul – at his or her inner self or individuality. The soul is 'the prison of the body' (Foucault 1977) and prisons are places for the training of souls.

Nonetheless, Foucault, typically perhaps, does not provide much further explanation about what he means by the soul. However, it is perhaps precisely the lack of clarity and definition that is essential to the concept of a soul, namely, that it is inherently personal and unpredictable. In its essence, a soul is something individual, personal and private. Trond Berg Eriksen (2000b: 349) argues that the soul is essentially an *'anti-thing'*. He describes the soul as a 'fundamental protest against objectification' and against the many social forces that, today, strive to 'transform the world into objects of control and exploitation' (2000b: 348).[12] In an antimetaphysical gesture, Gilbert Ryle in *The Concept of Mind* (1949) calls the soul 'the ghost in the machine'. As Eriksen (2000) points out, this is the natural consequence if one sees human nature as a mechanism or a machine – the soul then becomes a ghost, the inexplicable that is left in the machinery. By insisting on objectivity and predictability, contemporary sentencing reforms come closer to these automatic and machine-like features. They are, therefore, at odds with the Foucaultian delinquent and the concept of the soul. The categorical individual is, to a large extent, deprived of the possibility of having a distinct individuality and, one could also say, a strong sense of moral responsibility. Eriksen points out that a consequence of the diminishing space for the soul is a certain concept of the self that, because of its abstractness, has difficulty accounting for moral responsibility and a stable identity (2000: 349). Furthermore, he suggests that the acknowledgment of the soul, and the individuality that comes with it, gives people a certain protection against possible encroachment, control and exploitation. Soul has to do with acknowledgment and respect for the other. Eriksen's understanding of the role of the soul is quite different from Foucault's. The latter, in fact, sees the soul as an essential tool and a product of power and control. However, they both seem to agree that the concept of the soul has been central for conceptualising people as unique and conscious beings with a distinct sense of their own individuality.

In *The DNA Mystique: The Gene as a Cultural Icon*, Dorothy Nelkin and Susan Lindee (1995) suggest that today DNA, which in its essence is not unlike a computer program, has taken on some important social and cultural functions of the soul. Furthermore, Lyon points out that DNA data is increasingly used not only for medical but also for surveillance purposes – for so called *body surveillance*. 'It is the

12 My own translation.

co-opting of the body itself as a means of identification and of predicting behaviour and conditions' (2001: 70). Body surveillance (fingerprints, retinas, voice recognition, face and genetic clues, etc) represent a shift from verbal forms of identification (what one *knows*) to checking what one is (body parts). They can therefore be illustrative of the shift from the 'soul' or consciousness to the surface, described here. In the case of body surveillance (or biometrics) the body is used as a source of standardised information, rather than as a 'prison of the soul' as described by Foucault.

If one would follow Foucault, diminishing focus on the soul might have some liberating effects. To free one's self from the state, he writes, is to free oneself from the individuality it tries to impose on us. These were probably the wishes of the liberal critics in the 1970s who tried to turn sentencing into a more objective activity, and take away from the state the right to judge individuals according to what they are (their life), instead of what they do (the offence). However, 30 years later, with the massive increases in imprisonment and popular punitiveness, it seems that the soul may have been one more barrier which had to fall in order to 'give free hands to the contempt' (Eriksen 2000b) – to understand less and to punish more.

## Signs of change

The sentencing reforms described in this book can, therefore, compel us to question the relevance of the Foucaultian model of a delinquent. Penal models and strategies are not static phenomena. They change with time and place. *Discipline and Punish* was, after all, first published in 1975, almost 30 years ago, and Foucault's analysis of prison is mainly situated in the 19th century, which makes it necessary to question its relevance to contemporary penalty. As Anthony Bottoms suggests:

> it surely is possible that the change in the nature of society from 1800 to 1980 ... may also be affecting other penal developments. On the face of it, therefore, simple extrapolations from Foucault's description of the penal system from the early nineteenth century to the present are very unlikely to be adequate. (Bottoms 1983: 187)

The question is, therefore, what are the objectives of contemporary penality? Is penal power still punishing a delinquent and trying to reach his 'soul'? To talk about a soul seems at odds with the modern vocabulary of penal terms. Furthermore, is contemporary penality still attempting to change offenders' individuality and adjust it to the needs of the state? What are its techniques, and how prominently do disciplinary methods feature among them? Is the individual still in focus, or does the focus of penal strategies lie somewhere else? And even more so, what kind of image of offenders' identity does contemporary penal power have, and how does this process of identity-construction take place? It is important to note that Foucault's work appeared prior to the widespread technological change that has taken place in the past 30 years. Understandably, he does not study information technology, and his analysis of 'power/knowledge' does not reach the context of the so called information society. Yet, there is no doubt that information and communication technologies have had a significant impact on social relations in late modern societies. A growing body of research argues for the importance of the new technologies in shaping human identity and social action. Electronic databases, CCTV, electronic monitoring, biometric identification etc are the new modes of control that penal theory is now trying to come to terms with. It is beyond the scope of this book to address them all. They each need to be understood in their own particularity. In addition, although some have argued that the new electronic technologies can simply be viewed as a proliferation of the panopticon, they, in important aspects, depart from Foucault's descriptions. The new electronic technologies seem to have different objectives and employ a different model of individuality from that of traditional disciplines.

As early as 1983, Bottoms suggested that some significant developments in recent penal practice – the greatly increased use of fines, community service and compensation – are not essentially disciplinary in character, precisely because they lack the element of 'soul-training'. He argues that this is made possible by the implementation of more effective social control measures (including technological) within general society, and that the criminal justice system is only the last resort – and thus, juridical rather than disciplinary in nature. Bottoms builds on Foucault's distinction between disciplines as the individualising *'anatomo-politics of the human body'* and the more general bio-power (*'bio-politics of the population'*):

> [W]hat may therefore have been happening in contemporary western penal systems is that, as societal power in the form of 'the bio-politics of the population' has developed (through welfarism, corporatism, technological developments, and so forth), so individual discipline ('the anatomo-politics of the human body') has become less necessary to the penal apparatus. (Bottoms 1983: 195)

Similarly, Zygmunt Bauman argues that today's maximum security prisons are not simply high-tech versions of the panopticon, as may appear at first sight. They fundamentally differ from their predecessors because they 'lack the key qualities of work-related discipline and resubjectification that characterised the latter' (2000: 205). Panoptical institutions were conceived above all as *houses of correction*. Their purpose was to bring the inmates 'back from the road to moral perdition' and subject them to habits that would eventually permit their return to 'normal' society. Instead, prisons today operate as 'factories of exclusion' with few possibilities and illusions of return and reintegration in mind. Of course, one should be wary of suggesting that rehabilitative programmes are on the way out in contemporary prisons. A more accurate description would probably be to say that there has been a certain rearrangement of discourses and objectives when it comes to rehabilitation. As Kevin Haggerty writes:

> While rehabilitation programs certainly continue, they are decidedly scaled down, and public advocacy of the value and possibilities of rehabilitation has markedly diminished. To the extent that the individual continues to be the focus of reform ambitions, these efforts now often concentrate on developing genetic or biochemical interventions. (2004: 217)

What the above-mentioned authors have in common is that they doubt the adequacy of existing pictures of panopticon and disciplination. The French philosopher Gilles Deleuze (1995), a friend of Foucault's, goes as far as to suggest that, in the 1990s, we witnessed a transition from disciplinary societies to *societies of control*. He claims that disciplinary institutional forms such as prisons, schools, hospitals are breaking down and new forms of punishment, education, health care are now being introduced. Comparing the emerging new forms of power with discipline, Deleuze argues that a key feature of 'disciplinary spaces of enclosure', such as the prison, school and factory, is that they are architecturally and hence operationally separate from one another. In societies of control, on the other hand, the various control mechanisms are 'inseparable variations, forming a system' (Jones 2000: 9). The social system is, to a certain extent, unified through its shared language of numbers, a language which is *digital*. Deleuze suggests that in contemporary societies, all social fields are becoming determined by a single, deep, organising logic (Jones 2000: 9). Accordingly, these new institutional forms bring with them fundamental changes in the way in which we understand ourselves and others. The language of electronic databases, numbers and PIN codes brings about a different understanding of people than, for example, a handwritten or a typed file of the previous epochs does. As we shall see later, Deleuze describes this understanding as essentially 'anti-humanist' (Jones 2000), meaning anti-humanist, not only in an ethical sense, but more importantly, that the new technologically driven world brings into question the wholeness and unity of individual human beings themselves.

Deleuze, together with an increasing number of authors (Lyon 1994, 2001, Bottoms 1983, Mathiesen 2000, Norris 2002), points out that the emergence of new technologies has had an important impact on forms of social control and individualisation. The digital language of contemporary technologies seems to create different images and objectives of disciplination and the panopticon. The electronic panopticon, or super-panopticon as Poster (1990) calls it, emerges from a different society with a new set of objectives when it comes to deviance. As Rose describes it:

> In disciplinary societies it was a matter of procession from one disciplinary institution to another – school, barracks, factory ... each seeking to *mould* conduct by inscribing enduring corporeal and behavioural competences, and persisting practices of self-scrutiny and self-constraint into the soul. Control society is one of constant and never-ending modulation where the *modulation* occurs within the flows and transactions between the forces of and capacities of the human subject and practices in which he or she participates. (1999: 234, original emphasis)

Rose's choice of terminology points to a vital distinction between the terms *mould* and *modulate*. The word mould means 'to work into a required shape or form'. To modulate, on the other hand, can be explained as 'to regulate by or adjust to a certain measure or proportion; soften; tone down' (*Webster's Encyclopaedic Dictionary* 1989). It is, therefore, the difference between shaping a person in a fundamentally productive way versus adjusting a person's (pre-existing) shape to a certain level of conduct:

> In our societies of control, it is not a question of socializing and disciplining the subject *ab initio*. It is not a question of instituting a regime in which each person is permanently under the alien gaze of the eye of power exercising individualizing surveillance. It is not a matter of apprehending and normalizing the offender *ex post facto*. Conduct is continually monitored and reshaped by logics immanent within all networks of practice. Surveillance is 'designed in' to the flows of everyday existence. (Rose 1999: 234, original emphasis)

Similarly, the analysts of risk management and actuarial justice point out that the focus of penal policies has shifted from individuals to groups, sorted according to their perceived risk and danger. The purpose is no longer to correct and transform, but rather to categorise and *predict*. As early as 1985, in *Visions of Social Control: Crime, Punishment and Classification*, Stanley Cohen described a reality that, in some aspects, is notably different from Foucault's individualising disciplination:[13]

> '[T]he game is up' for all policies directed to the criminal as an individual, either in terms of detection (blaming and punishing) or causation (finding motivational or causal chains). The technological paraphernalia previously directed at the individual, will now be invested in cybernetics, management, systems analysis, surveillance, information gathering and opportunity reduction. (1985: 147)

A similar point has also been made by, among others, Mathiesen (1983) and Shearing and Stenning (1998), who argue that the growth of private security and private control systems represents an attention shift away from the morally culpable individual to the *categories* of people who create opportunities for disorder. Surveillance has thus become increasingly embedded in other structures and functions of the environment.

## Beyond Foucault

According to Shearing and Stenning (1998), the shift of focus from individuals to categories does not mean that modern systems of social control are not disciplinary. In their view, the concept of 'discipline' does not necessarily involve the element of individualised soul-training. The latter was characteristic only for a historically *specific* concept of carceral disciplination, to be distinguished from Foucault's *general* concept of disciplination. Foucault certainly tends to describe discipline as a general rather than a historically and institutionally specific technology. However, viewed in that way, one is faced with the difficulty of distinguishing between the meaning of discipline and control in general. Is nearly every form of modern control then disciplinary? The crucial issue here seems to be how we define the meaning of disciplination, and whether discipline is a term that should be connected exclusively to Foucault's work. The term discipline usually signifies 'training to act in accordance with rules' (*Webster's Encyclopaedic Dictionary* 1989). In this respect, one can support Stenning and Shearing's argument.

However, contemporary forms of disciplination clearly exhibit tendencies which differ from the ones described by Foucault. At the same time, through the enormous influence of Foucault's work, the words disciplination and panopticon have become almost synonymous with the meanings he has ascribed to them. There is therefore a need for clarification. In addition to the conceptual clarifications, there is also a need to re-evaluate the meaning of disciplination and the applicability of Foucault's work to the present social conditions. Whether or not we name contemporary penal practices disciplinary may be, in the end, of no more than semantic importance. However, what I wish to focus on at this point are the aspects whereby the individual ceases to be the main focus of penal control and is increasingly being replaced by the category. A question that I wish to ask is: what does this 'disappearance of the individual' really mean? Penal institutions are naturally still dealing with people and often see themselves as performing 'helping professions'. However, the language in which they address their clients makes in a number of

13 Cohen (1985), in a number of other aspects, supports Foucault's thesis.

cases individuals' social and cultural characteristics, their distinctly human qualities, less and less distinct.

It should be pointed out that my purpose here is not to describe a coherent 'post-disciplinary' control strategy. The new strategies of control often coexist with the old, disciplinary ones. As Rose writes:

> The diagnostician of control is thus faced with a bewildering complexity rather than a simple shift from discipline to control or from individualization and normalization to actuarial government of groups and populations ... There appears, then, to be no overarching 'post-disciplinary' logic, but rather a multiplication of possibilities and strategies deployed around different problematizations in different sites and with different objectives. (1999: 238, 240)

Contemporary penal strategies seem to be a versatile collection of various (often seemingly incompatible) objectives, ideologies and portrayals of the criminal: from situational crime prevention and zero-tolerance policies to incapacitation and expansion of prisons, electronic surveillance and cognitive skills programmes, to name just a few. Furthermore, there is nothing to indicate that in contemporary societies the subjectifying dimensions of the power of expert knowledge, so vividly described by Foucault, have diminished – quite the opposite. They seem to be exceedingly relevant when it comes to analysing the effects of advertising, consumerism, body politics, etc. The ever growing Foucaultian literature on these subjects seems to support this. The coupling of the individual, body, power and knowledge without doubt continues to be a powerful image in contemporary imagination. The argument, here, is that the subjectifying and individualising dimensions may be weaker in some more recent penal developments.

However, while there are important points of discontinuity and difference between Foucault's 'delinquent' and the categorical individual, there are, at the same time, important points of *continuity*. Most importantly, they are both products of the so called 'power/knowledge' nexus (Foucault 1980). In a similar way as the delinquent's identity was determined by the official scientific norms regarding what is normal and abnormal, so also is the categorical individual defined by official knowledge formats. Categorisation (scientific classification, statistical knowledge, etc) had a prominent place in the disciplinary regime. One may well argue that the trend towards categorisation described above represents nothing radically new. From the late 18th century onwards, penal policies have been characterised by increasing rationalisation, bureaucratisation and systematisation (Garland 1990). These trends are perhaps merely more visible and pronounced now. As Garland (1999) argues, the procedures of examination, assessment and classification that were characteristic of disciplinary regimes did not disappear with the fall of rehabilitation. They were simply used for different purposes, such as measuring security risks or criminal career profiles. In other words, there is perhaps no change, merely 'business as usual', a continuation of certain historic trends that have always been characteristic of modern penality.

Furthermore, it is difficult to overemphasise the influence Foucault's writing carries for contemporary penal research. Foucault's work on governmental rationalities (Foucault 1980, Burchell, Gordon and Miller 1991) has encouraged a widely diverse field of so called governmentality studies which has had considerable impact also in criminology (see, for example, Rose 1999, Garland 1997,

2001). Thus, as some aspects of Foucault's analysis seem to be fading, others remain and are gaining in prominence: most importantly, his power/knowledge concept. Today, official knowledge categories have gained even greater prominence in the functioning of power relations and in defining offenders' subjectivity, sometimes almost creating the impression that life outside the knowledge formats does not exist. This is also suggested in Poster's *Critical Theory and Poststructuralism: In Search of a Context* (1989), where he argues that some aspects of Foucault's methodology are becoming increasingly relevant for analysing power relations in the information age. Foucault's connection between knowledge and power, or better, his refusal to see knowledge and power as two separate entities, is vital for understanding contemporary mechanisms of control. Foucault points to the fact that power relations are essentially exercised through the production of discourse. This, Poster argues, is even more the case today, when it is becoming obvious that contemporary surveillance and the functioning of various social institutions are based on information processing – and therefore an essentially linguistic (discursive) experience.

Therefore, when assessing the relevance of the Foucaultian delinquent, and Foucault's work in general, for contemporary penality, one should keep in mind both the lines of continuity as well as discontinuity. While the paradigms of power/knowledge persist; while scientific classification still thrives, the *nature of knowledge*, however, is undergoing a process of fundamental change. The changes have taken place not only on the level of criminological discourse and official goals, but more importantly in the reforms of decision-making. The penal reforms of the past 30 years have introduced new forms of decision-making and thinking about offenders' identities; they institutionalise and demand a radically different relationship between criminal justice professionals (judges, probation workers) and offenders. One could, of course, suggest that the reforms merely institutionalised 'a power without narrative' which had already existed before, but was not admitted by the official ideology of care and help. An argument can be made that judges, for example, have never really had the time to pay attention to offenders' needs and treat each case according to its merits. However, the systematic acceptance of the 'ideology of categorisation' leads to the creation of a qualitatively (as well as quantitatively) different penal system. The technological incentive behind the standardisation of knowledge in penal systems is a relatively new force that offers different solutions to existing dilemmas and focuses on different problems. Contemporary societies are crucially dependent on, as well as controlled through, their production of knowledge – which is nothing radically new. However, knowledge today is produced and transmitted in computerised form, a fact that needs to be taken into account when exploring contemporary forms of control. Scott Lash makes a similar point:

> [T]he work of Michel Foucault may no longer have as much purchase on the social world as it once had. Power was once largely discursive; it is now largely informational. Power is still very strongly, as Foucault suggested, tied to knowledge, but informational knowledge is increasingly displacing narrative and discursive knowledge. (2002: 3)[14]

---

14 Here, Lash's (2002) understanding of discourse somewhat differs from Poster's (1989), mentioned above. While Poster sees databases as discourses, Lash seems to refer to discursive knowledge in terms of scientific discourses and narratives.

Thus, even though power is still tied to knowledge, this knowledge is now different. While Foucault locates power in the discourse and sees it, therefore, as linear, Lash suggests that the nature of power has changed in the information order: it has become *non-linear*. 'It lies no longer in discourse but in the much shorter and more transient bits and fragments of information' (2002: 189).[15] One of the crucial aspects of disciplinary power was that it thrived on and produced an abundance of explanatory scientific discourses and narratives concerning crime and criminals (legal, medical, psychiatric, etc). On the other hand, contemporary penal power, as represented in the guidelines, no longer asks the questions described by Foucault:

> What *is* this act, what is this act of violence or this murder? To what level or to what field of reality does it belong? ... How can we assign the causal process that produced it? Where did it originate in the author himself? Instinct, unconscious, environment, heredity? ... What would be the most appropriate measure to take? How do we see the future development of the offender? What would be the best way of rehabilitating him? (1977: 19)

Judges were previously bound to do something other than judge (Foucault 1977) – they had to refer to the scientific discourses, define judgments not only in terms of law, but also in terms of scientific knowledge. Now, judicial power no longer seems to be ashamed to punish. It seems to have ceased to look for alternative sources of justification other than its own, pre-defined norms. At the same time, it is losing interest in those who were previously the object of such fervent inquiries – namely the offenders.

Similarly, O'Malley (1992) writes that situational crime prevention theories also replace the disciplines' *biographical* individual with a polar opposition – the abstract *abiographical* individual – the rational choice actor. Garland, in fact, describes the shift from the interest in depth to the focus on the surface as a general trend in contemporary penal theory and practice:

> In criminological discourse, and indeed in crime control policies, there is evidence of what one might term a shift from depth to surface. It was an article of faith for criminological modernism that crime is a symptom of deeper psychological and social problems that must be investigated and treated; that the truth of crime lay deep in the offender's biography and circumstances. Nowadays prominent criminologists are losing interest in criminological depth, and indeed, in criminological truth. (Garland 1999: 524)

While disciplinary power was characterised by its focus on causes of crime, the new penal strategies of risk thinking, just deserts and situational crime prevention refrain from any such considerations. Consequently, considerations of class, gender, ethnicity, poverty, etc are not deemed to be relevant, except in their role as risk-enhancing factors. 'If bothered with at all they are taken to be predictive of behaviours, not explanatory of meaningful actions' (O'Malley 1992: 265). Even though disciplinary power attempted to redefine political dimensions of criminality

15 Lash suggests that Donna Haraway (1996, *Modest Witness*) presents a better picture of the new regime where power and knowledge cannot be separated. They are *fused* together into a technoscientific regime. Here the semiotic (knowledge) cannot circulate in the material, because the semiotic and material are already fused. Systems (both organic and others) thus have to be understood as technological systems they become 'cybernetic systems of information management with military-like structures of command, control, intelligence and communication' (Lash 2002: 190).

into questions of individual abnormality, it still retained certain social dimensions.[16] Crime and criminals were always situated in a certain social context. Contemporary penal policies, on the other hand, see criminal offenders as a-biographical agents and the problem of crime as essentially disconnected from the questions of social justice.

A similar observation has been made by Castel (1991) when writing about a new mode of surveillance based on risk evaluations. Castel suggests that, by replacing the old notion of dangerousness with objective, pre-described risk factors, state institutions are gaining an ability to supervise not only individuals, but are able to develop a general policy for the supervision of large groups. The traditional notion of dangerousness, misplaced as it was, was thought of as an *internal* quality of a subject. One came to it by diagnosis, that is by direct observation of, and a relationship with, a concrete individual. Risk factors, on the other hand, are abstract factors that are deduced from a general definition of the dangers one wishes to prevent. 'To intervene no longer means, or at least not to begin with, taking as one's target a given individual, in order to correct, punish or care for him or her' (Castel 1991: 288). Therefore, what intervention policies address are no longer individuals but factors, statistical correlations of risk. In fact, individuals may not even need to be present. Risk policies, writes Castel (1991: 281), *dissolve the notion of a subject* they deconstruct a concrete individual and reconstruct a combination of signs – a strategy that is essentially similar to the sentencing guidelines' approach. In the context of actuarial justice, individuals are first and foremost related to as members of statistically determined risk groups, and while disciplines are concerned with guilt and other personal faults, risks are highly impersonal (Feeley and Simon 1992).

My objective in summarising the work of the theorists referred to above is to indicate that a number of contemporary penal policies reveal a different strategy of subjection and a different dynamic of power and knowledge from Foucault's disciplinary power. This is perhaps because, as Bottoms contends, controls in other areas of social life have become more efficient. Or perhaps, as Bauman (2000) suggests, because the kind of individuality that was produced by disciplinary training is no longer needed in the context of the information society. Disciplination was, after all, meant first and foremost to control the working class as a precondition of industrialisation. However, the point here is that the offender's 'inner self', so important in previous epochs, seems no longer to be in focus. Now, the question that comes to mind is whether we are dealing with the notion of a self in the first place. The meaning of the word 'individual' was, after all, in its Latin origin *individuum* synonymous with 'indivisible' (Bagge 1998: 9). Are contemporary penal strategies then, by deconstructing offenders' subjectivities, redefining the meaning of individuality? The next chapter, therefore, explores how changes in the meaning of individuality are taking place on several levels in contemporary culture, and furthermore, how these changes may be connected to the cultural impact of the new, technologically-mediated, practices and knowledge.

---

16 This does not mean that categories concerning offenders' social conditions are not present in police databases, risk/needs assessment instruments, etc. On the contrary, Mathiesen (2000), for example, points to the increasing capabilities of contemporary police databases to collect large amounts of 'soft data' (regarding lifestyles, associations, movements of people). However, here, conditions such as unemployment and drug and alcohol use are used as abstract indicators of *risk*, rather than elements of a concrete biography.

# Chapter 5
# Data-vidual

## New technologies, new identities

'Identity' is a term which is probably in danger of becoming overused in contemporary social sciences. I can, for example, borrow at least 20 'identity readers' from my university library, a number of them addressing the issues of identity and cyber culture, virtual culture, the internet, etc. However, while books about identity and cyber culture are gradually filling the bookshelves, the question of how the new technologies reshape identities in everyday penal practices has received considerably less attention (see, for example, Ericson and Haggerty 1997, Jewkes 2003, Lyon 2001). Who are we and, more crucially, *who are the others*, when we communicate about crime and punish with the help of computers? The issue gains additional salience when we are faced with the growing technological paraphernalia used in the present 'war on terror'.

Due to the continuous efforts to fight crime, illegal immigration and terrorism, a large section of EU citizens will probably be carrying a biometric document, an ID card or a biometric passport in the coming years. Biometrics is measurement of the body. Practically, this means that instead of the usual procedure at the border, when we meet the passport officials and they look at our photograph to see if we really are the person on the document, now, a machine will read the document. Our passports will have a chip containing our biological data such as, for example, fingerprints, the shape of our heads or the pattern of our blood vessels in the iris. After reading the chip, a machine will scan our eyes or hands or measure our skulls and then compare the data with the information on the chip.[1] With biometrics, the question of establishing one's identity ceases to be an act of linguistic communication, but rather a question of whether one's body possesses the right 'code' or a 'password' which can be recognised by the technological systems. The point here is that translating human identity into information patterns, which is a task of biometric technologies, not only provides more information and quicker ways of identifying people, it also creates new conceptions of identity. Now, the 'coded body' (Lyon 2003) itself becomes the source of truth and identification. The individual who owns the body is, in fact, seen as unnecessary and, even more importantly, insufficient for identification. Now, only the body can talk in the required ways, through the unambiguous and cryptic language of codes.

I obtained a further glimpse into the changing modes of identification when recently reading an article about the future of written signatures. For most of us, our signature has been the quintessential mark of personal identity, confirming to banks, shops, postmen and marriage registrars that we really are who we claim to be. However, the handwritten signature has always been not only a certificate of identification but also a unique expression of one's personality. The handwritten

---

1 Fingerprinting is today commonly used in Europe for identification of illegal immigrants and asylum seekers, most notably in the EURODAC systems.

signature is an 'extension of the self', rather than simply an external, separate guarantee of one's authenticity. Precisely because of that, some suggest that handwritten signatures will probably not survive the digital age as a means of identification. They will be replaced by digital signatures:

> The pen signature is, it seems, too homemade to survive modernity. It is too human and irregular to match up to the ID standards technology demands, yet not human enough, not reliably irregular enough, to be a natural signature like a fingerprint. (Meek 2000: 20)

As a consequence, the process of identifying oneself to other people and organisations will be essentially altered. No longer does one need to rely purely on one's own memory and skill for identification. Digital signatures, on the other hand, rely on the electronic memories of machines and one's ability to remember passwords. From a means of identification that was an 'extension of the self', reflecting small personal whims and peculiarities, we move to the digital signature which is 'not quite your own, but manufactured elsewhere, written in code too complex to understand, and lent to you on the surface' (Meek 2000: 20).

The question here is whether penal systems, just as border controls, banks and shops, are creating new ways to construct offenders' identities and using new technologies for that purpose. Just as we may be 'losing' our signatures, are we not perhaps losing other attributes that used to tell others who we are? If previously, one tried to express one's personality and social status through handwriting, such personal clues are now far less visible through the impersonal letters of a computer-generated text. How, then, are these clues constructed now? Put another way, to borrow Bøhme's question: 'What possibilities or characteristics must an individual possess in order to participate in the life of society as a whole?' (1992: 46). What are the 'clues' according to which our identities are constructed? Which are the senses that are used in the process? And crucially, are penal systems in some ways adjusting their images of offenders to the limitations and possibilities offered by technology?

Poster suggests that 'a critical understanding of the new communication systems requires an evaluation of the type of subject it encourages' (2001b: 1). He argues that our technically advanced societies are going through a transformation similar to the one that the feudal societies of the middle ages went through with the emergence of an urban, merchant culture. At that stage in history, the exchange of commodities required individuals to act and speak in new ways, which were drastically different from the aristocratic code of honour with its face-to-face encounters based on trust and hierarchical bonds. In merchant cultures, interacting with total strangers, sometimes at great distances, required written documents as an objective guaranteeing of spoken promises, as well as an arm's length attitude even when face-to-face with the other, so as to afford a 'space' for calculations of self-interest:

> A new identity was constructed, gradually and in a most circuitous path to be sure, among the merchants in which a coherent, stable sense of individuality was grounded in independent, cognitive abilities. In this way the cultural basis for the modern world was begun, one that eventually would rely upon print media to encourage and disseminate these urban forms of identity. (Poster 2001b: 1)

Similarly, electronic media today enhance and enable new ways of constructing identities. These, as we shall see, often seem to break with the 'coherent and stable sense of individuality, grounded in independent cognitive abilities' (Poster 2001b: 1).

## Subjects that can be processed as information

> Criminal justice staffs increasingly seek to control offenders using the same techniques they use to control themselves. (Garland 2001: 189)

Looking at the issue of sentencing and categorical identity, presented in the previous chapter, one can notice numerous points of coincidence and similarity with studies into the issues of information technology and identity. Bottoms (1983), for example, points out that habitual exposure to technology does have important implications on everyday consciousness and, furthermore, social control. Among other notions that accompany the use of technology, he also names anonymous social relations, *componentiality* and a componential self. Componentiality is precisely one of the main characteristics that distinguish sentencing guidelines and risk assessment forms from the *holistic* approach of the previous, disciplinary regimes. While the Foucaultian delinquent was being punished for his life – for who he was, rather than what he did – the faith of a categorical individual is decided on the basis of partial, predetermined objective factors.

Furthermore, the decontextualised nature of a categorical individual – the lack of interest in the broader social and personal circumstances and causes of crime – fits into the so called 'data processing model of thought'. Here, the tendency is to make thought processes and communication explicit and clearly defined. The objective and technical understanding of offenders' identities can therefore be seen as part of their transformation into *data* – into formalised information – which, precisely because of its standardised form, is capable of being stored, analysed and communicated in the system. One could say that inherent in the process of categorisation is, not unlike that found in electronically mediated communication, a certain *coding* of language. Creation of a code restricts meaning by closing the semantic field. Code is composed of strong, clear, durable signs. This clarity and stability of language is made possible by the *standardisation* of objects that are described by the code (Poster 2001b). A categorical individual is in many ways a standardised offender – 'a two-dimensional crime and criminal history amalgam' (Tonry 1996: 20). Only by standardising and limiting the number of aspects according to which individuals are evaluated, are contemporary sentencing systems able to create the consistency and rationality that they so highly prioritise. As we have seen earlier, sentencing guidelines exhibit the same striving for sentencing to be a precise science, governed by rules characteristic of computer programs. They share an essential similarity, since they are both characterised by abstractness and decontextualisation. The effectiveness of a database, and one could say the same about the guidelines, lies in its non-ambiguous structure and the elimination of cultural context.

## Data-viduals

> The cultural function of databases is not so much the institution of dominant power structures against the individual as it is the restructuring of the nature of the individual.

> ... [K]nowledge itself is a form of linguistic power, the culturally formative power of subject constitution. (Poster 1996: 190)

In the context of the information society, the database becomes an important cultural form in its own right, just as a narrative was before. As such, the design and qualities, the ontology of the database referred to by Manovich (2001b) may give us some clues as to the process of identity construction. Social actors and agencies that use databases adjust their images of individuals to the fact that these images have to be handled by the database. Thus, the qualities of the database become essential to the process of identity construction. As Bøhme puts it: 'social actors must be disciplined in a way that makes their behaviour amenable to data collection' (1992: 42). In a similar way, the images of offenders handled by sentencing guidelines and sentencing information systems have to be adjusted to the ontologies of these two structures – which share a number of similarities with a database.

Poster describes databases as 'electronic lists' or, using Foucault's term, 'grids of specification' which classify their objects and, in the process, give them additional social identities. The vertical and horizontal fields which constitute the database thus construct individual identities in 'highly caricatured yet immediately available form' (Poster 1990: 96). 'Speed and efficiency of the database varies directly with the fixity of the form in which information appears in it' (1990: 96). The agency which collects information *constitutes individuals* according to these parameters. Poster contends that, just as databases operate by creating relationships among pieces of information which otherwise would not exist outside of the database, so too are individuals constituted through this process of manipulating relationships between bits of information (1990: 96). Therefore, the qualities that render the creation of information possible are also central to the constitution of identity, namely, the fixed definition of symbols and their abstract nature. As already mentioned, computer symbols have to have a fixed, exactly defined meaning to be operable. At the same time, they are always only simulations of reality, which makes it possible further to manipulate and work on them. For that reason, the subject image created in a database is always an abstract simulation open to further manipulation.

As with databases, sentencing guidelines and risk assessment instruments also assign values to various bits of information and create relations between them to achieve a 'score'. A score assigns numerical value to identity. This evaluation is achieved by combining pieces of information in a fundamentally different way from through speech or writing. The database imposes a new language on top of those already existing – a language removed from the context of face-to-face conversation and written narration – an 'impoverished, limited language, one that uses the norm to constitute individuals and define deviants' (Poster 1990: 95). As Sean Cubitt suggests:

> Databasing renders the person as a '*data-image*', a statistically coherent version of the messy human self. It is an engraving of power which, notably in police surveillance of ethnic minorities, inscribes identity. At the same time, if 'it is not that the beautiful totality of the individual is amputated, repressed, altered by our social order, [but] rather that the individual is carefully fabricated in it, according to a whole technique of forces and bodies' (Foucault 1977: 217), then we have to ask whether the data-image is not at all a reduction of the full, 'real' self to 'mere' writing, but the constitution of a new, statistical and distributed self, a deconstructed, fully textual, rewritable file. Is that

> rewrite facility then a door to freedom, or one which, in the malleable form of electronic records, makes us more manipulable and so more predictable? (1998: 20, emphasis added)

For Cubitt, the database brings a 'statistically coherent' version of the self, as well as turning the self into a distributed and deconstructed, fully textual, rewritable file – qualities that may force us to ask where we can draw the line between human subjectivity and objectivity.

In criminology, the 'data-image' of individuality resonates with what Garland (1997) terms 'a *statistical individual*' on an actuarial table. Here, the individual is not viewed as a distinct, unique person, to be studied in depth, but rather as a point on an actuarial table, understood through his relation to the population. The statistical individual is part of so called risk management, primarily focused on dealing with 'risk factor analysis' and 'risk profiles' rather than focusing on individualised intervention. Poster (1996) further argues that the process of subject formation in the database discourse is significantly different from the modern, conscious and 'coherent' subject, exemplified by Foucault's disciplines. In disciplinary power, Poster argues, subjects were constituted through 'subjectification', which gave them 'a (false) sense of their own interiority'. With the database, on the other hand, the process is the opposite, namely that of '*objectification*', of 'producing individuals with dispersed identities, identities of which individuals might not even be aware' (1996: 190).

It needs to be pointed out, however, that the technological developments obviously open up an array of additional issues regarding identity and the self. It is beyond the scope of this book to explore them all. Rather, the focus shall be on those aspects that can be relevant for understanding the shifts in contemporary penalty. Here, the 'data image' of subjectivity may figure more prominently than other, more flexible and playful aspects enabled by the new technological possibilities. Bolter (2001), for example, points out that, unlike the database, other uses of information technology, such as computer games, encourage the spontaneous, playful, personal and social nature of the self – rather than its abstraction and deconstruction. Similarly, Sherry Turkle (1995) describes how new technological developments permit the 'trying on' of different identities, without the demand for authenticity. The experimentation with identity on the internet can be experienced as positive and potentially liberating. It is liberating because, in this world of simulation and experimentation, the self can now be created free from the traditional social divisions of class, race and gender. The field of technology and identity studies, therefore, opens up a vast array of possibilities, where the data-image is only one of many. However, it is the 'data-vidual' that seems to be the most salient for understanding the issues of identity construction within contemporary penality, while the more playful and liberating aspects may be reserved for other social spheres.

## Subjects in a world of objects

> For if the mind is a 'structure' or a 'system' that can be brought within a framework of scientific explanation, what becomes of the distinctively human and free subject or 'self' we take ourselves to be? (Barglow 1994: 12)

Poster (1990) observes that computer-based writing has a number of effects on the subject:

- they [forms of computer writing] introduce new possibilities for playing with identities;
- they degender communication by removing gender rules;
- they destabilize existing hierarchies in relationships and rehierarchizes communications according to criteria that were previously irrelevant; and above all
- they disperse the subject, dislocating it temporally and spatially.

Poster draws our attention to two themes that usually come up in discussions about information technology and identity, namely the possibilities of experimentation with various identities and the dislocation of the subject of communication. Computer communication is marked by a certain anonymity that enables its users to experiment with identities (Turkle 1995), as well as bringing about the notion of having an identity that is somehow unstable and dispersed. A 'long or intensive experience with computer mediated electronic communication is associated with a certain fluidity of identity'.[2] Poster (1990) argues that while modernity tends to constitute identities as autonomous and (instrumentally) rational, the age of information encourages subjects that are unstable, multiple and diffuse. The speed of communication today is such that people now 'float' in an excess of electronically mediated communication. In a media saturated environment, the self becomes unstable and *fragmented*.[3] The internet in particular has raised a number of related questions. As Rheingold asks:

> [A]re relationships and commitments as we know them even possible in a place where identities are fluid? ... We reduce and encode our identities as words on a screen, decode and unpack the identities of others. (Quoted in Poster 2001b)

However, what may be interesting at this point is that contemporary sentencing reforms too are driven by a similar tendency to disconnect the sentencing process from the individual identities of both offenders and decision-makers. This move towards abstractness and anonymity represents a strong break with the sentencing philosophies of the previous epochs, where both the offender's and decision-maker's individuality was the focal point of the sentencing process. Poster's observations are therefore even more relevant: 'What is striking ... is that freedom is now being associated not with the assertion of individual identity in either the public or the private spheres but with complete anonymity' (1990: 119).

---

2 Poster: www.hnet.uci.edu/mposter/writings/internet.html (p 7).

3 There are, however, numerous other accounts of the fragmentation of identity in contemporary life. In *The Corrosion of Character: The Personal Consequences of Work in a New Capitalism*, Richard Sennett, for example, shows how global capitalism frustrates individuals' attempts to achieve a stable sense of identity. Due to constant uncertainty, short-term work, flexible institutions, risk taking and the demands for constant flexibility, it is almost impossible to retain a permanent sense of self and a coherent life narrative. A similar point is also made by Zygmunt Bauman in a series of books about the postmodern self, including *Postmodern Ethics* (1993), *Life in Fragments: Essays in Postmodern Morality* (1995) and *Postmodernity and its Discontents* (1997).

Several authors[4] have suggested that in some respects, the computer calls into question the Cartesian subject (active, unified and integrated by reason), traditionally seen as the cornerstone of modern law, science and democracy. Of course, the Cartesian subject has been justifiably criticised from a number of perspectives. Feminism, post-colonial studies and postmodern theorists have pointed out that its universality has traditionally been constructed on a model of white, Western male, thus suppressing the voices of women, non-whites, the mad and the poor. Now, with the computer, 'I think therefore I am' seems to acquire new undertones. As Poster argues:

> [I]n the Cartesian world, only individual minds have knowledge; the rest of nature is dumb. Now, however, when the subject has access to a database he or she is confronted by a machine that appears to 'know' more than the subject. In a sense, the database is no more than a library, a material world of mental traces. But the speed with which the data is available to the subject in the computerized database changes the subject's experience. (1989: 138)

We have seen that in sentencing information systems (SISs), a decision-maker is faced with a similar dilemma. He or she is faced with an information system that seems to have a far better and more systematic overview of sentencing practice than an individual judge will ever be able to have. This raises the question of whether it is justifiable to protect the model of an autonomous and independent decision-maker, or whether responsibility should be handed over to the man/machine symbiosis. Part of the answer certainly lies in the nature of tasks, which are asked of individual decision-makers. It seems that, as the focus is shifting towards topics that machines are better at, or even exclusively capable of, providing answers to, the insistence on a model of an autonomous decision-maker becomes increasingly difficult. As judges and other decision-makers are required to take into account not only individual but also systematic aspects of their cases, their deficiencies become more obvious, compared with the technological potential.

A similar point is also argued by Raymond Barglow in *The Crisis of the Self in the Age of Information* (1994). Combining critical theory and psychoanalysis, Barglow highlights the paradox that, while contemporary technological environments increase human powers of organisation, they also subvert the traditional Western notion of a unified, independent and sovereign self. For Barglow and his interviewees, the computer brings a technical understanding of individuals and renders superfluous the idea of a distinctly human subject; the 'computer provides a perfect metaphor here: as a model of detached, ownerless cognitive processing, the machine symbolizes an *absent* subject' (1994: 89). He suggests that in computer mediated interactions:

> people not only work with abstractions, but also view themselves and others abstractly. A computer program, whether as simple as a mailing-list application or as complex as an ICBM delivery system, typically works in a context-independent and person-independent way: it is indifferent to the identity of those who operate, benefit or suffer from its operations. (1994: 205)

Barglow points out the possible psychological consequences of the computer's abstract and senseless nature. He presents a fascinating analysis of the dreams and feelings of people working in high-tech environments in San Francisco in the 1990s.

4 See, for example, Barglow (1994), Poster (1989).

Resonating throughout the book is an image of a self that is weak and unstable, almost lost in the highly technological environment. As one person's dream reveals:

> Image of a head … and behind it is suspended a computer keyboard. The keys are being depressed, you can see them going up and down like the keys on a player piano, but *no one is there operating them*. (Barglow 1994: 53, emphasis added)

> I cannot feel warm or cold but have to read the temperature out of the machine. As if someone had to consult a table of numbers to know whether they are hungry or thirsty. At least the Ancient Mariner knew that much about himself! I too am thirsty, thirsty to understand these symbols. I might be hot or cold and not know it. (Barglow 1994: 88)

The experience is similar to that of the workers interviewed by Zuboff (1988) when their jobs had been computerised.[5] In both cases, we witness a 'divorce of rationality from sense experience', where a person 'depends entirely on the computer for contact with his surroundings. An intellectual system filters all the input that crosses the interface between the self and the world' (Barglow 1994: 88). One consequence is a diminished sense of self and trust in one's own judgment, and thus also a diminished sense of personal responsibility.

The divorce of rationality from sense experience seems also to be characteristic of contemporary sentencing reforms. In a way, one could describe sentencing guidelines and information systems as yet another system for filtering inputs and dissociate thinking from lived experience. As with computers, guidelines are also a technical device that helps individuals assess the experiences they have of their environments and people in their surroundings. In both cases, we see an absent subject(ivity) – both on the side of those who operate the abstract system, and on the side of those who are affected by it. At this point, I shall not proceed into the question of a judge's role in the sentencing guideline system and rather focus on offenders' subjectivity – however, the impersonality of the guideline system may have important implications for the ethical nature of sentencing. Defining the world in objective, technical terms that a database can store – as guidelines do – may lead to fragmentation of the shared social context within which ethical issues can make sense in the first place.

As argued earlier, the language of the guideline system is coded and dissociated from the cultural context from which it emerges. It takes little account of the fact that a phenomenon such as bribery, for example, has a different meaning in the cultural context of South Korean society than in US culture. Sentencing guidelines make no distinction. They give the same sentence to a Korean businessman who tries to bribe an official and sees this as a natural and necessary way of doing business, and to an American who is fully aware of other possible options (Forer 1994). For the guidelines, bribery exists as an *objective* category, without a context. As an objective category, bribery, or any other category of criminal acts, is based on

5 As outlined in Chapter 2, Zuboff (1988) describes how the introduction of IT is based on the process of explicating knowledge, and transforming it from a *personal* skill to the impersonal performance of a computer. The implicit knowledge of a worker is gathered and analysed and then translated into a computer program. Knowledge, once bound to the personal experience of concrete, immediate objects, is now 'lifted entirely out of the body's domain' into the abstract domain of information. The computer thus disturbs the unity of experience and knowledge. Work becomes the ability to manipulate data symbols, and workers can no longer 'feel and touch' their work (1988: 63). The statement could be compared to Judge Lasker's complaint regarding the 'desensitising' effects of sentencing guidelines.

what Albert Borgmann (1999) describes as 'technological information' – as opposed to cultural or natural information. Technological information is characterised by its *self-sufficiency* and self-realisation. It can function autonomously and independently from human intelligence and context. As information technology is increasingly used in new domains, these domains transform natural and cultural information into technological information. Borgmann, for example, reports that in agriculture, information technology delivers 'precision agriculture', where activities are measured, monitored and controlled and data gathering automated. However, this kind of transfer has consequences for the nature of knowledge and human competence:

> What in any event is likely to get lost is the symmetry of natural information and human competence that is reflected in this observation: 'My husband knows his cattle personally by working with them and has a memory for traits, problems and style. His father had that trait and so he does and our son seems to have it also.' (Borgmann 1999: 217)

Borgmann argues that something gets lost when technological information displaces natural and cultural information. One important aspect of this loss is the loss of experience:

> '[T]he more knowable the world came to seem as *information*, the more remote and opaque it came to be seen as *experience*.' … In our serious dealings with the world, we generate and possess more information than ever. But reality itself gets ever more deeply buried under all the information we have about it … [T]he reality of persons and things seems offensively heavy and crude. (Borgmann 1999: 218)

Now, the machine is consulted if we want to know whether we are hot or cold (as in the case reported by Barglow), or if a farmer wants to know if his cattle are hungry or thirsty. Are we also in danger then of consulting machines and machine-like systems in order to know what is just or unjust? One can particularly imagine that in sentencing, where decisions are often (emotionally and intellectually) challenging, a seemingly self-assured and infallible machine-driven system may be experienced as a welcome relief from responsibility.

## Government-at-a-distance

> Information technology is good for number crunching, but you don't know the face. (A police officer quoted in Chan 2001: 154)

According to Christie (1993, 2004), one important element that makes (legal and other) forms of categorisation easier is the *distance* between a decision-maker and an offender. Categorising people as criminals and their acts as crime is much less likely in a world where people are personally familiar with each other. Christie points out that when people possess a wealth of contextualised knowledge concerning the circumstances of events and persons, that knowledge breaks down the objectivity of legal categories. However, a vital aspect of information technology is precisely the ability to communicate information over long *distances* and store it in time. This ability to stretch social ties and live life at a distance has considerably changed the way social institutions, including penal systems, function, and the way they are being governed. Garland (2001), for example, talks about 'punishment-at-a-distance' (also Simon 1999). The concept is based on a term, most notably developed by Rose (1996): *government-at-a-distance*, which describes how the technologies of modern government transcend traditional state structures. Contemporary governmental technologies are based on a multitude of networks that link actors at distant sites. As Garland describes it:

> Action-at-a-distance requires that the whole chain of actors can communicate in ways that will be mutually intelligible, that messages or information will not be badly distorted in the process of being translated from centre to locality and back. 'Forms of inscription' – standardized statistical representations, units of measurement, categories, tables, accounting processes, etc – become important as means of enumerating, stabilizing and transmitting knowledge in regularized ways. The development of these standardized units (similar to what Giddens (1990) calls 'symbolic tokens') allow information to be compared, consolidated and combined across time and space. It thus links locales where action occurs to centres of calculation where knowledge can be accumulated and from which action may be directed and orchestrated … (1997: 182–83)

In this model, individual local actors are governed through certain common rationalities and objectives, such as economic success, crime reduction, efficient use of resources, etc. Government-at-a-distance today is essentially 'governance through information' (information having the objective and disembodied qualities described in Chapter 2). In this context, the essence of control and governance has come to be seen as collecting and analysing increasing amounts of information concerning the activities of the various agents and directing their actions through unambiguous messages. In order to gain a better understanding of how government-at-a-distance in fact operates, one needs to look not only at the various discourses (ie, their content), but also at the nature of knowledge and information (ie, the form) upon which these techniques are based.

Communication at a distance is essentially carried out through the process of coding and objectification of language: information should have the same meaning independent of space and time. 'Information at all places at all times,' in fact, means information having the same meaning regardless of context. The individual relationship between the knower and the object of knowledge, therefore, needs to be broken. In the context of a penal system that means that a decision-maker is no longer encouraged to produce data that only he or she, with personal knowledge of persons or events, can interpret. Rather, the system focuses on standardised items that 'can travel' without difficulty. Offenders, therefore, have to be made independent of their social context and dissociated from the decision-maker, in order to be handled by the computer. Or, as in the case of biometrics mentioned in the beginning of this chapter, individuals' identities need to be turned into coded items of information, such as fingerprints, which can be understood by passport officials and police officers anywhere in the world. Most importantly, they can be understood by computers. With biometric technologies, deviance of individuals, or better their risk, are defined by a singular sign or a combination of signs that require no communication with the holder of these signs. All these procedures are in fact designed precisely to minimise the need for any such communication.

Castel (1991) argues that by making intervention policies impersonal, and by breaking the direct relationship between a practitioner and a subject of control, practitioners tend to be reduced to suppliers of information to management. With the help of computerised data processing, administrators achieve almost complete autonomy from practitioners (judges, social workers, police officers, etc). Castel observes that practitioners' roles become auxiliary to that of the manager to whom they simply provide information, which is then processed and distributed in the system. Thus, '[t]hey no longer control the usage of the data they produce' (1991: 293). 'The relation which directly connected the fact of possessing a knowledge of a subject and a possibility of intervening upon him or her (for better or for worse) is shattered' (1991: 293).

Haggerty (2004) argues that the changes in the knowledge structure of penal systems, and the consequent growth of 'technoscientific knowledge' (2004: 222), may be an important reason behind the diminishing power of criminological expertise to influence penal policy. Criminological expertise traditionally focused on addressing individual and social problems, is now replaced by 'technical expertise applied on a routine basis by low-ranking professionals' (2004: 218). The focus is on information gathering, efficient system management and resource allocation. Haggerty describes the case of the New York City Probation Department where low-level probationers now report to computerised information kiosks rather than to human beings:

> Such technologies assist in transforming what was originally envisioned as a 'helping' profession into an agency engaging in routine forms of technological surveillance, with individual officers taking it on trust that their monitoring tools accurately depict the physical location (and occasionally the sobriety) of their *virtual charges*. (2004: 223, emphasis added)

An argument can be made, of course, that there is no substantial difference between probationers reporting by filling out paper forms, as was the case in the past, or reporting to computers (Jacobson 2004). In a way, computerisation is simply one further step in institutionalisation of faceless decision-making and virtual identity.

It seems that the increasing impersonality of contemporary penal decisions is, to a considerable extent, aided by the technological framework in which they are executed, as well as by prevailing philosophical and political beliefs. This development raises a number of questions. Lyon (1988), for example, observes that extending language over space may reduce its capacity to serve as an instrument for emotive meaning. Does the disembodied information that is abstracted from its various social contexts make a penal system less able to respond directly to individual conflicts and emotional situations? If so, how does this change our definitions of justice and conflict resolution? Are we on our way to constructing 'justice-at-a-distance', just as we have 'culture-at-a-distance'? Justice that is impersonal and blind has, after all, always been one of our Western ideals. Would such blindness and impersonality still have the same positive resonance if we describe it as justice-at-a-distance or justice that stays on the surface?

## Staying on the surface

In *Life on the Screen: Identity in the Age of the Internet* (1995), Sherry Turkle suggests that the computer is a driving force behind a new culture of *simulation*, where a computer screen becomes a world in itself and 'reality just one more window, and usually not the best one'. In this cultural environment of simulation, the focus is on surface manipulation, rather than on in-depth understanding. 'Staying on the surface' therefore becomes a cultural phenomenon (Cubitt 2001) and not without resonance in the field of crime control. Computer culture represents a move away from the modernist culture, from the so called 'epistemologies of depth', that saw reality as something logical, having 'depths' that could be understood (Turkle 1995: 47). The modernist view of the world can be characterised as linear, logical, hierarchical, etc. The new technologies, on the other hand, bring into everyday life a set of ideas that are associated with postmodernism.[6] The postmodern world is focused on exploration of surfaces. Turkle contends that computers bring postmodernism into everyday life. Epitomised in the Macintosh, computers introduced a way of thinking that limits itself to surface manipulation, working in ignorance of the underlying mechanisms. A computer screen becomes a world in itself. It encourages people to act, rather than analysing the underlying processes. 'We have learned to take things at interface value. We are moving toward a culture of simulation in which people are increasingly comfortable with substituting representations of reality for the real' (Turkle 1995: 23).

Bolter (1984) makes a similar proposition. He contends that 'men of the computer age seem destined to lose Faustian concern with depth'. 'The rejection of depth for considerations of surface and form, long a feature of modern art, is now spreading throughout our intellectual life' (1984: 220). While previously, the Western character was fascinated with depth and possessed the desire to penetrate the surface of reality (like the traditional Christian preoccupation with the soul as something deep and mysterious, as well as psychology's preoccupation with the unconscious), a computer programmer, on the other hand, is characterised by a dislike for mystery:

> Unexplained and unknown lines of code do not add variety or give his work a pleasant unpredictable turn; they simply mean failure to perform ... A Faustian sense for depth, for understanding, adds nothing to a program's operational success. Turing's man analyses not primarily to understand, but to act. (Bolter 1984: 221, 222)

The soul thus really does become a 'ghost in the machine', a superfluous entity that cannot be grasped with the rationalist vocabulary or represented as a set of easily understood icons. As Bolter somewhat ironically writes, established belief is that 'man is all surface, that there is nothing dark or mysterious in the human condition, nothing that cannot be lit by the even light of operational analysis' (1984: 221).[7] With technology life gets '*flattened* and lifted out' (Lash 2001: 108). I would like to suggest that this is precisely how one could describe categorical identity represented in sentencing guidelines and information systems. The absence of a soul has made the categorical individual flat, and furthermore, the eschewing of social context has 'lifted him out' of his concrete network of social relations.

---

6 I do not wish to suggest, however, that postmodernism should be the preferred theoretical framework for understanding sentencing reforms. While being able to provide some useful images, such as the ones described above, there exists a large body of research pointing to the modernist traits of contemporary penal systems (Christie 1993, Garland 1999).

7 Simon and Feeley (1995: 173) report that the new penology 'has trouble with the concept of humanity'. Similarly to the concept of the soul or the concept of justice, humanity is an idea that can never be fully explicated, made predictable and put into words. Its meaning cannot be represented by following formal procedures, but rather needs to be (internally) understood and experienced.

In the previous chapters, we saw how focus on surface manipulation and the move away from in-depth understanding differs from previous epochs in penal reasoning. While previously penal systems were characterised by the desire to 'penetrate the surface' and to back up its decisions with psychological, psychiatric and criminological knowledge of causes of crime, the focus now appears to be on system management and predictability of decisions. As Garland describes, there has been a more general shift from depth to surface in contemporary crime control policies:

> Pragmatic considerations prompt a return to surface phenomena – to choices and opportunities and rational calculations ... The fact that such policies do not address the 'root causes' or deep-lying problems is not perceived as a failing. Pragmatic considerations prefer available, manipulable surface to hard-to-reach depth ... In these perspectives, the category of the criminal shifts from deep subject to shallow opportunist, from psychological man to situational actor, from a *specific individual* with a history that has to be explored to a *universalized decision-maker* whose behavior can be statistically predicted. (Garland 1999: 524, emphasis added)

Turkle contends that the tendency to work on the surface has become characteristic of many other intellectual domains, thus creating a new cultural sensibility – and our conceptions of human identity are changing accordingly. A number of postmodern theorists have argued that the subject, today, is not alienated, but fragmented. The self is decentred and multiple. Garland (1999), however, doubts that this apparent move away from depth can be regarded as the end of penal modernism and a sign of postmodernism. He warns against 'overstating the resemblances between criminology and broader cultural trends'. However, rather than categorising the concepts at hand as modern, postmodern or late modern, I want to examine here why these developments are taking place. Are we staying 'on the surface' because the technological environments in which we work encourage us to do so; because an exploration of the soul 'would add nothing to a program's operational success'?

Baudrillard (1996) tells us that to celebrate his victory in the first Gulf War, General Schwartzkopf, commander of the allied forces, organised a massive party in Disneyworld. This apparently irrelevant fact resonates with symbolism and irony to many observers[8] of that war. For many, including myself, the Gulf War in 1991 was the first powerful reminder of modern technological capacity for simulation, disembodiment, and consequently, also dehumanisation. Baudrillard's statement (2001): 'The Gulf War did not take place,' still remains one of the most resonating descriptions of that war. As Barglow writes:

> The war seemed to be less a physical then a mental enterprise, fought by smart bombs from a distant aerial perspective that prevented detailed observation of the havoc wreaked below. Wounded and dead were excluded from consciousness, although they might be mentioned for certain strategic purposes. (1994: 26)

The first Gulf War served as an illustration of how modern technology brings a different experience of the battlefield and its victims. Information technology renders the battlefield abstract and remote. A soldier today processes data and

8 The use of the term 'observer', however, may be somewhat misleading with regard to the fact that access to and production of images of war was highly restricted and politically controlled.

images on the screen, remote from the physical realities of war. Images are separated from reality and technological actions from the human consequences they produce. The differences between flying a real plane or throwing real bombs and doing the same thing on a flight simulator (or even playing a computer game) become increasingly smaller. It may be, therefore, no coincidence that a video game called 'America's Army' has become one of the most effective recruiting tools for the US Army (CBS News 2004). Information-processing systems can thus result in the distancing of actors from the consequences of their actions. The abstract nature of technology can lead to the denial of the realities of war, and can thus have profoundly dehumanising consequences (Barglow 1994).[9] Naturally, the growing tide of images, presenting the carnage and atrocities of the present war in Iraq, expose the futility of any attempts to put a humane face on warfare. While the designers of the first Gulf War may have to some extent succeeded in translating warfare into a computer game, this is far from being the case in Iraq today.

Nevertheless, the irony of celebrating the first Gulf War in Disneyland must have been even greater for Baudrillard himself, who describes Disneyland as a perfect model of a simulated world – and which, in fact, typifies to him the consumerist postmodern experience. In this world, the subject's position is reduced to choosing between a number of predefined packages of meaning that require a minimum of creative effort on the part of the individual. He or she has no need to explore the world in order to make sense of it. The themes of Disney-style worlds[10] offer prefabricated and coherent stories that are easy to understand (a trait they obviously share with sentencing guidelines). Here, decontextualisation is of vital importance:

> By pulling meanings out of their contexts and repackaging them in bounded information packets, decontextualisation makes it difficult for people to maintain their coherent understanding about how things work ... In this context, the subject loses its hold on its power to independently make sense of the world, to establish meaning. Specific 'meanings' are presented ready-made, *without negotiation*, and the subject becomes a *consumer of meanings*. (Rodaway 1995: 262, emphasis added)

Is not a judge in the sentencing guideline system, similarly, merely a consumer of meanings about punishment that others have created and prepackaged, leaving him little space for negotiation as well as reducing the need for independent understanding? Now, understanding can be delivered by a 'hotline' or a training manual. As a consumer, the subject is not defined by an individual biography, social history and experiences. He or she does not look for identity within himself or herself, but from the outside. The subject is not a creative and knowing agent, but a passive, insufficient entity, depending on a constant supply of ready-made

9 The dehumanisation present in every form of warfare may in this case be accentuated by the abstract nature of the medium through which the war is conducted. The computer and technical environments in which it operates represent a divorce of rationality from sensory experience. By mapping the world into graphic images on a screen, human individuals are turned into abstract data, distant from their physical and sensory reality. As a consequence, the distinction between human subjects and technological objects seems to diminish. The process of dehumanisation, of denying the subjective qualities of the enemy and turning him into an object, is an essential element of warfare and of war propaganda. However, information technology seems to achieve a similar effect simply by obscuring the physical realities of war.

10 See Shearing and Stenning (1998) about security in Disneyworld.

identities. The subject in itself has, therefore, no coherence; it is just a *collection of characteristics*, gaining a temporary sense of coherence from a growing flow of signs and commodities around it (Rodaway 1995). This passive subjectivity, fragmentation and lack of biography are certainly traits which consumers also share with categorical offenders, described above.

## Di-viduals

Richard Jones (2000) suggests that contemporary control societies tend to foster an understanding of people that is essentially 'anti-humanist'. He builds on Deleuze's (1995) contention that there has been a break with the modernist understanding of individuality. For the modernists, the individual was the smallest possible socio-political unit, not able to be subdivided any further, the social 'atom'. Now, on the other hand, further division is possible and indeed happening. Deleuze suggests that we are no longer dealing with the old dichotomy between the mass and the individual. Masses today have become samples, data and markets, and individuals have become 'dividuals'. They are something that can be divided further, that is not whole, thus negating a centred notion of subjectivity. As Rose suggests:

> [W]e are not dealing with 'individuals' but with 'dividuals': not with subjects with a unique personality that is the expression of some inner fixed quality, but with elements, capacities, potentialities. These are plugged into multiple orbits, identified by unique codes, identification numbers, profiles of preferences, security ratings and so forth … (1999: 234)

If the Foucaultian delinquent was characterised by his uniqueness and the importance of his biography, the contemporary (in)dividual seems to be quite the opposite. Often, penal strategies appear to dispense with the notion of a subject altogether. There is no clear link or connection which would provide the various parts of identity (the so called 'factors') with a sense of unity, or even less, uniqueness. Where the previous epoch looked for the underlying psychological or environmental causes of crime, today it is no longer clear that an individual is a 'unit' of discourse in the first place (or that he or she has a biography which can provide a certain sense of continuity and meaning).

Lianos and Douglas make a similar point. They suggest that contemporary systems of social control, based on automation and the use of information and communication technologies, dispense with the need for dealing with an integrated and coherent self:

> An integrated, coherent self is not necessary for dealing with an automated system because the system has its own unshakeable coherence into which it incorporates the acts of its users on a strictly delineated domain; the rest of the user's identity is simply meaningless each time. The fact that ASTE [Automated Socio-Technical Environments] are one-faceted, monosemic environments turns their users from coherent actors into mere fragmentary 'activators'. (2000a: 265)

The unity and coherence of the system now appears to replace the unity and coherence that an individual used to represent.[11]

However, it could be argued that the notion of a coherent self is itself a social construction and, in fact, an illusion. It has been pointed out that the idea that people live (and should live) their lives as coherent and internalised life stories or narratives has in itself distinctly modern traits, rather than being an ahistoric characteristic of human identity. In an essay entitled 'The biographical illusion', Pierre Bourdieu writes that 'one cannot evade the question of the social mechanisms which favour or permit the ordinary experience of life as a unity and a totality':

> The social world which tends to identify normality with identity understood as the constancy to oneself of a responsible being that is predictable, or at least intelligible, in the way of a well-constructed history (as opposed to a history told by an idiot), has available all sorts of institutions of integration and unification of the self. (2000: 299)

The tendency to consider human identity in terms of a coherent life history (with a meaning) is certainly evident in the long literary tradition of the modern novel, particularly in biography and autobiography as a genre, as well as in cinema stories and in a number of discourses in the social sciences and the humanities. Giddens, for example, sees the autobiographical narrative as an essential part of self-identity in modern life, which needs constantly to be worked on and reinforced (1991: 76).[12]

## Virtual identity

By contrast, the world represented on the computer screen is a world which introduces a different experience of identity. It is a world where coherent narratives and stable meanings give place to fluctuating information patterns, and where one is accustomed to dealing with representations instead of reality:

> With computers we can simulate nature in a program or leave nature aside and build second natures limited only by our powers of imagination and abstraction. The objects on the screen have no simple physical referent. In this sense, life on the screen is without origins and foundation. It is a place where signs taken for reality may substitute for the real. Its aesthetic has to do with manipulation and recombination. (Turkle 1995: 47)

A question can be asked whether decontextualised offenders in the world of sentencing guidelines similarly represent mere simulations of nature. They resemble two-dimensional crime and criminal history constructs rather then three-dimensional human beings. One could say that their identity has been manipulated in order to fit into the design of an abstract system. Has not a subjectivity which has been dissolved into factors and taken out of the social world entered a new level of objects which 'have no simple physical referent' (Turkle 1995)? The world of sentencing guidelines and sentencing information systems in many ways resembles the new culture of information where digital symbols replace concrete, embodied entities, and where decision-makers simply become 'symbolic analysts'. Are we then approaching a 'condition of virtuality'?

11 A similar observation is made by Simon (1993) in his study of parole in the US.

12 For a forceful argument for the importance of narratives and 'narrative studies' in understanding criminal offending and desistance, see Maruna (2001).

Katherine Hayles describes virtuality as the 'cultural perception that *material objects are interpenetrated by information patterns*' (1999: 13, emphasis added):

> [L]iving in a condition of virtuality implies we participate in the cultural perception that information and materiality are conceptually distinct and that information is in some sense more essential, more important, and more fundamental than materiality. (Hayles 1999: 18)[13]

Hayles raises a crucial question concerning whether embodiment is essential to understand human beings, and how essential is embeddedness in the material world for governing social life? If we accept the view that people can be dematerialised into information patterns, disembodied and decontextualised symbols become the primary point of reference for a penal system when it comes to constitution of identity. The influx of personal and unformatted language and experience is limited. As a consequence, the need for an individual's presence is reduced. He or she can be acted upon at-a-distance. As Poster points out, the subject becomes 'capable of being acted upon by computers at many social locations without the least awareness by the individual concerned, yet just as surely as if the individual were present somehow inside the computer' (1996: 185).

Creation of a 'virtual identity' is, according to a number of authors, a necessary condition for the functioning of contemporary society, and consequently an increasingly important part of contemporary forms of social control. As Rose writes:

> It is impossible to participate in almost any contemporary practice without being prepared to demonstrate identity in ways that inescapably link individuation and control. The modes of identification are multiple: computer-readable passports, driving licenses with unique identification codes, social insurance numbers, bank cards, credit cards ... Each card identifies the bearer with a *virtual identity* – a database record storing personal details – whilst at the same time allowing access to various privileges. Each access to such a privilege, for example the purchase of an item using a credit card, entails a further entry upon the database, a further accretion to the virtual identity. (1999: 240–41, emphasis added)

Rose draws our attention to the fact that virtuality cannot be understood fully without grasping its usefulness to the exercise of contemporary power and control. Even though the extent to which our everyday lives are penetrated by information technology may be in many ways quite limited (and to some social groups almost irrelevant), its influence on the exercise of power is nevertheless considerable. As Hayles points out, it is no accident that the condition of virtuality is most pervasive and advanced where centres of power are most concentrated. Power relations in the technologically advanced societies seem to be intrinsically connected to the processes of creation of virtual identities – that can be handled by, and are compatible with, the new information and communication technologies. Furthermore, through the move towards increasing categorisation (rather than individualised normalisation), contemporary penality too may be coming closer to the condition of virtuality: a condition where individuals are 'interpenetrated by

13 However, virtuality is a wide concept which has been used in a number of contexts, particularly with reference to the internet. It will be used here as a term to describe the disembodied and decontextualised approach to the self – especially with respect to providing better understanding of the processes of identity construction in contemporary penality. See, for example, Jones (1997).

information patterns' and where, in fact, these information patterns are more important and more essential than individuals themselves.

Hayles argues that if we wish to contest what these technologies signify, we need histories that show the erasures which went into creating the condition of virtuality, in this case the erasures which went into creating decontextualised offenders or offenders seen as essentially information patterns as well as visions arguing for the *importance of embodiment*. Hayles therefore sees the contextualised individuality (and narrative identity) as one way of working against and balancing off the dominance of information patterns.[14] However, Baudrillard (1983, 2001) goes beyond the simple division between the real and the virtual, and paints a slightly more pessimistic picture. He points out that in contemporary simulation culture, the real becomes almost superfluous. He contends that, unlike previous epochs, ours no longer creates abstract models in order to mirror and explain the real. Baudrillard goes a step further. Today, the objective is to make the real coincide with the simulation models. The real is therefore produced in the process of simulation.[15] The real is produced from miniaturised units, from matrices, memory banks and command models – and with these it can be reproduced an indefinite number of times:

> It is no longer a question of imitation, nor of reduplication, nor even of parody. It is rather a question of *substituting the signs of the real for the real itself*; that is, an operation to deter every real process by its operational double, a metastable, programmatic, perfect descriptive machine which provides all the signs of the real and short-circuits all its vicissitudes. (Baudrillard 2001: 170, emphasis added)

Baudrillard's writing may at first seem too far-fetched to provide any insight into contemporary penal practice. However, it may also serve as a provocation to ask whether, in some cases, contemporary penal practice is not 'substituting the signs of the real for the real itself', and whether sentencing guidelines, risk assessment instruments and SISs are in some aspects not models which replace 'real process by its operational double that short-circuits all its vicissitudes' (2001: 170). According to Baudrillard's somewhat exaggerated description, contemporary culture is not only in danger of replacing the territory with the map (ie, the real with the simulation). We have gone a step further and are in danger of taking the 'map', the simulation, for the real thing. Thus, the metaphysical effort that went into understanding the dialectics between abstraction and reality – between the universal and the concrete, now becomes unnecessary. Contemporary information systems are tools for action rather than deep understanding. In contemporary sentencing practice, this would mean that a decision-maker is no longer 'doomed' to the eternal dichotomy between universal norms and concrete cases that never seem to 'fit'. Sentencing

14 I wish to point out here that, despite the critical tone, I do not wish to be seen as regretting that past concepts are undergoing change. As Foucault vividly points out, the delinquent and the concept of subjectivity he or she was based on was deeply entwined with relations of domination and oppression. A critical view of the present, therefore, does not carry a hope for the restitution of the past, but rather one of raising awareness and promoting discussion concerning the contours of a future that is becoming visible in the present.

15 It may be argued, of course, whether there is any such thing as 'the real', referred to by Baudrillard. While Baudrillard frequently uses the term reality, I prefer to use terms such as concrete, embodied and contextualised.

guidelines fit by definition, because they simply replace the 'territory with the map', or, as Hayles would put it, the material with the information patterns.

In fact, in a number of areas today, physical presence is no longer necessary to the purpose of social action.[16, 17] We pay our bills on the internet or with credit cards, borrow books, work and make conversations at-a-distance. Increasingly, we may notice that banks, airline companies, university administrations and various government agencies experience the embodied presence (even a voice on a telephone) from their customers as a nuisance, and prefer their online selves. To repeat Bøhme's question: '[W]hat possibilities or characteristics must an individual possess in order to participate in the life of society as a whole?' (1992: 46). One can say that, in a number of contexts, also when it comes to social control, these characteristics do not have to include an embodied self.

## Power to create a self

My intention is not to argue that the new type of social control described here operates with no notion of an individual at all, or that it has no effect on the individual. Quite the opposite. Mark Poster, when analysing data surveillance (the so called 'superpanopticon'), makes an important point. Whether the individual is aware of it or not, the database does in fact *create a self* for each individual. Jon Bing describes this self created in databases as the 'electronic double' (1991: 12).[18] The double may share certain qualities with an embodied individual, such as name, age, address, etc, but it is also quite different. The average Norwegian would probably have at least 100 electronic doubles in the various databases (1991: 12). Bing suggests that in some ways, these doubles are more important than the real person. Without the information recorded in databases, an individual could not vote, obtain a bank loan or a driving licence, etc.

In the same way, this replicated self is also effective for the purposes of social control. As Poster suggests:

> If Bentham's panopticon strove to alter the prisoner, to change one centered subject (the criminal) into another (the bourgeois), the superpanopticon *supplements* and complicates the self by *constituting another self* for that individual, one that may be as socially effective as the self that walks in the street. (Poster 1989: 123, emphasis added)

One could thus say that the replicated self replaces the soul-searching and examination of individuality for the purposes of social control. Therefore, even if

---

16 Jones (2000) suggests that as classical mechanisms such as work lose their power to integrate, integration by means of data and networks will become more important. We are on the way from a work society to a *registration society*. In technological civilisation, physical presence is increasingly becoming superfluous to social action – the social existence of the individual has been transferred to a juncture of terminals, connections and credit cards. Consequently, new forms of social control (at-a-distance monitoring) are taking form, where decisions are made automatically by the system, forming what Jones terms a *'digital rule'*.

17 It may be interesting to remember, however, that as early as the beginning of the 19th century, the Russian writer Gogol, in his *Dead Souls*, described the possibility of a person existing only for bureaucratic purposes, regardless of their physical presence, or indeed, existence.

18 'Elektroniske dobbeltgjenger' in Norwegian.

penal systems are not interested in 'genuine' individuality,[19] ie, individuals in the flesh – even if what they operate with no longer resembles reality – they still create their own models of subjectivity, which are quite adequate, and probably even better suited for the purpose of certain governmental strategies. At the same time, we need to remember that both models of the self presented here – the Foucaultian delinquent and the categorical individual – are models created for the purpose of social control. The Western preoccupation with depth, with the human soul, has its origins in the Christian tradition of confession. According to Foucault (1978), this preoccupation with the soul and the need to go beneath the façade of human behaviour was later taken over by psychology and psychiatry in their preoccupation with the unconscious. In both cases, Foucault points to the control strategies implicit in these conceptions of individuality.

It has often been pointed out that Foucault's analysis of power lacked a coherent strategy for fighting domination. The omnipresence of power which he described often inspired readers with a sense of pessimism. One possible strategy of resistance, indicated by Foucault himself, was that to fight against state power is to fight against the individuality which has been imposed on us, since the comprehensive web of state controls go hand in hand with increasing specification of individuality:

> [T]he political, ethical, social, philosophical problem of our days is not to try to liberate the individual from the state, and from the state's institutions, but to liberate us both from the state and from the type of individualization which is linked to the state. We have to promote new forms of subjectivity through the refusal of this kind of individuality which has been imposed on us for several centuries. (Foucault 1983: 216)

However, contemporary penal strategies hardly show the same interest in individuals' identities as before. Today, institutions of social control are capable of creating their own individuality without the direct participation of those being controlled. As Poster writes regarding data surveillance:

> the individual is 'spoken' about in the communication between memory banks of agencies, without knowing anything about the 'conversation' ... The individual is politically controlled because decisions are made ... in which the individual has lost the power to respond directly. (1989: 136)

Similarly, in sentencing guidelines, a judge no longer needs to examine an individual's lifestyle. If a criminal is turned into a 'two-dimensional crime and criminal history amalgam', a database can contain all the information a judge needs (Tonry 1996: 20). One might wonder whether the presence of an individual in the flesh is still necessary. Simon points to the interesting fact that, in the sentencing guideline system, many defence lawyers allow their clients to go unaccompanied to the interview with a probation officer (1995: 17). They believe that the facts

19 My point here is not to claim that anything we might call 'real' or 'genuine' individuality in fact exists. Rather, what I am interested in is how penal systems construct the notion of individuality and how they use it in their control strategies. Even though the 'real self' may be described as a socially and historically specific construction, even an illusion, there still exist culturally specific notions of the self. These are the objects of this study.

produced by this oral examination about the offender's background do not matter under the current system. By contrast, information relevant to evaluating criminal conduct and history is tightly controlled by the defence lawyers, who communicate directly with the probation officer – in writing. Therefore, the point may no longer be to rebel against our individuality – against 'who we are' – as was Foucault's message.[20] Today, penal strategies are increasingly gaining the ability to bypass having to deal with individuality.

In *The Rise of the Network Society*, Manuel Castells refers to Alain Touraine, who suggests that in post-industrial societies '[i]t is the defense of the subjects, in its personality and in its culture, against the logic of apparatuses and markets, that replaces the idea of class struggle' (1996: 23). Castells suggests that this distance between the abstract nature of power relations and concrete identities of individuals is a general trait of contemporary social relations, driven by the force of so called 'informationalism'. While acknowledging the effects that informationalism (and the emerging network society) have on people's identities, Castells also underlines the increasing *distance* between '*the Net and the Self*', between globalisation and identity:

> [It follows] a fundamental split between abstract, universal instrumentalism, and historically rooted, particularistic identities. Our societies are increasingly structured around a bipolar opposition between the Net and the Self. (Castells 1996: 3)

Castells, therefore, unlike Barglow (1994), points to identity as a sphere outside the network's influence – even more, as a place of possible resistance against globalisation, markets and networks:

> When the Net switches off the Self, the Self, individual or collective, constructs its meaning without global, instrumental reference: the process of disconnection becomes reciprocal, after the refusal by the excluded of the one-sided logic of structural domination and social exclusion. (Castells 1996: 25)

Therefore, perhaps a new line of critique and resistance needs to be directed at placing the embodied individual back on the social stage – a stage increasingly being overtaken by the technological.

---

20 This at least seems less to be the point of penal strategies. However, individualising techniques are present in other spheres of contemporary social life, such as advertising, popularised medicine, psychology, television, etc, and are perhaps more intrusive than ever.

# Chapter 6
# From Faust to Macintosh

## The story of Faust

The figure of Faust has held a special place in people's imagination for centuries. Faust was reputedly a German fortune-teller and magician. He lived in the 16th century, in various university cities in Germany, and travelled around the country performing tricks. Several scholars of his own time described him as a charlatan, while others reported that he was a respected citizen, under the patronage of the archbishop of Cologne. By the late 16th century, the stories of Faust's supernatural powers were widely told and believed by his contemporaries, including Martin Luther and Melanchton.[1] Faust is not primarily known for the actual events of his life, but rather for the legends about him that later formed the basis for a number of literary and musical works. The first story was printed in 1587 by Johann Spies and published in Frankfurt. According to this narrative, Faust made a pact with the devil, called Mephistopheles, and exchanged his soul for 24 years of pleasure, power and knowledge of magic. After 24 years, the devil carried Faust to hell, and Faust repented for having made the pact. In this version, Faust's story represented the old myth about the struggle between good and evil for a man's soul.

The story was then retold many times, most notably in 1832 by the German poet and playwright Johann Wolfgang von Goethe.[2] Goethe's version differs from the previous narratives in that Faust makes the pact with the devil because he genuinely desires to extend the limits of his knowledge and the general progress of society. In the end, Goethe saves Faust by bringing about his redemption. Goethe transformed the story of Faust from a morality play about the fight between good and evil into a symbolic drama of modern man seeking self-realisation and creativity. With his self-consciousness and identity crisis, Faust's character appealed to the Romantic age, and the story was retold several times throughout the 19th and 20th centuries. Goethe's Faust also powerfully represented the thirst in his age for new knowledge, and the dangers that came with it. It is perhaps no coincidence that the first story of Faust was published at the time of important scientific and geographical discoveries, and Gutenberg's invention of print, threatening the then acknowledged religious and social order. In a way, Faust was the embodiment of the dangers that new secular knowledge represented to Christianity. In fact, Faust was long identified with Gutenberg's collaborator Johann Faust, thus unconsciously representing the dangers that printing seemed to bring.

Marshall Berman (1988) has persuasively argued that Faust is in fact a *tragedy of development* and represents a potent image of the contradictions of modern science and development. Faust envisions and strives to create a world of unlimited social

---

1 Sources: WorldAlmanac: http://firstsearch.oclc.org/WebZ/.

2 After Goethe's text, there are three other works that should be mentioned: the dramatic epic *Faust* by Nikolaus Lenau (1835), Heinrich Heine's *Faust* (1851) and the novel *Doktor Faustus* (1948) by Thomas Mann.

growth and scientific progress. However, this development does not come without a price. This is the meaning of Faust's relationship with the devil: 'human powers can be developed only through what Marx called "the powers of the underworld", dark and fearful energies that may erupt with a horrible force beyond all human control' (Berman 1988: 40). Only by working with and through the destructive powers (the devil) was Faust able to create anything in the world. The message is that progress, science and knowledge do not come without a price. They involve tragic acts such as the disposing of certain categories of people who are in the way of progress and who are regarded as obsolete – personified most obviously in Goethe's inclusion of the figures of Philemon and Baucis (from Greek mythology) in his *Faust*.[3]

The story of Faust, therefore, brings the awareness that every act of creation will also be an act of destruction and that this inevitably has its human cost. Society (personified in Faust's drive for development) has to pay a price for development and progress. It has to enter a 'Faustian bargain' where its soul is at stake. Berman points out that Goethe's *Faust* presents one of the earliest and most potent critiques of modernity (represented in socialism and capitalism), with its unlimited belief in material and scientific progress. The Faustian science and technology are driven by guilt, anguish and contradictions. They are a Faustian bargain in which something is created but something else is destroyed.

## Turing's man

The essential aspect of Faust's contract with the devil is that he, as a person, is changed in the process of obtaining knowledge. This is why the allusion to the soul is vital. According to David Bolter (1984), Faust's story symbolises the fact that, traditionally, learning in Western culture has been seen as a long and painful process, which brings with it the personal transformation of the person involved. The most important answers and the most profound truths have always seemed difficult and remote. The knowledge to which Faust aspired demanded years and years of study and a pact with the devil. Learning was a long and painful personal effort, a spiritual and physical journey, or as Bolter argues – *a quest*. The quest for knowledge (as well as God) has been one of the central themes of Western European literature. 'The man on a quest had to go to the ends of the world to learn his difficult lesson; in general, he changed in the process' (Bolter 1984: 223).

The same, Bolter says, cannot be said of the computer (or Turing's) man. The nature and expectations of knowledge have changed in contemporary, computer mediated culture. Now, the goals that we set for ourselves are not something remote, hidden and deep, where we are at risk of the ultimate failure. Computer programs take place in a restricted universe, where one looks for solutions to well defined problems in accordance with a strict set of rules. The computer programmer:

3 Philemon and Baucis are an old couple who own a small piece of land and a cottage on the coast. They offer aid and hospitality to shipwrecked sailors and wanderers. Faust views them as an obstacle in his path to creating a large observation tower on the coast. He offers them money to resettle, but they refuse to move. At last, he has to call in Mephisto's men and orders them to get the old couple out of the way (Berman 1988).

> remains in the confined logical universe of his machine, rearranging the elements of that universe to suit the current problem. The programmer remains the same and the world changes around him. Self-knowledge is not particularly his goal; self-improvement may be a goal, but this is understood in practical terms as increased efficacy … In the process, he learns nothing more than he put there himself, for he *does not discover* his world so much as *invent it*. (Bolter 1984: 223, 224, emphasis added)

Throughout this book, the question has been raised and argued that some contemporary sentencing reforms, most notably represented in numerical sentencing guidelines and sentencing information systems, bear an essential similarity to this restricted universe of computer programming. A vital part of the project of achieving consistency and proportionality in sentencing has been to specify in advance and, therefore, limit the number of factors that are the basis for sentencing decisions. Like computer programs, sentencing guidelines and sentencing information systems (SISs) wish to limit the influx of new terms and experiences. The goal of proportionality in sentencing is a well-defined goal. It is based on a belief that there is 'no mystery' in sentencing; that it can be made transparent and implemented within the matrix-framework.

In that context, a sentencing judge is not, to use Bolter's terms, a person on a quest, but rather the user of an algorithm invented by others. He or she is not meant to enter a process of 'discovery' (with the possibility of failure), but rather resembles Bolter's Turing's man, who plays games over and over again, saved from the dangerous paths and the possibility of ultimate failure. For Turing's man, and one can say the same about sentencing guidelines, SISs and risk instruments, knowledge is a *process*. It is defined primarily by its form, not its content. The objective is not primarily to understand, but to act:

> In his own way, computer man retains and even extends the Faustian tendency to analyze. Yet the goal of Faustian analysis was to understand, to 'get to the bottom' of a problem; it divided an issue painstakingly into parts in order to build a clear picture of the interrelations. Turing's man analyzes not primarily to understand but to act. (Bolter 1984: 221)

Similarly, we have seen that Foucault's delinquent, and the scientific and correctional apparatus around him, was trapped in the compulsion to 'know the truth', to know the individual and his 'inner workings' and to understand the causes of crime. On the other hand, the knowledge apparatus built around the categorical individual seems to be free of such compulsions. However, this inability to get 'to the bottom' of things does not prevent penal systems from acting as if they did. Categorical identity is, therefore, more of an operational concept, a conscious 'simulation of reality', that can be constructed and deconstructed in accordance with the wishes of its creators.

Lash (2002) observes that the technological culture represents an important change in the nature of reflexivity: traditionally, reflection was intended to gain some deeper knowledge of ontological structures (aimed at deep meaning, as distinct from the trivial). It presupposed the distancing of the reflector from everyday life and a separate *space for reflection*. However, in technological forms of life, Lash argues, knowledge no longer reflects on doing – doing is at the same time knowing (2002: 17). Nowhere is this more obvious than in the case of contemporary penal forms and guidelines. These are instruments of action, where the questions addressed to a decision-maker are not (deep) ontological and ethical questions (such as deciding about 'good and bad'), but rather empirical questions of the type 'how many prior convictions' and 'association with predominantly pro-criminal peers'. Unlike Faust's story, where there is a place for words such as good and bad, God and the devil, the new, technologically mediated world tends to eschew moral considerations of acts and individuals and replaces them with partial, technical evaluations. As one probation officer said in conversation: 'We no longer ask "Is he a good lad or is he a bad lad?" Now, it's all about evaluating risk and filling in the forms.' It seems as if human interaction is never long enough and unregulated enough to allow space for value judgments (Lash 2002). Interaction is no longer spontaneous, but rather tends to be interrupted, divided into units, and mediated by scientific instruments that further analyse these units of interaction and prescribe further action.

Furthermore, it is easy to see that answering questions such as 'age of first substance use?' does not really require a large amount of experience or represent a challenge to the mind. To paraphrase Lash, such reflexivity is close to becoming a 'reflex' (2002: 17). It does not involve a dialectic between theory and practice, but rather a fusion of theory and practice. As a result, a decision-maker's role is fundamentally changed. He or she is no longer a person who reflects, who discovers meaning and makes sense – who possesses an 'expressive subjectivity'. He or she becomes an 'account-giver':

> [S]ense-making loses its interiority. There is flattening of the interiority of the subject … Expressive subjectivity presumed consciousness as an interior monologue. Meaning was somehow in consciousness. One made meaning for oneself. In technological forms of life, sense-making is for *others*. Sense-making is account-giving, it is 'glossing', it is *communication*. Sense-making or knowledge is the glossing, the account-giving of everyday activities that is inseparable from those activities. Reflexivity in the technological culture is not a separate process of reflection. There is no time, no space for such reflection. (Lash 2002: 17–18)

The focus of judicial activity, therefore, shifts from reflection on the concrete circumstances of a case and the legal and ethical principles involved, to communication (account-giving) concerning judges' own decisions to the system. The question is not primarily whether a decision was appropriate or just, but rather whether it follows the prescribed procedural standards and is properly accounted for.

Here, we can detect a certain cultural move from a condition where 'the transcendental was the essential part of human culture and thought' to a state where everything is swept into 'the general plane of immanence' (Lash 2002: 9). There is nothing more to aspire to than concern with procedures, systems and goals. Sentencing, like computer programming, is, to borrow Bolter's (1984) words, becoming a *finite* activity. While the traditional Western or Faustian quest for knowledge (as well as God, beauty or justice) was characterised by its striving for the transcendence of the present, the computer culture is not able to cope with this possibility. Computer programs are finite sets of rules. They always proceed to a predetermined goal, achieved by a finite number of steps. The problems that programmers choose, the goals they set, are those that are accessible – those that can be handled by logical calculus, by repetition and in a limited period of time. The future is simply being determined by the present.

While transcendence is based on the existence of certain space for (critical) reflection and a conception of reality that is different from the one at hand, contemporary penal systems seem to be systematically closing off this possibility and are instead building upon the immanence of information. In many ways, contemporary sentencing reforms that have resulted in sentencing guidelines and information systems are adjusting the idea of justice to this finite world of computational logic. While justness was previously a concept (perhaps an ideal) that somehow eluded pinning down and explication, the sentencing reforms of the past decades have done just the opposite. They have tried to pin down the idea of justness and often turn it into an exact combination of steps that judges need to follow. In the extreme, sentencing guidelines quite literally turned the idea of justice into an algorithm. To talk about 'infinite justice', therefore, becomes a paradox in more than one way. Perhaps 'transparent justice' would be a better expression?

## The story of Macintosh

> There was nowhere visible to dive. (Sherry Turkle)

Ever since its creation, the Macintosh seems to have had special meaning to its users – one could almost call them 'followers'. A number of my colleagues still fervently argue its superiority over other personal computers whenever the opportunity arises. When it first appeared 20 years ago, 'the Mac' was different from most computers of its time. It dispensed with complicated programming languages. With its user-friendly interface, easily navigated by the mouse, the Mac and its clones became widely adopted. As one of its users, writer Howard Rheingold, remembers:

> It was the first PC that was actually an extension of my mind. As a writer, I had forced myself to learn geeky command lines for CP/M and DOS. Now I could point and click. It was like turning on a whole new lobe of my brain. (*Wired News* 2004)

In fact, it can be said that 'every personal computer these days is essentially a Macintosh clone' (*Wired News* 2004).

Rheingold's statement points to a particular aspect of the Macintosh which illustrates one of the central arguments of this book, namely, its *transparency*. Webster's Dictionary defines 'transparent' as:

- having the property of transmitting rays of light through its substances so that bodies situated beyond or behind can be distinctly seen …
- open; frank; candid ...
- easily seen through, recognised, or detected.

The word 'transparent' is usually opposed to 'opaque' or 'secretive'. However, in *Life on the Screen: Identity in the Age of the Internet*, Sherry Turkle describes how transparency has gained a new meaning in contemporary culture. The arrival of the Macintosh computer has given transparency yet another meaning, besides openness and visibility. The Macintosh symbolises the ascendance of a different way of understanding and working; it symbolises a mode of thought based on working on the *surface* of things rather than on in-depth understanding. 'The Mac', unlike earlier computers:

> encouraged users to stay at a surface level of visual representation and gave no hint of inner mechanisms. The power of the Macintosh was how its attractive simulations and

> screen icons helped organize an unambiguous access to programs and data. The user was presented with a scintillating surface on which to float, skim, and play. There was nowhere visible to dive. (Turkle 1995: 34)

In this context, the term 'transparency' described this new visibility and ease of understanding:

> [W]hen, in the mid 1980s, users of the Macintosh began to talk about transparency, they were talking about seeing their documents and programs presented by attractive and easy-to-interpret icons. They were referring to *having things work without needing to look into the inner workings* of the computer. ... By the end of the decade, the word 'transparency' had taken on its Macintosh meaning in both computer talk and colloquial language. In a culture of simulation, when people say something is transparent, they mean that they can easily see how to make it work. *They don't necessarily mean that they know why it is working in terms of any underlying process.* (Turkle 1995: 42, emphasis added)

Turkle argues that the Macintosh aesthetic is part of a larger cultural shift in the meaning and importance of transparency. The Macintosh is a cultural object that symbolises a culture where things can get done without needing to analyse them in depth; a culture where work, to a large extent, consists of manipulating simulations of things and where one does not need to 'get one's hands dirty'. Turkle suggests that the cultural legacy of the Macintosh is that it has made us accustomed to staying on the surface. My concern in this book has been to explore whether and how the habits, exemplified by the Macintosh, may be transforming contemporary penal decision-making. Is it a coincidence that we expect penal systems (in similarity with schools, universities and health systems) to be transparent, just as our personal computers are? We expect our organisations to be fully defined and predictable, the output being a known function of the input, just as in a computer program. We even expect human thought to come a step closer to this ideal. In penal systems, a growing number of forms and guidelines are telling professionals how they should think, and thereby making their work transparent and open.

However, the issue of transparency opens a number of contradictions. On the one hand, the rise of information technology and various types of surveillance technologies raise concerns about too much visibility, transparency and surveillance. A number of critics have argued for the right to privacy, the right to remain, in a way, invisible to the 'technological eye'. On the other hand, the very same 'technological eye' can bring visibility and information concerning areas previously surrounded by secrecy, and therefore always vulnerable to prejudice and to the abuse of power. Technology can make more information accessible about government spending, the financial records of political parties or, as is the subject of this book, the nature of judicial decisions. Some authors argue that technology's ability to achieve transparency can be used to bring about 'reciprocal transparency': 'if police cameras watch us, shouldn't we be able to tune into police stations?' (Brin 1998). In this way, one might come closer to the pre-modern or village system, where people know each other in great detail. The right to privacy, the right to keep parts of one's life secret, is in many aspects a modern, bourgeois invention, where the public and the private spheres became two distinctly separate entities.

However, the issue of transparency cannot simply be reduced to the dichotomy between acceptance and refusal to provide information about one's activities. The right to deny information and refuse to be 'visible' is in itself a legitimate right.

What good comes from, for example, me or my employer knowing my IQ?[4] However, there is also the issue of what kind of transparency we are in fact talking about. If technology brings us 'glasses' to make things more visible, these glasses should be examined, because they are the result of human creation. Transparency, visibility, accountability are not neutral words. When we want to make things transparent and visible, we cannot simply make them appear in their 'true' nature. There will always be some aspects that are more visible than others. The question is therefore: what are we making visible when striving for transparency? What is illuminated when databases are sending their rays of light and illuminating the activities of teachers, doctors or judges?

At a closer look, transparency has two meanings: one is the opposite of secrecy, the illumination of darkness. The other one, however, has to do with enabling a certain ease of understanding, creation of order, distinguishing between what is worth noticing and what is not, and therefore, inevitably, reduction of complexity. This is the transparency mentioned by Turkle (1995) above: seeing documents and programs presented by attractive and easy-to-interpret icons; being able to see systems and processes in diagrams and flow-charts, or, as in the case of sentencing, guidelines and statistical distributions. In this sense, things are made transparent by creating a new 'map of the territory' that makes it easier to navigate and know where one is going. However, there is always a question of the relations between the map and the territory. The map can be wrong. It is, after all, only an interpretation of the territory. Or, the map can be so useful that it can, for all practical purposes replace the territory.[5] This text is therefore not simply a story about the creation of transparency in sentencing; it is a story about two transparencies: one, about combating secrecy and illuminating places that were invisible, the other, about creating new maps and structures of perception.

I have discussed a number of aspects concerning the striving for transparency in contemporary penal systems. One of the main preconditions for transparency is the existence of what I have called *disembodied information* – meaning information that is decontextualised and which can travel between the various penal actors without changing its meaning in a new context. It is information that can cross great distances and that thus enables governance, as well as 'sentencing-at-a-distance'. A transparent penal system also presupposes a concept of offenders' identity that is transparent. Categorical identity has certain Macintosh traits. 'There is nowhere visible to dive' in the world of sentencing guidelines and risk assessment instruments. These instruments can 'make things work' without needing to understand (Turkle 1995). They are instruments for action rather than understanding (Lash 2002). Categorical identity has qualities that are clear and predictable and that can be represented in digitised forms. Categorical offenders do not seem to be subjected to the 'soul-searching' gaze described by Foucault. To bring the soul into this context would mean the inconvenience of unpredictability, connotations of uniqueness, individuality and mystery, which would be at odds with the demands for transparency. Sentencing matrix and risk assessment forms

4 I am grateful to Thomas Hylland Eriksen for bringing this issue to my attention.

5 This is the point of Baudrillard's reference to Borges's tale of cartographers of the Empire who drew up a map so detailed that it ended up covering the territory. Baudrillard inverts the allegory and argues that the abstraction (the map) today no longer mirrors the concept (the territory), but rather replaces it. The 'present-day simulators try to make the real, all the real, coincide with their simulation models' (2001: 170).

are based on abstract factors amenable to processing by the technological framework at hand. The factors do not tell stories and create narratives. Factors, on the other hand, can travel at a distance and create order and visibility.

Furthermore, a transparent penal system implies a new role for penal professionals. The demands for transparency are closely connected to the disturbed relations of trust in the professional judgment of penal professionals (Garland 2001). The abstract and objective nature of the sentencing process can be seen as a protection from a prejudiced and arbitrary judiciary. To detach knowledge from the judiciary and turn it into an impersonal, predictable, information driven process was often seen as an act of political liberation. The use of information technology in penal systems, therefore, has important political dimensions. Sherry Turkle's study of people's attitudes towards hypothetical computer judges shows that the idea of having a computer as a judge looked more appealing to her interviewees when the legal system was seen as racist and prejudiced (1995: 292). When she interviewed college students, a number of them thought that having, for example, a computerised expert system decide cases was a bad idea. They came with objections such as: 'Judges have to be wise. Computers can be smart, only people can be wise.' Or: 'Judges have to have compassion for the particular circumstances of the people before them. Computers could never develop this quality' (Turkle 1995: 292). However, there were a number of students who saw the idea of a computer judge as appealing. They were mostly black, from inner city neighbourhoods and streetwise. Turkle here points to an important point that attitudes about computers often reflect fears about people. The minority students who were positive to the idea of computer judges did not necessarily have a different image of technology from the rest of the students. What they did have was a different image and experience of people and of the judicial system. The idea that justice would not depend on the personality, social class and skin colour of a judge, but rather that it would be a question of following a precise set of rules of a computer program, was reassuring to them. Therefore, it needs to be pointed out that the implementation of objective technological solutions also reflects the level of trust that judges and other decision-makers enjoy by the general public and by the political establishment. Contemporary penal systems seem to be particularly unwilling to trust. Part of the reason is surely that mistakes can have fatal and irreversible consequences that can quickly become the subject of public outrage and media scrutiny. Another reason may be that the demands for visibility and scrutiny of administrative procedures have become a defining part of our cultural environment.

The purpose of this book has been to present and explore some questions concerning what happens when individual (or better, professional) creativity is provided by a tool – by a set of rules for thought. I have argued that, as a tool for judicial thinking and communication, sentencing guidelines and sentencing information systems are far from unique. They are a product of contemporary computer mediated culture. The use of new technologies in sentencing redefines authority and changes the legitimate ways of interpreting social life. The issue is not only about using information in more rational ways. It is also about creating information. It is about constructing new lenses and ways of knowing and seeing. It is about giving preference to new skills and types of knowledge – such as the ability to see similarity where before there was none, and the ability to use models and rules when before there were individual narratives.

# Appendix

## Table 1: Minnesota Sentencing Guidelines Grid

### Presumptive Sentence Lengths in Months

Italicized numbers within the grid denote the range within which a judge may sentence without the sentence being deemed a departure. Offenders with non-imprisonment felony sentences are subject to jail time according to law.

**CRIMINAL HISTORY SCORE**

| SEVERITY LEVEL OF CONVICTION OFFENSE (Common offenses listed in italics) | | 0 | 1 | 2 | 3 | 4 | 5 | 6 or more |
|---|---|---|---|---|---|---|---|---|
| *Murder, 2nd Degree (intentional murder; drive-by-shootings)* | XI | 306 *299–313* | 326 *319–333* | 346 *339–353* | 366 *359–373* | 386 *379–393* | 406 *399–413* | 426 *419–433* |
| *Murder, 3rd Degree Murder, 2nd Degree (unintentional murder)* | X | 150 *144–156* | 165 *159–171* | 180 *174–186* | 195 *189–201* | 210 *204–216* | 225 *219–231* | 240 *234–246* |
| *Criminal Sexual Conduct, 1st Degree* [2] *Assault, 1st Degree* | IX | 86 *81–91* | 98 *93–103* | 110 *105–115* | 122 *117–127* | 134 *129–139* | 146 *141–151* | 158 *153–163* |
| *Aggravated Robbery 1st Degree Criminal Sexual Conduct, 2nd Degree ©,(d),(e),(f),(h)* [2] | VIII | 48 *44–52* | 58 *54–62* | 68 *64–72* | 78 *74–82* | 88 *84–92* | 98 *94–102* | 108 *104–112* |
| *Felony DWI* | VII | 36 | 42 | 48 | 54 *51–57* | 60 *57–63* | 66 *63–69* | 72 *69–75* |
| *Criminal Sexual Conduct, 2nd Degree (a) & (b)* | VI | 21 | 27 | 33 | 39 *37–41* | 45 *43–47* | 51 *49–53* | 57 *55–59* |
| *Residential Burglary Simple Robbery* | V | 18 | 23 | 28 | 33 *31–35* | 38 *36–40* | 43 *41–45* | 48 *46–50* |
| *Nonresidential Burglary* | IV | 12[1] | 15 | 18 | 21 | 24 *23–25* | 27 *26–28* | 30 *29–31* |
| *Theft Crimes (Over $2,500)* | III | 12[1] | 13 | 15 | 17 | 19 *18–20* | 21 *20–22* | 23 *22–24* |
| *Theft Crimes ($2,500 or less) Check Forgery ($200-$2,500)* | II | 12[1] | 12[1] | 13 | 15 | 17 | 19 | 21 *20–22* |
| *Sale of Simulated Controlled Substance* | I | 12[1] | 12[1] | 12[1] | 13 | 15 | 17 | 19 *18–20* |

☐ Presumptive commitment to state imprisonment. First Degree Murder is excluded from the guidelines by law and continues to have a mandatory life sentence. See section IIE Mandatory Sentences for policy regarding those sentences controlled by law, including minimum periods of supervision for sex offenders released from prison.

▒ Presumptive stayed sentence; at the discretion of the judge, up to a year in jail and/or other non-jail sanctions can be imposed as conditions of probation. However, certain offenses in this section of the grid always carry a presumptive commitment to state prison. These offenses include Third Degree Controlled Substance Crimes when the offender has a prior felony drug conviction, Burglary of an Occupied Dwelling when the offender has a prior felony burglary conviction, second and subsequent Criminal Sexual Conduct offenses and offenses carrying a mandatory minimum prison term due to the use of a dangerous weapon (eg, Second Degree Assault). See sections II.C. Presumptive Sentence and IIE Mandatory Sentences.

1 One year and one day.

2 Pursuant to MS § 609.342, subd. 2 and 609.343, subd. 2, the presumptive sentence for Criminal Sexual Conduct in the First Degree is a minimum of 144 months and the presumptive sentence for Criminal Sexual Conduct in the Second Degree – clauses c, d, e, f, and h is a minimum of 90 months (see II.C. Presumptive Sentence and II.G. Convictions for Attempts, Conspiracies, and Other Sentence Modifiers).

Effective August 8, 2003

## Table 2: US Federal Sentencing Guidelines Sentencing Table

**SENTENCING TABLE**
**(in months of imprisonment)**

| | | Criminal History Category (Criminal History Points) | | | | | |
|---|---|---|---|---|---|---|---|
| | Offense Level | I (0 or 1) | II (2 or 3) | III (4, 5, 6) | IV (7, 8, 9) | V (10, 11, 12) | VI (13 or more) |
| Zone A | 1 | 0-6 | 0-6 | 0-6 | 0-6 | 0-6 | 0-6 |
| | 2 | 0-6 | 0-6 | 0-6 | 0-6 | 0-6 | 1-7 |
| | 3 | 0-6 | 0-6 | 0-6 | 0-6 | 2-8 | 3-9 |
| | 4 | 0-6 | 0-6 | 0-6 | 2-8 | 4-10 | 6-12 |
| | 5 | 0-6 | 0-6 | 1-7 | 4-10 | 6-12 | 9-15 |
| | 6 | 0-6 | 1-7 | 2-8 | 6-12 | 9-15 | 12-18 |
| | 7 | 0-6 | 2-8 | 4-10 | 8-14 | 12-18 | 15-21 |
| | 8 | 0-6 | 4-10 | 6-12 | 10-16 | 15-21 | 18-24 |
| Zone B | 9 | 4-10 | 6-12 | 8-14 | 12-18 | 18-24 | 21-27 |
| | 10 | 6-12 | 8-14 | 10-16 | 15-21 | 21-27 | 24-30 |
| Zone C | 11 | 8-14 | 10-16 | 12-18 | 18-24 | 24-30 | 27-33 |
| | 12 | 10-16 | 12-18 | 15-21 | 21-27 | 27-33 | 30-37 |
| Zone D | 13 | 12-18 | 15-21 | 18-24 | 24-30 | 30-37 | 33-41 |
| | 14 | 15-21 | 18-24 | 21-27 | 27-33 | 33-41 | 37-46 |
| | 15 | 18-24 | 21-27 | 24-30 | 30-37 | 37-46 | 41-51 |
| | 16 | 21-27 | 24-30 | 27-33 | 33-41 | 41-51 | 46-57 |
| | 17 | 24-30 | 27-33 | 30-37 | 37-46 | 46-57 | 51-63 |
| | 18 | 27-33 | 30-37 | 33-41 | 41-51 | 51-63 | 57-71 |
| | 19 | 30-37 | 33-41 | 37-46 | 46-57 | 57-71 | 63-78 |
| | 20 | 33-41 | 37-46 | 41-51 | 51-63 | 63-78 | 70-87 |
| | 21 | 37-46 | 41-51 | 46-57 | 57-71 | 70-87 | 77-96 |
| | 22 | 41-51 | 46-57 | 51-63 | 63-78 | 77-96 | 84-105 |
| | 23 | 46-57 | 51-63 | 57-71 | 70-87 | 84-105 | 92-115 |
| | 24 | 51-63 | 57-71 | 63-78 | 77-96 | 92-115 | 100-125 |
| | 25 | 57-71 | 63-78 | 70-87 | 84-105 | 100-125 | 110-137 |
| | 26 | 63-78 | 70-87 | 78-97 | 92-115 | 110-137 | 120-150 |
| | 27 | 70-87 | 78-97 | 87-108 | 100-125 | 120-150 | 130-162 |
| | 28 | 78-97 | 87-108 | 97-121 | 110-137 | 130-162 | 140-175 |
| | 29 | 87-108 | 97-121 | 108-135 | 121-151 | 140-175 | 151-188 |
| | 30 | 97-121 | 108-135 | 121-151 | 135-168 | 151-188 | 168-210 |
| | 31 | 108-135 | 121-151 | 135-168 | 151-188 | 168-210 | 188-235 |
| | 32 | 121-151 | 135-168 | 151-188 | 168-210 | 188-235 | 210-262 |
| | 33 | 135-168 | 151-188 | 168-210 | 188-235 | 210-262 | 235-293 |
| | 34 | 151-188 | 168-210 | 188-235 | 210-262 | 235-293 | 262-327 |
| | 35 | 168-210 | 188-235 | 210-262 | 235-293 | 262-327 | 292-365 |
| | 36 | 188-235 | 210-262 | 235-293 | 262-327 | 292-365 | 324-405 |
| | 37 | 210-262 | 235-293 | 262-327 | 292-365 | 324-405 | 360-life |
| | 38 | 235-293 | 262-327 | 292-365 | 324-405 | 360-life | 360-life |
| | 39 | 262-327 | 292-365 | 324-405 | 360-life | 360-life | 360-life |
| | 40 | 292-365 | 324-405 | 360-life | 360-life | 360-life | 360-life |
| | 41 | [illegible] | 360-life | 360-life | 360-life | 360-life | 360-life |
| | 42 | 360-life | 360-life | 360-life | [illegible] | 360-life | 360-life |
| | 43 | life | life | life | life | life | life |

Source: Federal Sentencing Guidelines Manual 2004, available at: www.ussc.gov/GUIDELIN.HTM

## Table 3: ASSET Risk Assessment Profile Used by Youth Justice Board for England and Wales

Asset

**Final Warning Profile**

YOUTH JUSTICE BOARD

11 FINAL WARNING PROFILE

### Personal details

Surname ______________ First name(s) ______________

Other names ______________ Gender: Male / Female Date of birth ______________

*Unique ID ______________ *Police National Computer number ______________

*Address ______________________________

______________________________ *Postcode ______________

Phone numbers (home, mobile, work) ______________

***Ethnic classification (2001 census)** **Information not obtainable** ☐

| | | | | |
|---|---|---|---|---|
| **White** | British ☐ | Irish ☐ | Other White ☐ | |
| **Black/Black British** | Caribbean ☐ | African ☐ | Other Black ☐ | |
| **Asian/Asian British** | Indian ☐ | Pakistani ☐ | Bangladeshi ☐ | Other Asian ☐ |
| **Mixed** | White/Black Caribbean ☐ | White/Black African ☐ | White/Asian ☐ | Other Mixed ☐ |
| **Chinese/Other ethnic group** | Chinese ☐ | Any other ☐ | | |

Preferred language (other than English) ______________

### Information used for assessment **(Please tick all that apply.)**

| | | |
|---|---|---|
| Interview ☐ | Crown Prosecution Service ☐ | General practitioner ☐ |
| Case record ☐ | Solicitor ☐ | Mental health service ☐ |
| Family/carer ☐ | Previous convictions ☐ | Other health service ☐ |
| School ☐ | Residential home/hostel ☐ | Drug/alcohol service ☐ |
| Social Services Department ☐ | Housing association ☐ | Young Offender Institution ☐ |
| Victim ☐ | Local education authority ☐ | Secure unit ☐ |
| Police ☐ | Careers guidance service ☐ | Voluntary organisation ☐ |

Other (e.g. club, religious organisation, local youth projects) ______________

**Give details of any particular difficulties in obtaining information.**

**Specify any significant pieces of information still to be obtained.**

Assessment completed by ______________ Date completed ______________

## Offence details

| | | *Seriousness score (1-8) |
|---|---|---|
| *Primary index offence | | |
| Additional offences | | |

Outline of current offence(s)

***Victim/s (Please tick all that apply.)**

*Specific, targeted victim ☐ *Vulnerable victim ☐ Repeat victim ☐

Victim not known to him/her ☐ Racially motivated offence ☐

Impact and effect on victim

## Criminal history

| | 10 | 11 | 12 | 13 | 14 | 15 | 16 | 17 | N/A | Don't know |
|---|---|---|---|---|---|---|---|---|---|---|
| Age at first Reprimand/Caution | ☐ | ☐ | ☐ | ☐ | ☐ | ☐ | ☐ | ☐ | ☐ | ☐ |
| Age at first Final Warning | ☐ | ☐ | ☐ | ☐ | ☐ | ☐ | ☐ | ☐ | ☐ | ☐ |

| | 3 months | 6 months | 12 months | 1 year + | N/A | Don't know |
|---|---|---|---|---|---|---|
| *Time since last Reprimand, Caution or Final Warning | ☐ | ☐ | ☐ | ☐ | ☐ | ☐ |

## Care history

| | Yes | No | Don't know |
|---|---|---|---|
| ***Is the young person known to Social Services?** | ☐ | ☐ | ☐ |

Details (Please explain reasons for any 'Don't know' responses.)

## Ratings

**Rate the extent to which the following factors are associated with the likelihood of further offending.**
(0 = not associated, 4 = very strongly associated)

1. **Living arrangements** (e.g. living with known offenders, deprived household, accommodation unsuitable for his/her needs, absconding/staying away, no fixed abode)

| 0 | 1 | 2 | 3 | 4 |
|---|---|---|---|---|

2. **Family and personal relationships** (e.g. family members involved in substance abuse or criminal activity, lack of interest shown in the young person, inconsistent supervision, abuse, loss)

| 0 | 1 | 2 | 3 | 4 |
|---|---|---|---|---|

Evidence (If you have rated 2 or above in either section 1 or 2, you must give evidence for your decision here.)

3. **Education, training and employment** (e.g. any identified special educational needs, instances of exclusion, truancy or bullying, difficulties with basic literacy/numeracy, poor relationships with teachers, current training/employment situation, level of qualifications/skills, attitudes towards employment)

| 0 | 1 | 2 | 3 | 4 |
|---|---|---|---|---|

Evidence (If you have rated 2 or above in section 3, you must give evidence for your decision here.)

4. **Neighbourhood** (e.g. level of crime in the area, obvious signs of drug-dealing and/or usage, lack of age-appropriate facilities, isolated location/lack of transport, racial or ethnic tensions)

| 0 | 1 | 2 | 3 | 4 |
|---|---|---|---|---|

5. **Lifestyle** (e.g. predominantly pro-criminal peers, non-constructive use of time, lack of legitimate income, lack of age-appropriate friendships, involvement in reckless activity)

| 0 | 1 | 2 | 3 | 4 |
|---|---|---|---|---|

Evidence (If you have rated 2 or above in either section 4 or 5, you must give evidence for your decision here.)

6. **Substance use** (e.g. use of alcohol/tobacco/solvents/drugs, substance use which has detrimental effect on education or relationships, offending to obtain money for substances)

| 0 | 1 | 2 | 3 | 4 |
|---|---|---|---|---|

7. **Physical health** (e.g. health condition which significantly affects everyday functioning, physical immaturity/delayed development, health put at risk through his/her own behaviour)

| 0 | 1 | 2 | 3 | 4 |
|---|---|---|---|---|

Evidence (If you have rated 2 or above in either section 6 or 7, you must give evidence for your decision here.)

8. **Emotional and mental health** (e.g. problems coming to terms with significant past events, contact with mental health services, any suicide attempts or instances of self-harm)

| 0 | 1 | 2 | 3 | 4 |
|---|---|---|---|---|

9. **Perception of self and others** (e.g. inappropriate levels of self-esteem, general mistrust of other people, displays a lack of understanding for other people, discriminatory attitudes)

| 0 | 1 | 2 | 3 | 4 |
|---|---|---|---|---|

10. **Thinking and behaviour** (e.g. does not understand the consequences of actions, acts impulsively, has a constant need for excitement, gives in easily to pressure from others, poor temper control)

| 0 | 1 | 2 | 3 | 4 |
|---|---|---|---|---|

Evidence (If you have rated 2 or above in either sections 8, 9 or 10, you must give evidence for your decision here.)

11. **Attitudes to offending** (e.g. lack of understanding about the impact of offending on victim or their family/carers, lack of remorse, belief that certain offences are acceptable, sees offending as inevitable)

| 0 | 1 | 2 | 3 | 4 |
|---|---|---|---|---|

12. **Motivation to change** (e.g. understands consequences of offending, can identify reasons to stop offending, likely to receive support from family/friends, willing to co-operate to achieve change)

| 0 | 1 | 2 | 3 | 4 |
|---|---|---|---|---|

Evidence (If you have rated 2 or above in either sections 11 or 12, you must give evidence for your decision here.)

## Summary of ratings

| | Rating | | Rating |
|---|---|---|---|
| 1. Living arrangements | | 7. Physical health | |
| 2. Family and personal relationships | | 8. Emotional and mental health | |
| 3. Education, training and employment | | 9. Perception of self and others | |
| 4. Neighbourhood | | 10. Thinking and behaviour | |
| 5. Lifestyle | | 11. Attitudes to offending | |
| 6. Substance use | | 12. Motivation to change | |
| | | **Total score from sections 1-12 (max. 48)** | |

## *Positive factors

(e.g. stable living arrangements/family relationships, school attendance, constructive leisure activities, resilience)

## *Indicators of vulnerability

**Please indicate if there is any possibility of harm being caused to the young person, e.g. being vulnerable as a result of bullying or intimidation, risk of self-harm/suicide.**

### Indicators of serious harm to others

**Please indicate any possibility of the young person causing serious physical or psychological harm to other people, e.g. any previous harm intended/caused, use of weapons, targeting victims, other disconcerting or disturbing attitudes or behaviour. (If issues are raised in this section please complete a *Risk of Serious Harm* form.)**

### Future Plans

**Is intervention being proposed at this stage?** Yes ☐ No ☐ Don't know ☐

If 'no', please explain reasons, e.g. she/he has already made reparation, circumstances leading to offence are unlikely to recur.

**Please complete the tables below if a Final Warning intervention is being proposed.**

| | Objectives | Method | Who (Yot, family, agencies) |
|---|---|---|---|
| 1. | | | |
| 2. | | | |
| 3. | | | |
| 4. | | | |
| 5. | | | |

FINAL WARNING PROFILE 11

**Summarise key positive factors that could be strengthened during intervention to reduce risk of reoffending.**

| |
|---|
| |

**Are there other issues – not directly related to offending – which need to be addressed?** Yes ☐ No ☐

| | Objectives | Method | Who (Yot, family, agencies) |
|---|---|---|---|
| 1. | | | |
| 2. | | | |
| 3. | | | |
| 4. | | | |
| 5. | | | |

## Final Warning Closure

**Give a brief summary of the work that has been undertaken with the young person during this intervention.**

| |
|---|
| |

***Has the young person engaged well with this intervention?** Yes ☐ No ☐

| Details |
|---|
| |

***Have there been any difficulties in arranging programmes or services?** Yes ☐ No ☐

| Details |
|---|
| |

***Have there been any referrals to other agencies?** Yes ☐ No ☐

| Details |
|---|
| |

***Are you aware of any reoffending by the young person?** Yes ☐ No ☐

| Details |
|---|
| |

**Please re-score the following sections based on your current knowledge of the young person.**

| | Rating | | Rating |
|---|---|---|---|
| 1. Living arrangements | | 7. Physical health | |
| 2. Family and personal relationships | | 8. Emotional and mental health | |
| 3. Education, training and employment | | 9. Perception of self and others | |
| 4. Neighbourhood | | 10. Thinking and behaviour | |
| 5. Lifestyle | | 11. Attitudes to offending | |
| 6. Substance use | | 12. Motivation to change | |
| | | **Total score from sections 1-12 (max. 48)** | |

| Evidence (Please provide evidence of any changes in your above assessment of the young person e.g. from positive outcomes relating to any intervention, further disclosure by the young person.) |
|---|
| |

**Have there been any changes in the assessment of vulnerability or risk of serious harm to others?** Yes ☐ No ☐

| Details |
|---|
| |

Signed (practitioner):____________________ Date of closure:__________

## Table 4: US Sentencing Commission's Sentencing Worksheet (Training Worksheet)

# Worksheet A (Offense Level)

Defendant ______________________ District/Office ______________________

Docket Number (Year-Sequence-Defendant No.) ___ ___-___ ___ ___ ___ ___-___ ___

Count Number(s) _______ U.S. Code Title & Section _______: ______________________

_______: ______________________

Guidelines Manual Edition Used: 20___ *(NOTE: worksheets keyed to the Manual effective November 1, 2001)*

Instructions:

For each count of conviction (or stipulated offense), complete a separate Worksheet A. Exception: Use only a single Worksheet A where the offense level for a group of closely related counts is based primarily on aggregate value or quantity (see §3D1.2(d)) or where a count of conspiracy, solicitation, or attempt is grouped with a substantive count that was the sole object of the conspiracy, solicitation, or attempt (see §3D1.2(a) and (b)).

1. **Offense Level** (See Chapter Two)
Enter the applicable base offense level and any specific offense characteristics from Chapter Two and explain the bases for these determinations. Enter the sum in the box provided.

| Guideline | Description | Level |
|---|---|---|
| | | |
| | | |
| | | |
| | | |
| | | |

Sum ☐

2. **Victim-Related Adjustments** (See Chapter Three, Part A)
Enter the applicable section and adjustment. If more than one section is applicable, list each section and enter the combined adjustment. If no adjustment is applicable, enter "0." § _______ ☐

3. **Role in the Offense Adjustments** (See Chapter Three, Part B)
Enter the applicable section and adjustment. If more than one section is applicable, list each section and enter the combined adjustment. If the adjustment reduces the offense level, enter a minus (-) sign in front of the adjustment. If no adjustment is applicable, enter "0." § _______ ☐

4. **Obstruction Adjustments** (See Chapter Three, Part C)
Enter the applicable section and adjustment. If more than one section is applicable, list each section and enter the combined adjustment. If no adjustment is applicable, enter "0." § _______ ☐

5. **Adjusted Offense Level**
Enter the sum of Items 1-4. If this worksheet does not cover all counts of conviction or stipulated offenses, complete Worksheet B. Otherwise, enter this result on Worksheet D, Item 1. ☐

---

☐ *Check if the defendant is convicted of a single count. In such case, Worksheet B need not be completed.*

☐ *If the defendant has no criminal history, enter criminal history "I" here and on Item 4, Worksheet D. In such case, Worksheet C need not be completed.*

# Worksheet B

## (Multiple Counts or Stipulation to Additional Offenses)

Defendant ______________________ Docket Number ______________________

**Instructions**

**Step 1:** Determine if any of the counts group. (Note: All, some, or none of the counts may group. Some of the counts may have already been grouped in the application under Worksheet A, specifically, (1) counts grouped under §3D1.2(d), or (2) a count charging conspiracy, solicitation, or attempt that is grouped with the substantive count of conviction (see §3D1.2(a)). Explain the reasons for grouping:

______________________________________________________________________

______________________________________________________________________

**Step 2:** Using the box(es) provided below, for each group of closely related counts, enter the highest adjusted offense level from the various "A" Worksheets (Item 5) that comprise the group (see §3D1.3). (Note: A "group" may consist of a single count that has not grouped with any other count. In those instances, the offense level for the group will be the adjusted offense level for the single count.)

**Step 3:** Enter the number of units to be assigned to each group (see §3D1.4) as follows:

- One unit (1) for the group of closely related counts with the highest offense level
- An additional unit (1) for each group that is equally serious or 1 to 4 levels less serious
- An additional half unit (1/2) for each group that is 5 to 8 levels less serious
- No increase in units for groups that are 9 or more levels less serious

1. **Adjusted Offense Level for the First Group of Closely Related Counts** ☐ ______(unit)
   Count number(s):____________

2. **Adjusted Offense Level for the Second Group of Closely Related Counts** ☐ ______(unit)
   Count number(s):____________

3. **Adjusted Offense Level for the Third Group of Closely Related Counts** ☐ ______(unit)
   Count number(s):____________

4. **Adjusted Offense Level for the Fourth Group of Closely Related Counts** ☐ ______(unit)
   Count number(s):

5. **Adjusted Offense Level for the Fifth Group of Closely Related Counts** ☐ ______(unit)
   Count number(s):____________

6. **Total Units** ______ (total units)

7. **Increase in Offense Level Based on Total Units (See §3D1.4)** ☐

| | | | |
|---|---|---|---|
| 1 unit: | no increase | 2 1/2 - 3 units: | add 3 levels |
| 1 1/2 units: | add 1 level | 3 1/2 - 5 units: | add 4 levels |
| 2 units: | add 2 levels | More than 5 units: | add 5 levels |

8. **Highest of the Adjusted Offense Levels from Items 1-5 Above** ☐

9. **Combined Adjusted Offense Level (See §3D1.4)** ☐
   Enter the sum of Items 7 and 8 here and on Worksheet D, Item 1

# Worksheet C (Criminal History)

Defendant ______________________ Docket Number ______________________

Enter the Date Defendant Commenced Participation in Instant Offense (Earliest Date of Relevant Conduct)______________

1. 3 Points for each prior ADULT sentence of imprisonment EXCEEDING ONE YEAR AND ONE MONTH imposed within 15 YEARS of the defendant's commencement of the instant offense OR resulting in incarceration during any part of that 15-YEAR period. (See §§4A1.1(a) and 4A1.2.)

2. 2 Points for each prior sentence of imprisonment of AT LEAST 60 DAYS resulting from an offense committed ON OR AFTER the defendant's 18th birthday not counted under §4A1.1(a) imposed within 10 YEARS of the instant offense; and

   2 Points for each prior sentence of imprisonment of AT LEAST 60 DAYS resulting from an offense committed BEFORE the defendant's 18th birthday not counted under §4A1.1(a) from which the defendant was released from confinement within 5 YEARS of the instant offense. (See §§4A1.1(b) and 4A1.2.)

3. 1 Point for each prior sentence resulting from an offense committed ON OR AFTER the defendant's 18th birthday not counted under §4A1.1(a) or §4A1.1(b) imposed within 10 YEARS of the instant offense; and

   1 Point for each prior sentence resulting from an offense committed BEFORE the defendant's 18th birthday not counted under §4A1.1(a) or §4A1.1(b) imposed within 5 YEARS of the instant offense. (See §§4A1.1(c) and 4A1.2.)

   NOTE: A maximum sum of 4 Points may be given for the prior sentences in Item 3.

| Date of Imposition | Offense | Sentence | Release Date** | Guideline Section | Criminal History Pts. |
|---|---|---|---|---|---|
| | | | | | |
| | | | | | |
| | | | | | |
| | | | | | |
| | | | | | |
| | | | | | |
| | | | | | |
| | | | | | |
| | | | | | |

* Indicate with an asterisk those offenses where defendant was sentenced as a juvenile.

** A release date is required in only three instances:

a. When a sentence covered under §4A1.1(a) was imposed more than 15 years prior to the commencement of the instant offense but release from incarceration occurred within such 15-year period;

b. When a sentence counted under §4A1.1(b) was imposed for an offense committed prior to age 18 and more than 5 years prior to the commencement of the instant offense, but release from incarceration occurred within such 5-year period; and

c. When §4A1.1(e) applies because the defendant was released from custody on a sentence counted under 4A1.1(a) or 4A1.1 (b) within 2 years of the instant offense or was still in custody on such a sentence at the time of the instant offense (see Item 6).

4. Sum of Criminal History Points for prior sentences under §§4A1.1(a), 4A1.1(b), and 4A1.1(c) (Items 1,2,3). ☐

# Worksheet C

Page 2

Defendant ____________________ Docket Number ____________________

5. 2 Points if the defendant committed the instant offense while under any criminal justice sentence (e.g., probation, parole, supervised release, imprisonment, work release, escape status). (See §§4A1.1(d) and 4A1.2.) List the type of control and identify the sentence from which control resulted. Otherwise, enter 0 Points.

6. 2 Points if the defendant committed the instant offense LESS THAN 2 YEARS after release from imprisonment on a sentence counted under §4A1.1(a) or (b), or while in imprisonment or escape status on such a sentence. However, enter only 1 Point for this item if 2 points were added at Item 5 under §4A1.1(d). (See §§4A1.1(c) and 4A1.2.) List the date of release and identify the sentence from which release resulted. Otherwise, enter 0 Points.

7. 1 Point for each prior sentence resulting from a conviction of a crime of violence that did not receive any points under §4A1.1(a), (b), or (c) because such sentence was considered related to another sentence resulting from a conviction of a crime of violence. *Provided*, that this item does not apply where the sentences are considered related because the offenses occurred on the same occasion. (See §§4A1.1(f) and 4A1.2.) Identify the crimes of violence and briefly explain why the cases are considered related. Otherwise, enter 0 Points.

Note: A maximum sum of 3 Points may be given for Item 7.

8. **Total Criminal History Points** (Sum of Items 4-7)

9. **Criminal History Category** (Enter here and on Worksheet D, Item 4)

| Total Points | Criminal History Category |
|---|---|
| 0-1 | I |
| 2-3 | II |
| 4-6 | III |
| 7-9 | IV |
| 10-12 | V |
| 13 or more | VI |

# Worksheet D (Guideline Worksheet)

Defendant ______________________ District ______________________

Docket Number ______________________

1. **Adjusted Offense Level** (From Worksheet A or B)
If Worksheet B is required, enter the result from Worksheet B, Item 9. Otherwise, enter the result from Worksheet A, Item 5.

2. **Acceptance of Responsibility** (See Chapter Three, Part E)
Enter the applicable reduction of 2 or 3 levels. If no adjustment is applicable, enter "0". —

3. **Offense Level Total** (Item 1 less Item 2)

4. **Criminal History Category** (From Worksheet C)
Enter the result from Worksheet C, Item 9.

5. **Terrorism/Career Offender/Criminal Livelihood/Armed Career Criminal/Repeat and Dangerous Sex Offender**
(see Chapter Three, Part A, and Chapter Four, Part B)

a. Offense Level Total

If the provision for Career Offender (§4B1.1), Criminal Livelihood (§4B1.3), Armed Career Criminal (§4B1.4), or Repeat and Dangerous Sex Offender (§4B1.5) results in an offense level total higher than Item 3, enter the offense level total. Otherwise, enter "N/A."

b. Criminal History Category

If the provision for Terrorism (§3A1.4), Career Offender (§4B1.1), Armed Career Criminal (§4B1.4), or Repeat and Dangerous Sex Offender (§4B1.5) results in a criminal history category higher than Item 4, enter the applicable criminal history category. Otherwise, enter "N/A."

6. **Guideline Range from Sentencing Table**
Enter the applicable guideline range from Chapter Five, Part A. Months

7. **Restricted Guideline Range** (See Chapter Five, Part G)
If the statutorily authorized maximum sentence or the statutorily required minimum sentence restricts the guideline range (Item 6) (see §§5G1.1 and 5G1.2), enter either the restricted guideline range or any statutory maximum or minimum penalty that would modify the guideline range. Otherwise, enter "N/A." Months

☐ Check this box if §5C1.2 (Limitation on Applicability of Statutory Minimum Penalties in Certain Cases) is applicable.

8. **Undischarged Term of Imprisonment** (See §5G1.3)

☐ If the defendant is subject to an undischarged term of imprisonment, check this box and list the undischarged term(s) below.

# Worksheet D

Page 2

Defendant ______________________ Docket Number ______________________

9. **Sentencing Options** (Check the applicable box that corresponds to the Guideline Range entered in Item 6.) (See Chapter Five, Sentencing Table)

☐ Zone A If checked, the following options are available (see §5B1.1):

- Fine (See §5E1.2(a))
- "Straight" Probation
- Imprisonment

☐ Zone B If checked, the minimum term may be satisfied by:

- Imprisonment
- Imprisonment of at least one month plus supervised release with a condition that substitutes community confinement or home detention for imprisonment (see §5C1.1(c)(2))
- Probation with a condition that substitutes intermittent confinement, community confinement, or home detention for imprisonment (see §5B1.1(a)(2) and §5C1.1(c)(3))

☐ Zone C If checked, the minimum term may be satisfied by:

- Imprisonment
- Imprisonment of at least one-half of the minimum term plus supervised release with a condition that substitutes community confinement or home detention for imprisonment (see §5C1.1(d)(2))

☐ Zone D If checked, the minimum term shall be satisfied by a sentence of imprisonment (see §5C1.1(f))

10. **Length of a Term of Probation** (See §5B1.2)

If probation is authorized, the guideline for the length of such term of probation is: (Check applicable box)

☐ At least one year, but not more than five years if the offense level total is 6 or more

☐ No more than three years if the offense level total is 5 or less

11. **Conditions of Probation** (See §5B1.3)

List any mandatory conditions ((a)(1)-(9)), standard conditions ((c)(1)-(14)), and any other special conditions that may be applicable:

______________________________________________________________________

______________________________________________________________________

______________________________________________________________________

______________________________________________________________________

______________________________________________________________________

______________________________________________________________________

# Worksheet D

Page 3

Defendant ______________________ Docket Number ______________

12. **Supervised Release** (See §§5D1.1 and 5D1.2)

a. A term of supervised release is: (Check applicable box)

☐ Required because a term of imprisonment of more than one year is to be imposed or if required by statute

☐ Authorized but not required because a term of imprisonment of one year or less is to be imposed

b. Length of Term (Guideline Range of Supervised Release) (Check applicable box)

☐ Class A or B Felony: Three to Five Year Term

☐ Class C or D Felony: Two to Three Year Term

☐ Class E Felony or Class A Misdemeanor: One Year Term

c. Restricted Guideline Range of Supervision Release

☐ If a statutorily required term of supervised release impacts the guideline range, check this box and enter the required term. ______________________

13. **Conditions of Supervised Release** (See §5D1.3)
List any mandatory conditions ((a)(1)-(7)), standard conditions ((c)(1)-(15)), and any other special conditions that may be applicable:
______________________

14. **Restitution** (See §5E1.1)

a. If restitution is applicable, enter the amount. Otherwise enter "N/A" and the reason: ______________________

b. Enter whether restitution is statutorily mandatory or discretionary: ______________________

c. Enter whether restitution is by an order of restitution or solely as a condition of supervision. Enter the authorizing statute: ______________________

15. **Fines** (Guideline Range of Fines for Individual Defendants) (See §5E1.2)

| | Minimum | Maximum |
|---|---|---|
| a. Special fine provisions<br>☐ Check box if any of the counts of conviction is for a statute with a special fine provision. (This does not include the general fine provisions of 18 USC § 3571(b)(2), (d)) | | |
| Enter the sum of statutory maximum fines for all such counts | | $________ |
| b. Fine Table (§5E1.2(c)(3))<br>Enter the minimum and maximum fines | $ | $ |
| c. Guideline Range of Fines:<br>(determined by the minimum of the fine table (Item 15(b)) and the greater maximum above (Item 15(a) or 15(b))) | $________ | $________ |

d. Ability to Pay

☐ Check this box if the defendant does not have an ability to pay.

*U.S. Sentencing Commission*
*December 17, 2001*
*H:\TAS\TRAINING\Worksheets\worksheets.DECEMBER001.wpd*

# Worksheet D

Page 4

Defendant ______________________ Docket Number ______________________

16. **Special Assessments** (See §5E1.3)

Enter the total amount of special assessments required for all counts of conviction:

- $25 for each misdemeanor count of conviction
- Not less than $100 for each felony count of conviction

$__________

17. **Additional Factors**

List any additional applicable guidelines, policy statements, and statutory provisions. Also list any applicable aggravating and mitigating factors that may warrant a sentence at a particular point either within or outside the applicable guideline range. Attach additional sheets as required.

Completed by ______________________ Date ______________________

# Bibliography


Ackroyd, S, Harper, R, Hughes, JA, Shapiro, D and Soothill, K (1992) *New Technology and Practical Police Work*, Buckingham: The Open University Press

Alldridge, P (1997) 'Anoraks among the suits and jeans: computers, law and the legal academy', in *Journal of Law, Information and Technology*, Vol 2

Anderson, WT (2000) *Det Nye Selvet: identitet i det 21 århundre*, Oslo: Aschehoug

Apollon (2004) 'Når verden tenker i kulepunkter', Nr 01/2004

Ashworth, A (1992) 'Sentencing reform structures', in Tonry, M (ed), *Crime and Justice: A Review of Research*, Vol 16, Chicago and London: University of Chicago Press

Ashworth, A (1997) 'Sentencing', in Maguire, M, Morgan, R and Reiner, R (eds), *The Oxford Handbook of Criminology*, 2nd edn, Oxford: Clarendon Press

Auge, M (1995) *Non-Places*, London: Verso

Bagge, S (1998) *Det europeiske menneske: Individoppfatninger fra middelalderen til i dag*, Oslo: Ad Notam Gyldendal AS

Barglow, R (1994) *The Crisis of the Self in the Age of Information*, London and New York: Routledge

Barry, A (2001) *Political Machines: Governing a Technological Society*, London and New York: The Athlone Press

Baudrillard, J (1983) *Simulacra and Simulations*, Foss, P, Patton, P and Beitchman, P (trans), New York: Semiotext(e)

Baudrillard, J (1996) 'Disneyworld Company', in CTHEORY, www.chtheory.com/e25disneyworld_comp.html

Baudrillard, J (2001) *Selected Writings*, Poster, M (ed), 2nd edn, Cambridge: Polity Press

Bauman, Z (1992) 'Life world and expertise: social production of dependency', in Stehr, N and Ericson, R (eds), *The Culture and Power of Knowledge: Inquiries into Contemporary Societies*, Berlin and New York: Walter de Gruyter, pp 81–106

Bauman, Z (1993) *Postmodern Ethics*, Oxford: Blackwell

Bauman, Z (1995) *Life in Fragments: Essays in Postmodern Morality*, Oxford: Blackwell

Bauman, Z (1997) *Postmodernity and its Discontents*, Cambridge: Polity Press

Bauman, Z (2000) 'Social issues of law and order', in *The British Journal of Criminology*, Vol 40, pp 205–21

Bazelon, E (2003) 'With no sentencing leeway, what's left to judge?', in *The Washington Post*, 4 May

Beccaria, C ([1764] 1986) *On Crimes and Punishments*, Young, D (trans and notes), Indianapolis: Hackett Publishing

Beck, U, Giddens, A and Lash, S (1994) *Reflexive Modernization*, Cambridge: Polity Press

Bennett, LW and Feldman, MS (1981) *Reconstructing Reality in the Courtroom*, London and New York: Tavistock Publications

Berman, M (1988) *All That is Solid Melts into Air*, New York: Penguin Books

Berry, MF (1999) *The Pig Farmer's Daughter and Other Tales of American Justice*, New York: Knopf

Bing, J (1991) *Personvern i faresonen*, Oslo: Cappelen

Blumstein, A, Cohen, J, Roth, JA and Visher, CA (eds) (1986) *Criminal Careers and 'Career Criminals'*, Vol 1, Washington, DC: National Academy Press

Bøhme, G (1992) 'The techno-structures of society', in Stehr, N and Ericson, R (eds), *The Culture and Power of Knowledge: Inquiries into Contemporary Societies*, Berlin and New York: Walter de Gruyter, pp 39–50

Bolter, DJ (1984) *Turing's Man*, Chapel Hill: The University of North Carolina Press

Bolter, DJ (2001) *Writing Space: Computers, Hypertext, and the Remediation of Print*, 2nd edn, Mahwah, NJ: Lawrence Erlbaum Associates, Publishers

Borgmann, A (1999) *Holding on to Reality: The Nature of Information at the Turn of Millennium*, Chicago: University of Chicago Press

Bottoms, AE (1983) 'Neglected Features of Contemporary Penal Systems', in Garland, D and Young, P (eds), *The Power to Punish*, London and New Jersey: Humanities Press, pp 165–202

Bottoms, AE (1995) 'The philosophy and politics of punishment and sentencing', in Clarkson, C and Morgan, R (eds), *The Politics of Sentencing Reform*, Oxford: Clarendon Press

Bourdieu, P (2000) 'The biographical illusion', in du Gay, P, Evans, J and Redman, P (eds), *Identity: A Reader*, London: Sage

Braithwaite, J (1989) *Crime, Shame and Reintegration*, New York: Cambridge University Press

Bråten, S (1983) *Dialogens vilkår i datasamfunnet*, Oslo: Universitetsgorlaget

Brin, D (1998) *The Transparent Society*, Reading, Mass: Addison Wesley

Brown, JS and Duguid, P (2000) *The Social Life of Information*, Boston, Mass: Harvard Business School Press

Burchell, G, Gordon, C and Miller, P (eds) (1991) *The Foucault Effect: Studies in Governmentality*, London: Harvester Wheatsheaf

Calhoun, C (1995) *Critical Social Theory: Culture, History, and the Challenge of Difference*, Oxford, UK and Cambridge, USA: Blackwell

The Canadian Sentencing Commission (1987) *Sentencing Reform: A Canadian Approach*, Report of the Canadian Sentencing Commission, Ottawa: Canadian Government Publishing Centre

Caplow, T and Simon, J (1999) *Understanding Prison Policy and Population Trends*, Chicago: University of Chicago Press

Cardwell Hughes, R (1999) *Examining Our Commissions & Sentencing Policy*, Report from the National Association of Sentencing Commissions 1999 Annual Conference, Salt Lake City, Utah

Castel, R (1991) 'From dangerousness to risk', in Burchell, G, Gordon, C and Miller, P (eds), *The Foucault Effect: Studies in Governmentality*, London: Harvester Wheatsheaf

Castells, M (1996) *The Rise of the Network Society. The Information Age: Economy, Society and Culture*, Vol 1, Oxford: Blackwell

CBS News (2004) 'Army recruits video gamer', www.cbsnews.com/stories/2004/03/30/eveningnews/main609489.shtml

Chan, JBL (2001) 'The technological game: how information technology is transforming police practice', in *Criminal Justice*, Vol 1(2), pp 139–59

Christie, N (1976) 'Is it time to stop counting?', in *Evaluation Research in Criminal Justice*, Rome: United Nations, Social Defence Research Institute, Publ No 11, pp 63–76

Christie, N (1977) 'Conflicts as property', in *The British Journal of Criminology*, Vol 1, pp 1–15

Christie, N (1980) 'Nyklassisismens skjulte budskap', in Hecksner, S, Snare, A, Takala, H and Vestergaard, J (eds), *Straff og rattfardighet*, Stockholm: PA Norstedt & Soners Forlag

Christie, N (1985) *Den Gode Fiende – Narkotikapolitikk i Norden*, Oslo: Universitetsforlaget AS (German edn, 1991)

Christie, N (1993) *Crime Control as Industry: Towards GULAGS, Western Style*, London and New York: Routledge

Christie, N (1997) 'Four blocks against insight: notes on the oversocialization of criminologists', in *Theoretical Criminology*, Vol 1(1), pp 13–23

Christie, N (2002) 'On Mediation in hell: vengeance and peacemaking', in Vanacker, J (ed), *Herstel en detentie: Hommage aan Prof Dr Tony Peters*, Uiteverij: Politeia NV, pp 23–28

Christie, N (2004) *A Suitable Amount of Crime*, London: Routledge

Clarkson, C and Morgan, R (1995) 'The politics of sentencing reform', in Clarkson, C and Morgan, R (eds), *The Politics of Sentencing Reform*, Oxford: Clarendon Press

Coalition For Federal Sentencing Reform (1997) 'The case for reform', www.sentencing.org.reform.html (viewed 12 November 2003)

Cohen, S (1985) *Visions of Social Control: Crime, Punishment and Classification*, Cambridge: Polity Press

Couch, CJ (1996) *Information Technologies and Social Orders*, New York: Aldine de Gruyter

Cubitt, S (1998) *Digital Aesthetics*, London: Sage

Cubitt, S (2001) *Simulation and Social Theory*, London and Thousand Oaks: Sage

Dahlbom, B and Mathiassen, L (1993) *Computers in Context: The Philosophy and Practice of Systems Design*, Cambridge, MA and Oxford, UK: NCC Blackwell

Davis, J (2002) 'The science of sentencing: measurement theory and von Hirsch's new scale of justice', in Tata, C and Hutton, N (eds), *Sentencing and Society: International Perspectives*, Aldershot: Ashgate

Davis, KC (1969) *Discretionary Justice*, Baton Rouge: Louisiana State University

Deleuze, G (1995) *Negotiations: 1972–1990*, New York: Columbia University Press

Dreyfus, HL and Rabinow, P (1983) *Michel Foucault: Beyond Structuralism and Hermeneutics*, Chicago: University of Chicago Press

Dworkin, R (1977) *Taking Rights Seriously*, Cambridge, MA: Harvard University Press

Encyclopaedia Britannica Online (2002), http://search.eb.com/ebi/article?eu=295590& query=computer

Ericson, RV and Haggerty, KD (1997) *Policing the Risk Society*, Oxford: Clarendon Press

Eriksen, TB (2000a) *Budbringerens overtak: Perspektiver på skriftkulturen*, Oslo: Universitetsforlaget

Eriksen, TB (2000b) 'Postmoderne Identitetsproblemer', in Walter Truett Anderson, *Det Nye Selvet*, Oslo: Ascheoug

Federal Sentencing Guidelines Research Center (1999) *Calculating Sentencing Guidelines With the Federal Sentencing Guide Research Center*, Version 1.05, System Design by McCann, DG, WhiteHorse Solutions Inc

Feeley, MM and Simon, J (1992) 'The new penology: notes on the emerging strategy of corrections and its implications', in *Criminology*, Vol 30(4), pp 449–73

Feeley, MM and Simon, J (1994) 'Actuarial justice: the emerging new criminal law', in Nelken, D (ed), The Futures of Criminology, London and Thousand Oaks: Sage

Finnemann, NO (1999a) *Hypertext and the Representational Capacities of the Binary Alphabet*, www.hum.au.dk/ckulturf/pages/publications/nof/hypertext.htm

Finnemann, NO (1999b) *Thought, Sign and Machine – The Computer Reconsidered*, www.hum.au.dk/ckulturf/pages/publications/nof/tsm/abstract.html

Fjellman, S (1992) *Vinyl Leaves: Walt Disney World and America*, West View Point: Boulder, CO: Westview Press

Fletcher, J (1966) *Situation Ethics: The New Morality*, Louisville, KY: Westminster John Knox Press

Forer, LG (1994) *A Rage to Punish: The Unintended Consequences of Mandatory Sentencing*, New York and London : WW Norton & Company

Foucault, M (1970) *The Order of Things: An Archaeology of the Human Sciences*, London: Tavistock Publications

Foucault, M (1977) *Discipline and Punish; The Birth of the Prison*, Sheridan, A (trans), New York: Vintage Books

Foucault, M (1978) *History of Sexuality: An Introduction*, Hurley, R (trans), London: Penguin Books

Foucault, M (1980) *Power/Knowledge: Selected Interviews and Other Writings 1972–1977*, Gordon, C (ed), New York: Pantheon Books

Foucault, M (1983) 'The subject and power', afterword in Dreyfus, HL and Rabinow, P, *Michel Foucault: Beyond Structuralism and Hermeneutics*, Chicago: University of Chicago Press, pp 208–26

Foucault, M (1997) *The Essential Works of Michel Foucault, 1954–1984*, Rabinow, P (ed), Hurley, R *et al* (trans), London: Allen Lane, The Penguin Press

Frankel, ME (1972) *Criminal Sentences: Law Without Order*, New York: Hill and Wang

Freed, DJ (1992) 'Federal sentences in the wake of guidelines: unacceptable limits in the discretion of sentencers', in *Yale Law Journal*, Vol 101, pp 1,681–754

Fussel, P (1975) *The Great War and Modern Memory*, New York: Oxford University Press

Garland, D (1990) *Punishment and Modern Society: A Study in Social Theory*, Oxford: Clarendon Press

Garland, D (1997) '"Governmentality" and the problem of crime', in *Theoretical Criminology*, Vol 1(2), pp 173–214

Garland, D (1999) 'Penal modernism and postmodernism', in Mathews, R (ed), *Imprisonment*, Dartmouth: Ashgate

Garland, D (2001) *The Culture of Control: Crime and Social Order in Contemporary Society*, Oxford: Oxford University Press

Giddens, A (1985) *The Nation State and Violence: Volume Two of a Contemporary Critique of Historical Materialism*, Cambridge: Polity Press

Giddens, A (1990) *The Consequences of Modernity*, Cambridge: Polity Press

Giddens, A (1991) *Modernity and Self-Identity*, Stanford: Stanford University Press

Goethe, JW (2001) *Faust: A Tragedy*, Arndt, W (trans), Hamlin, C (ed), Norton Critical Edition, New York: WW Norton & Company

Goffman, E (1969) *Strategic Interaction*, Philadelphia: University of Pennsylvania Press

Gottfredson, DM and Tonry, M (eds) (1987) *Prediction and Classification: Criminal Justice Decision Making*, Chicago and London: University of Chicago Press

Grey, V (2000) *Web Without a Weaver: The Meaning of the Internet*, unpublished manuscript, reference in Anderson, WT, *Det Nye Selvet: identitet i det 21. århundre*, Oslo: Aschehoug

Haggerty, KD (2004) 'Displaced expertise: three constraints on the policy-relevance of criminological thought', in *Theoretical Criminology*, Vol 8(2), pp 211–31

Hanners, U (1992) *Cultural Complexity*, Columbia: Columbia University Press

Haraway, D (1996) *Modest_Witness@Second_Millennium*, London: Routledge

Hayles, NK (1999) *How We Became Posthuman: Virtual Bodies in Cybernetics, Literature, and Informatics*, Chicago and London: University of Chicago Press

Heidegger, M (1977) *The Question Concerning Technology and Other Essays*, New York: Harper & Row

Hekman, S (1983) *Weber, the Ideal Type, and Contemporary Social Theory*, Notre Dame: University of Notre Dame Press

Henden, G (2004) *Intuition and its Role in Strategic Thinking*, Oslo: Norwegian School of Management BI

Hennum, R (2002) *Domstolenes utmåling av straff – en undersøkelse av rettspraksis*, Oslo: Justis og politi departement

Home Office (2001) *Making Punishments Work: Report of a Review of the Sentencing Framework for England and Wales*, London: Home Office Communications Directorate

Hudson, BA (1995) 'Beyond proportionate punishment: difficult cases and the 1991 Criminal Justice Act', in *Crime, Law and Social Change*, Vol 22, pp 59–78

Hudson, B (2002) 'Punishment, poverty and responsibility: the case for a hardship defence', in Tata, C and Hutton, N (eds), *Sentencing and Society: International Perspectives*, Aldershot: Ashgate

Hutchby, I (2001) *Conversation and Technology: From the Telephone to the Internet*, Cambridge: Polity Press

Hutton, N (1995) 'Sentencing, rationality, and computer technology', in *Journal of Law and Society*, Vol 22(4), pp 549–70

Hylland Eriksen, T (2001) *Tyranny of the Moment: Fast and Slow Time in the Information Age*, London and Sterling, Virginia: Pluto Press

*The Independent* (2002) 'Analysis: secretive, elitist, self-serving: why Britain's legal system needs radical reform', http://news.independent.co.uk/uk/legal/story.jsp?story=340503 (viewed 8 October 2002)

*International Journal of Law and Information Technology* (1998), Vol 6(2), Special Issue on Judicial Decision Support Systems

Jacobson, M (2004) 'Reply to Kevin D Haggerty', in *Theoretical Criminology*, Vol 8(2), pp 233–38

Jenkins, BS (2002) 'For thinking press 1, for compassion press 2, for judgment press 3', in *Vital Speeches of the Day*, 15 January

Jenkins, R (1996) *Social Identity*, London and New York: Routledge

Jewkes, Y (ed) (2003) *Dot.cons: Crime, Deviance and Identity on the Internet*, Cullompton: Willan Publishing

Jones, C (1993) 'Auditing criminal justice', in *The British Journal of Criminology*, Vol 33(2), pp 187–202

Jones, R (2000) 'Digital rule: punishment, control and technology', in *Punishment & Society*, Vol 2(1), pp 5–22

Jones, SG (ed) (1997) *Virtual Culture*, London and Thousand Oaks: Sage

Judicial Commission of New South Wales (2002) *Welcome to the Sentencing Information System*, www.judcom.nsw.gov.au/sisdemo/ (viewed 15 February 2002)

JURIX (1992) *Legal Knowledge Based Systems: Information Technology and the Law: JURIX 1992 Conference*, Gruetters, CAFM *et al* (eds), Lelystad: Koninklijke Vermande

Kemp, P (1996) *Det uerstattelige: en teknologi – etikk*, Oslo: Gyldendal

Kern, R (1999) *Examining Our Commissions & Sentencing Policy*, Report from the National Association of Sentencing Commissions 1999 Annual Conference, Salt Lake City, Utah

Kling, R and Allen, JP (1996) 'How the marriage of management and computing intensifies the struggle for personal privacy', in Lyon, D and Zureik, E (eds), *Computers, Surveillance, and Privacy*, Minneapolis and London: University of Minnesota Press

Kramer, JH and Ulmer, JT (1996) 'Sentencing disparity and departures from the Guidelines', in *Justice Quarterly*, Vol 13, pp 81–106

Lakoff, G and Johnson, M (1980) *Metaphors We Live By*, Chicago: University of Chicago Press

Lash, S (2001) 'Technological forms of life', in *Theory, Culture & Society*, Vol 18(1), pp 105–20

Lash, S (2002) *Critique of Information*, London, Thousand Oaks, New Delhi: Sage

Lasker, ME (1997) 'Remarks of Morris E Lasker, US District Judge for the Southern District of New York', before Symposium on Sentencing Guidelines, 9 September, www.vcl.org/Judges/Lasker_J.htm

Leith, P (1998) 'The judge and the computer: how best "decision support"?', in *Artificial Intelligence and Law*, Vol 6(2/4), pp 289–309

Lianos, M and Douglas, M (2000a) 'Dangerisation and the end of deviance', in *The British Journal of Criminology*, Vol 40, pp 261–78

Lianos, M and Douglas, M (2000b) 'Dangerisation and the end of deviance', in Garland, D and Sparks, R (eds), *Criminology and Social Theory*, Oxford: Oxford University Press, pp 103–25

Lubitz, RL and Ross, TW (2001) 'Sentencing guidelines: reflections on the future', in *Sentencing & Corrections, Issues for the 21st Century*, National Institute of Justice

Luhmann, N (1995) *Social Systems*, Bednarz, J with Baecker, D (trans), Stanford, California: Stanford University Press

Luna, E (2002) 'Misguided guidelines: a critique of federal sentencing', *Policy Analysis*, Vol 458, 1 November

Lyon, D (1988) *The Information Society: Issues and Illusions*, Cambridge: Polity Press

Lyon, D (1994) *The Electronic Eye: The Rise of Surveillance Society*, Cambridge: Polity Press

Lyon, D (1995) 'The roots of the information society idea', in Heap, N, Thomas, R, Einon, G, Mason, R and Mackay, H (eds), *Information Technology and Society*, London: Sage in association with The Open University Press

Lyon, D (2001) *Surveillance Society: Monitoring Everyday Life*, Buckingham: The Open University Press

Lyon, D (ed) (2003) *Surveillance and Social Sorting*, London and New York: Routledge

Lyotard, J-F (1999) *The Postmodern Condition: A Report on Knowledge*, Manchester: Manchester University Press

Mackay, H (1995) 'Theorising the IT/Society relationship', in Heap, N, Thomas, R, Einon, G, Mason, R and Mackay, H (eds), *Information Technology and Society*, London: Sage in association with The Open University Press

Mann, M (ed) (1983) *The Macmillan Student Encyclopaedia of Sociology*, London: Macmillan

Manning, P (1992a) 'Information technology and the police', in Tonry, M and Morris, N (eds), *Modern Policing*, Chicago: University of Chicago Press, pp 349–98

Manovich, L (2001a) *From the Externalization of the Psyche to the Implementation of Technology*, www.manovich.net (viewed 20 September 2001)

Manovich, L (2001b) *The Language of New Media*, Cambridge, Mass and London: MIT Press

Martinson, R (1974) 'What works? – questions and answers about prison reform', in *The Public Interest*, Vol 10, pp 22–54

Maruna, S (2001) *Making Good: How Ex-Convicts Reform and Rebuild Their Lives*, Washington, DC: American Psychological Association

Mathiesen, T (1983) 'The future of social control systems – the case of Norway', in Garland, D and Young, P (eds), *The Power to Punish: Contemporary Penalty and Social Analysis*, Atlantic Highlands, NJ: Humanities

Mathiesen, T (1987) 'The eagle and the sun: on panoptical systems and mass media in modern society', in Lowman, J, Menzies, RJ and Palys, TS (eds), *Transcarceration: Essays in the Sociology of Social Control*, Aldershot: Gower

Mathiesen, T (1999) *Industrisamfunn eller informasjonssamfunn? Inspill til belysning av den høymoderne tid*, Oslo: Pax Forlag AS

Mathiesen, T (2000) *Siste ord er ikke sagt: Schengen and globalisering av kontroll*, Oslo: Pax Forlag AS

Mathiesen, T (2001) *Retten I samfunnet: En innføring i rettssosiologi*, Oslo: Pax Forlag AS

McCormick, KRE and Visano, LA (1992) 'Technology and control: generic trends', in McCormick, KRE and Visano, LA (eds), *Canadian Penology: Advanced Perspectives and Research*, Toronto: Canadian Scholars' Press

McLaughlin, E, Muncie, J and Hughes, G (2001) 'The permanent revolution: New Labour, new public management and the modernization of criminal justice', in *Criminal Justice*, Vol 1(3), August

McLuhan, M (1998) *Understanding Media: The Extensions of Man*, Cambridge, Mass: MIT Press

Meek, J (2000) 'Signing off', *Guardian Weekly*, 21–27 September, p 20

Meyer, S (1993) *Menneske eller maske?Refleksjoner over kunst, vitenskap og individ*, Bergen: Universitet I Bergen

Meyrowitz, J (1986) *No Sense of Place: The Impact of Electronic Media on Social Behavior*, New York: Oxford University Press

Miller, J (2001) 'Bringing the individual back in', *Punishment & Society*, Vol 3(1), pp 153–60

Minnesota Sentencing Guidelines Commission (2003) *Minnesota Sentencing Guidelines and Commentary*, revised 8 August 2003

Morgan, N (2002) 'A sentencing matrix for Western Australia: accountability and transparency or smoke and mirrors?', in Tata, C and Hutton, N (eds), *Sentencing and Society: International Perspectives*, Aldershot: Ashgate

Morris, N (1974) *The Future of Imprisonment*, Chicago: University of Chicago Press

Moser, I (2001) 'Med semiotikk som brobygger – oversettelsesarbeid i et prosjekt om subjektivitet i teknososiale praksiser', in Liestøl, G and Morrison, A (eds), *Tverfaglighet og Digitale Medier*, Rapport 2000–01, Oslo: InterMedia UiO

Mumford, L (1963) *Myth of the Machine*, Vol 2, New York: Harcourt Brace Jovanovich

Nelkin, D and Lindee, S (1995) *The DNA Mystique: The Gene as a Cultural Icon*, San Francisco and New York: WH Freeman

Norris, C (2002) 'From personal to digital: CCTV, the panopticon and the technological mediation of suspicion and social control', in Lyon, D (ed), *Surveillance and Social Sorting*, London: Routledge

Oakeshott, M (1967) 'Learning and teaching', in Peters, RS (ed), *The Concept of Education*, London: Routledge and Kegan Paul

O'Malley, P (1992) 'Risk, power and crime prevention', in *Economy and Society*, Vol 21(3), pp 252–74

Ong, W (1988) *Orality and Literacy: The Technologizing of the World*, London: Methuen

Orlikowski, W and Robey, D (1991) 'Information technology and the structuring of organizations', in *Information Systems Research*, Vol 2, pp 143–69

Østerberg, D (1988) *Metasociology: An Inquiry into the Origins and Validity of Social Thought*, Oslo: Universitetsforlaget

Østerberg, D (1993) *Fortolkende sosiologi I*, Oslo: Universitetsforlaget

Pattenden, R (1990) *Judicial Discretion and Criminal Litigation*, Oxford: Clarendon Press

Polanyi, M (1966) *The Tacit Dimension*, Garden City, NY: Doubleday

Porter, T (1996) *Trust in Numbers: The Invention of Objectivity*, Princeton: Princeton University Press

Poster, M (1989) *Critical Theory and Poststructuralism: In Search of a Context*, Ithaca and London: Cornell University Press

Poster, M (1990) *The Mode of Information: Poststructuralism and Social Context*, Cambridge: Polity Press

Poster, M (1995) *The Second Media Age*, Cambridge: Polity Press

Poster, M (1996) 'Databases as discourse; or, electronic interperllations', in Lyon, D and Zureik, E (eds), *Computers, Surveillance, and Privacy*, Minneapolis and London: University of Minnesota Press, pp 175–93

Poster, M (2001a) *Interview with Mark Poster: Community, New Media, Post-Humanism*, darkwing.uoregon.edu/~ucurrent/2-Poster.html (viewed 9 October 2001)

Poster, M (2001b) *Postmodern Virtualities*, www.hnet.uci.edu/mposter/writings/internet.html (viewed 9 October 2001), also published as Chapter 2 in Poster, M (1995) *The Second Media Age*, Cambridge: Polity Press

Postman, N (1985) *Amusing Ourselves to Death: Public Discourse in the Age of Show Business*, New York: Penguin Books

Postman, N (1993) *Technopoly: The Surrender of Culture to Technology*, New York: Vintage Books

Power, M (1999) *The Audit Society: Rituals of Verification*, Oxford: Oxford University Press

President's Commission on Law Enforcement and Administration of Justice (1967) *The Task Force Report on Science and Technology*, Washington, DC: US Government Printing Office

Provine, DM (1998) 'Too many black men: the sentencing judge's dilemma', in *Law and Social Inquiry*, Vol 23, pp 823–56

Raine, JW (2001) 'Modernizing courts or courting modernization?', in *Criminal Justice*, Vol 1(1), pp 105–28

Rasmussen, T (2000) *Social Theory and Communication Technology*, Aldershot: Ashgate

Rasmussen, T (2004) *Media of the Self: Reflections on the Personal Web Page*, www.media.uio.no/personer/terjer (viewed 30 March 2004)

Reich, RB (1991) *The Work of Nations: Preparing Ourselves for 21st Century Capitalism*, New York: Alfred A Knopf

Reitz, KR (2001) 'The disassembly and reassembly of US sentencing practices', in Tonry, M and Frase, RS (eds), *Sentencing and Sanctions in Western Countries*, New York: Oxford University Press

Rex, S and Tonry, M (eds) (2002) *Reform and Punishment: The Future of Sentencing*, Cullompton: Willan Publishing

Robins, K and Webster, F (1999) *Times of the Technoculture: From the Information Society to the Virtual Life*, London: Routledge

Rodaway, P (1995) 'Exploring the subject in hyper-reality', in Pile, S and Thrift, N (eds), *Mapping the Subject*, London and New York: Routledge

Rose, N (1996) 'Governing "advanced" liberal democracies', in Barry, A, Osborne, T and Rose, N (eds), *Foucault and Political Reason: Liberalism, Neo-Liberalism and Rationalities of Government*, Chicago: University of Chicago Press

Rose, N (1999) *Powers of Freedom: Reframing Political Thought*, Cambridge: Cambridge University Press

Rose, N (2000) 'Identity, genealogy, history', in du Gay, P, Evans, J and Redman, P (eds), *Identity: A Reader*, London: Sage

Rose, N and Miller, P (1992) 'Political power beyond the state: problematics of government', *The British Journal of Sociology*, Vol 43(2), pp 172–205

Roszak, T (1994) *The Cult of Information: A Neo-Luddite Treatise on High Tech, Artificial Intelligence, and the True Art of Thinking*, London: University of California Press

Rothman, DJ (1991) *Strangers at the Bedside: A History of How Law and Bioethics Transformed Medical Decision Making*, New York: Basic Books

Rothman, DJ (1994) 'The crime of punishment', in *The New York Review of Books*, 17 February, pp 34–38

Ryle, G (1949) *The Concept of Mind*, New York: Barnes

Sarat, A and Simon, J (2003) *Cultural Analysis, Cultural Studies, and the Law: Moving Beyond Legal Realism*, Durham and London: Duke University Press

Sartor, G, Sartor, L and Branting, K (1998) 'Introduction: judicial applications of artificial intelligence', in *Artificial Intelligence and Law*, Vol 6, pp 105–10

Schmatt, E (2001) 'The sentencing information system of the Judicial Commission of New South Wales', paper presented at the Seventh National Court Technology Conference, Baltimore, August

Sennett, R (1998) *The Corrosion of Character: The Personal Consequences of Work in New Capitalism*, New York: WW Norton

Shearing, C and Stenning, P (1998) 'From the panopticon to Disney World: the development of discipline', in O'Malley, P (ed), *Crime and the Risk Society*, Aldershot: Ashgate

Shore, C and Wright, S (2000) 'Coercive accountability: the rise of audit culture in higher education', in Strathern, M (ed), *Audit Cultures: Anthropological Studies in Accountability, Ethics and the Academy*, London: Routledge

Silver, E (2000) 'Actuarial risk assessment: reflections on an emerging social-scientific tool', in *Critical Criminology*, Vol 9(1/2), Autumn, pp 123–43

Simon, E and Gaes, G (1989) 'ASSYST – computer support guidelines sentencing', in *Proceedings from the 2nd International Conference on AI and Law*, New York: ACM Press

Simon, J (1993) *Poor Discipline: Parole and the Social Control of the Underclass, 1890–1990*, Chicago: University of Chicago Press

Simon, J (1995) *Disciplining Punishment: The Re-Form of Sentencing*, unpublished manuscript

Simon, J (1999) 'On their own: delinquency without society', in *The University of Kansas Law Review*, Vol 47(5), pp 1001–19

Simon, J and Feeley, MM (1995) 'True crime: the new penology and public discourse on Crime', in Bloomberg, TG and Cohen, S (eds), *Punishment and Social Control: Essays in Honor of Sheldon L Messinger*, Aldine de Gruyter: New York

Smith, MJ (1998) *Social Science in Question*, London, Thousand Oaks and New Delhi: Sage in association with The Open University Press

Somers, MR (1994) 'The narrative constitution of identity: a relational and network approach', in *Theory and Society*, Vol 23, pp 605–49

Sparks, R and Newburn, T (eds) (2002) 'How does crime policy travel?', in *Criminal Justice*, Vol 2(2)

Spohn, CC (2002) *How Do Judges Decide? The Search for Fairness and Justice in Punishment*, Thousand Oaks, CA: Sage

Sporkin, S (1997) 'Statement of the Honourable Stanley Sporkin', in *Impact of Sentencing Guidelines on Federal Courts: Symposium on 10th Anniversary of Sentencing Guidelines*, Judiciary Committee, Washington, DC, www.sentencing.org/sporkin.html (viewed 20 January 1998)

Stith, K and Cabranes, JA (1997) 'Judging under the federal sentencing guidelines', in *Northwestern University Law Review*, Vol 91(4), pp 1,247–83

Stith, K and Cabranes, JA (1998) *Fear of Judging*, Chicago: University of Chicago Press

Stone, J (1966) *Social Dimensions of Law and Justice*, Stanford, CA: Stevens & Sons

Strathern, M (1999) *Property, Substance and Effect: Anthropological Essays on Persons and Things*, London: The Athlone Press

Strathern, M (2000a) 'Abstraction and decontextualisation: an anthropological comment or: e for ethnography', paper given at *Virtual Society? Get Real!* Conference, May 2000, http://virtualsociety.sbs.ox.ac.uk/GRpapers/strathern.htm

Strathern, M (ed) (2000b) *Audit Cultures: Anthropological Studies in Accountability, Ethics and the Academy*, London: Routledge

Stenbore, E (2003) Påföljdsbestämningen i Sverige och Straffeulmålingen i Norge: Med en studie av rättsfall från Högsta domstolen och Hoyesterett, Lund: Lunds Universitet

Tait, D (1998) 'Judges and jukeboxes: sentencing information systems in the courtroom', in *International Journal of Law and Information Technology*, Vol 6(2), pp 167–89

Tait, D (2002) 'Sentencing as performance: restoring drama to the courtroom', in Tata, C and Hutton, N (eds), *Sentencing and Society: International Perspectives*, Aldershot: Ashgate

Tak, PJ (2001) 'Sentencing and punishment in the Netherlands', in Tonry, M and Frase, R (eds), *Sentencing and Sanctions in Western Countries*, Oxford: Oxford University Press, pp 151–87

Talbott, SL (1995) *The Future Does Not Compute: Transcending the Machines in Our Midst*, Sebastopol, CA: O'Reilly & Associates Inc

Tata, C (1997) 'Conceptions and representations of the sentencing decision process', in *Journal of Law and Society*, Vol 24(3), pp 395–420

Tata, C (1998) '"Neutrality", "choice", and "ownership" in the construction, use, and adaptation of judicial decision support systems', in *International Journal of Law and Information Technology*, Vol 6(2), pp 143–66

Tata, C (2000) 'Resolute ambivalence: why judiciaries do not institutionalize their decision support systems?', *International Review of Law, Computers & Technology*, Vol 14(3), pp 297–316

Tata, C (2002) 'So what does "and society" mean?', in Tata, C and Hutton, N (eds), *Sentencing and Society: International Perspectives*, Aldershot: Ashgate

Tata, C and Hutton, N (eds) (2002) *Sentencing and Society: International Perspectives*, Aldershot: Ashgate

Tata, C, Wilson, JN and Hutton, N (1996) 'Representations of knowledge and discretionary decision-making by decision – support systems: the case of judicial sentencing', in *International Journal of Law and Information Technology*, http://elj.warwick.ac.uk/jilt/ArtifInt/2tata/default.htm

Thorpe, S (2001) *Online Legal Information in Denmark, Norway and Sweden*, www.llrx.com/features/scan.htm (viewed 17 September 2003)

Tonry, M (1992) 'Judges and sentencing policy – the American experience', in Munro, C and Wasik, M (eds), *Sentencing, Judicial Discretion and Training*, London: Sweet & Maxwell

Tonry, M (1994) 'Proportionality, parsimony and interchangeability of punishments', in Duff, A *et al* (eds), *Penal Theory and Practice: Tradition and Innovation in Criminal Justice*, Manchester: Manchester University Press

Tonry, M (1995) 'Sentencing reforms across national borders', in Clarkson, C and Morgan, R (eds), *The Politics of Sentencing Reform*, Oxford: Clarendon Press, pp 267–82

Tonry, M (1996) *Sentencing Matters*, New York: Oxford University Press

Tonry, M (2001) 'Symbol, substance and severity in western penal policies', in *Punishment & Society*, Vol 3(4), pp 517–36

Tonry, M (2002) 'Setting sentencing policy through guidelines', in Rex, S and Tonry, M (eds), *Reform and Punishment: The Future of Sentencing*, Cullompton: Willan Publishing, pp 75–104

Tonry, M and Frase, RS (eds) (2001) *Sentencing and Sanctions in Western Countries*, Oxford: Oxford University Press

Turkle, S (1984) *The Second Self: Computers and the Human Spirit*, New York: Simon & Schuster

Turkle, S (1995) *Life on the Screen: Identity in the Age of the Internet*, London: Phoenix

US Sentencing Commission (November 2003) *Guidelines Manual*, Washington, DC

Von Hirsch, A (1976) *Doing Justice: The Choice of Punishments*, New York: Hill and Wang

Von Hirsch, A (1985) *Past or Future Crimes: Deservedness and Dangerousness in the Sentencing of Criminals*, New Brunswick, NJ: Rutgers University Press

Von Hirsch, A (2002) 'Scaling punishments: a reply to Julia Davis', in Tata, C and Hutton, N (eds), *Sentencing and Society: International Perspectives*, Aldershot: Ashgate

Walker, N (1993) *Taming the System: The Control of Discretion in Criminal Justice 1950–1990*, New York: Oxford University Press

*The Washington Times* (2002) 'Analysis: sentencing rules often unjust', 11 January

Weber, M (1968) *Economy and Society: An Outline of Interpretative Sociology*, Roth, G and Wittich, C (eds), New York: Bedminster Press

*Webster's Encyclopedic Unabridged Dictionary of the English Language* (1989), Portland House: New York

Webster, F (1999) 'What information society?', in Mackay, H and O'Sullivan, T (eds), *The Media Reader: Continuity and Transformation*, London: Sage

Weinstein, JB (1992) 'A trial judge's second impression of the Federal Sentencing Guidelines', in *Southern California Law Review*, Vol 66, pp 357–66

Weizenbaum, J (1976) *Computer Power and Human Reason: From Judgment to Calculation*, San Francisco: Freeman

White, EG (1976) *The American Judicial Tradition: Profiles of Leading American Judges*, New York: Oxford University Press

Williams, R (1974) *Television, Technology and Cultural Form*, London: Fontana

Winston, B (1998) *Media Technology and Society – A History: From the Telegraph to the Internet*, London and New York: Routledge

Wired News (2004) *We're All Mac Users Now*, www.wired.com/news/print/0,1294,61730,00.html (viewed 6 February 2004)

Wolfgang, M and Riedel, M (1973) 'Race, judicial discretion and the death penalty', in *Annual of American Political & Social Science*, Vol 407

World Almanac: http://firstsearch.oclc.org/WebZ/

Zuboff, S (1988) *In the Age of the Smart Machine: The Future of Work and Power*, New York: Basic Books

# Index